LIBERATE AND LEAVE

LIBERATE AND LEAVE

FATAL FLAWS IN THE EARLY STRATEGY FOR POSTWAR IRAQ

DON EBERLY
Senior Advisor to the
Coalition Provisional Authority

ZENITH PRESS

First published in 2009 by Zenith Press, an imprint of MBI Publishing
Company, 400 1st Avenue North, Suite 300, Minneapolis, MN 55401 USA.

Zenith Press titles are also available at discounts in bulk
quantity for industrial or sales-promotional use. For details
write to Special Sales Manager at MBI Publishing Company,
400 1st Avenue North, Suite 300, Minneapolis, MN 55401 USA.

Designer: Diana Boger
Front cover photo: AP Photo/Saurabh Das
Interior photos: Author's collection
Maps: Philip Schwartzberg, Meridian Mapping, Minneapolis

Library of Congress Cataloging-in-Publication Data

Eberly, Don E.
 Liberate and leave : fatal flaws in the early strategy for postwar Iraq / Don
Eberly.
    p. cm.
  ISBN 978-0-7603-3680-9
1. Postwar reconstruction--Iraq. 2. Iraq--Politics and government--2003-
I. Title.
 DS79.769.E235 2009
 956.7044'3--dc22

                            2008042852

Printed in the United States of America

Contents

Preface

THE FOLLOWING IS A COMBINATION of personal story and professional analysis of what I observed during the two years of my life I spent working on Iraq—the first two years of the war.

My time covered every phase of the operation, including serving in the Pentagon in the lead-up to war, and on the civilian planning team led by Gen. Jay Garner that camped out in Kuwait City when the war got underway. I served four months under General Garner and the rest of my time in Iraq as senior advisor to Ambassador Paul Bremer. After returning to Washington, I served in positions at both the Pentagon and State Department.

As a nonpartisan advisor to presidents and national leaders on the subject of civil society and economic development, and a member of the White House staff under two presidents, Ronald Reagan and George W. Bush, I was invited to be one of the first civilian senior ministry advisors under General Garner, part of a small team who flew into Baghdad right after the city fell. My fellow advisors and I spent the first four months in the Republican Palace, which had been previously occupied by Saddam Hussein.

My specific authority was for the Ministry of Youth and Sport, an operation that was formerly presided over by Uday Hussein. When we first arrived in the emergency environment of liberated Baghdad, it was "all hands on deck." For the first month, we had only forty civilians to start rebuilding a nation the size and population of California. My first reconstruction assignment under Jay Garner had nothing to do with Youth and Sport, the position for which I had originally signed up. The more urgent need was to restore basic services. Following the collapse of Saddam's regime, I was the first American civilian to arrive at a totally emptied Baghdad municipal building, where I had to search the neighborhoods to find and reassemble the team of city managers who functioned under Saddam. There was simply no other way to get water, sanitation, and street cleaning services restored.

A group of poor children from Baghdad's slums gather with me as I survey the bombed remains of the Olympic Committee building.

Dozens of books on the war in Iraq have emerged over the past few years, each capturing some piece of the large complex operation we were all a part of. Any examination is partial, both in scope and perspective. Although I offer many personal perceptions and conclusions, they are not merely subjective. My account is informed by hundreds of conversations with colleagues and Iraqis that occurred during every phase of the Iraq operation.

I write neither as a war planner nor as a member of the military. The members of the Office of Reconstruction and Humanitarian Assistance (ORHA) team were sent to Baghdad to help with reconstruction, as the organization's title suggests. My background has been in the fields of international economic development, civil society, and post-disaster stabilization and reconstruction.

When we arrived in Baghdad, the city was, from a law-and-order standpoint, in a state of meltdown. That fact—more than any other combination of factors—made it feel like the deck was stacked against us from the get-go. To have served during the early days is to comprehend just how deeply wounded the Iraqis were and how broken Iraq was as a nation. Iraq was a collapsed state, and the lawlessness and lack of authority were akin to a Hobbesian "state of nature." The only order that existed was order we created, and most of my colleagues and I believed we had about one third the troops needed to maintain security in the country.

Everyone up to and including the president of the United States has admitted to serious miscalculations, costly blunders, and crippling breakdowns during the early phases of the Iraq war. Given history's need to settle on a plausible theory about the failure to execute an effective postwar rebuilding effort, the Washington debate today is mostly looking for individual culprits, like the men I worked for—Jay Garner or Paul Bremer. Or it searches for a single decision, like "disbanding" Saddam's army or "de-Ba'athifying" Saddam's senior government managers.

None of those theories comes close to capturing the deeper issues of Iraq.

Those who didn't serve on the ground in Iraq, especially during the early days, have a hard time appreciating just how devastated the country was after thirty years of dictatorship—socially, politically, and psychologically—and how unprepared it was to shoulder the burden of constructing a democracy. For me, the culprit is not so much a particular person as much as it is a profoundly flawed premise about postwar realities—what I capture in the book's title as the naive hope held by many top senior civilians in Washington during the lead-up to the war that we could somehow "liberate and leave."

I have my own fairly straightforward thesis, which is as follows: The risks of the postwar realities in Iraq were well known when the decision to liberate was made; the prudent thing would have been to offer a postwar rebuilding plan based on the worst-case scenario, which obviously did not happen. Most critically, absent a sound plan and absent an immediate correction of course by Washington during the early days of postwar Iraq, the die was pretty well cast, and the trajectory was set for years to come. For every passing month that an adequate response was not forthcoming from Washington, the number of years it would take for security, political stability, and economic recovery to be achieved would multiply.

Introduction
The Confused Early Days

I WAS PROUD OF THE CIVILIAN RECONSTRUCTION TEAM I worked with as a senior advisor to the Office for Reconstruction and Humanitarian Assistance (ORHA), first in Kuwait City during the planning phase and then in Baghdad. They were highly capable people with lots of solid ideas and plans. But they were mostly empty-handed when it came to the essential resources needed to do the job. All of us had assumed that a serious plan covering all the major decisions had been laid months before the war by the massive policy office that exists at the Pentagon.

It took months for Washington to slowly realize that postwar plans and resources were wholly inadequate. It would take years to realize that nothing could be accomplished without adequate security. The "surge" that finally came in early 2007 was needed in the summer of 2003.

In many cases, we had to build new ministries almost completely from scratch—in the midst of chaos and looting. At no point from the beginning to the present were there adequate troops to manage the security fallout from a collapsed state. Having been liberated, Iraq was ours to manage and re-order. No phrase ever offered by a senior government official better captured this reality than when Secretary of State Colin Powell compared Iraq to a piece of glassware in a pottery shop: "you break it, you own it."

The senior advisors served as interim ministers because in most cases there were no senior officials from the previous Iraqi regime who could be trusted to take on the role. Each of us was given broad authority under occupation law: authority to reorganize, to hire and fire, to deal with bad people and bombed buildings, to provide emergency cash payments to tens of thousands of former workers to prevent destitution and rebellion, to secure sites in the midst of profound security shortcomings, and basically to do what was necessary to get operations restored.

A sample of erotic art found in Uday's "concubine" palace. Uday's palace revealed that he was a man of multiple vices, including extensive drug and alcohol use, pornography, and the abuse of women.

As one colleague describes, it was "assembling the vehicle while driving."

In my case, I inherited a cluster of functions that had been carried out by Uday Hussein, including the Ministry of Youth and Sport and the National Olympic Committee of Iraq, both of which he presided over with unthinkable cruelty. Uday had tortured or imprisoned thousands of talented athletes, and turned the basement of an otherwise modern-looking Olympic Committee building into a torture chamber. He had huge business dealings in the Baghdad area, and many of his corrupt henchmen were still lurking in the background trying to figure out what was left of their stake in his personal empire. Uday also had three sizable palaces of his own, including a so-called "concubine palace," where he kept women against their will. Sorting through the remains of Uday's estate and business dealings, along with rebuilding the Ministry of Youth and Sport, fell to me for the simple reason that no one else was available to take on the challenge.

We would need to recruit and train entirely new ministry teams, and—since the Ministry of Youth and Sport building was bombed and looted beyond repair—locate and supply new offices. We had to hobble together a new national ministry, reorganize hundreds of community centers across

Iraq, and resupply sports clubs with equipment from some of the donations that were pouring in.

In spite of the difficulty, there were real successes during the summer of 2003 across every sector of society, many unreported by the media. Even with the instability and violence surrounding us, a new civil society began to emerge with a flourishing of independent media outlets and political parties. New civic and advocacy-based organizations representing women, students, and professionals of various kinds began emerging.

During the summer of 2003, there were modest signs of hope. Small businesses were beginning to flourish. Within months, markets were full of produce, and downtown sidewalks were lined with businesses hawking new appliances and satellite dishes. The streets became clogged with hundreds of thousands of new automobiles rapidly imported from Jordan and elsewhere to meet demand. Within weeks, satellite dishes were seen popping up on rooftops, with wires stretching haphazardly from house to house. The fact that there was significant economic growth by the second year, without currency problems or severe inflation, was no small feat—a tribute to American competence. None of these early spurts of progress would prove sustainable, however, because the American government never supplied the necessary security.

In many ways we were able to produce results in spite of the brutal environment and practical obstacles. Every senior advisor across the twenty-four Iraqi ministries was able to perform miracles. My own and my successor's team managed to get Iraqi athletes to the 2004 Olympics against considerable odds. Obviously, that was a great boost to Iraqi pride and morale. This required completely replacing the old abused system under Uday Hussein with a nationally representative temporary committee to reorganize sports and put the pieces together of a new organization in accordance with international procedures.

This required that we preside over hundreds of local club elections all across Iraq, all within five months, and in an insecure environment. Only after that step was completed could a national assembly be convened that would produce a legitimately elected National Olympic Committee of Iraq. Iraqi sports teams were prepared to make a heroic effort on the field; it would fall to us to carry the organizing task, legally and diplomatically.

That meant we had to help the Iraqis organize and fund teams, and send them off to distant places for training and regional competition, all with limited finances and under severe security constraints. My team and that of my able successor, Mounzer Fatfat, were able to achieve what felt impossible at the time. The Iraqi soccer team, under the most trying conditions, managed to qualify for the 2004 games in Athens, just missing a bronze medal. With that achievement alone, the Iraqis had made a comeback; it was arguably their proudest moment in decades. The streets erupted with celebratory gunfire.

While still in Kuwait City with the war proceeding, at General Garner's suggestion, I worked with U.S. businessman Phil Anchutz and the American soccer community to get eighty thousand soccer balls donated to the kids of Iraq. That may seem trivial until you consider how powerful a gift it was during the early days in reaching hearts and minds among the youth. Few things generated more sincere enthusiasm in Iraq than when, a month later, Garner's successor, Paul Bremer, unveiled the soccer ball distribution campaign at the newly restored Olympic village in downtown Baghdad.

For this work, we had no choice but to leave the Green Zone regularly and move around the country. Most of us would encounter hostilities and take our turns hitting the ground to avoid gunfire. Most of us experienced the trip to the Baghdad airport at ninety miles an hour with military aides pointing machines out each car window hoping to deter sniper fire from the bushes by the roadside. Many of us were caught in traffic jams in downtown Baghdad surrounded at close range by faces often filled with hostility, and endured the sinking feeling that we were "sitting ducks." It was odd to have gone from Washington desk jobs to sitting in meetings in army boots and flak jackets and listening to machine gun fire outside on the streets.

My successor, Mounzer Fatfat, had several close encounters with life-threatening danger. Shortly after I left Iraq, the office space I occupied took a direct mortar hit, and Fatfat narrowly escaped mortal attacks three times.

Many who signed up to serve in Iraq shared the doubts and concerns that were being intensely debated in the media. They signed up anyway because they believed that if their country was going to liberate Iraq, it had to be done right. They wanted to see the American liberation succeed. And they gave it their all. They wanted to be proud.

The American people also wanted it to succeed. After returning home from Baghdad, I continued through the first year coordinating social programs and private donations, first in the Coalition Provisional Authority (CPA) office at the Pentagon, then at the State Department after CPA dissolved in June

2004. I will never forget the outpouring of interest. Private donations, whose values ranged into the hundreds of millions, flooded into Iraq, including sporting equipment, medical textbooks, gifts for children, and offers of assistance from universities.

Neither will I ever forget the smiles of the hundreds of children I met. I still think about them every day; and as I do, I worry, and whisper a prayer for their safety and for a more hopeful future. There is no telling how they are doing or what their futures hold. They've seen difficult days, but I still think the children of Iraq have a more promising future because of what America has done.

Many media reports have suggested that America's reconstruction money was squandered. In fact, most of it was not, at least not during the time period in which I served when Americans were in charge of the money. Though there certainly was significant mismanagement on some projects, and lots of money was diverted to cover security, thousands of projects involving water and sewage, police stations, border posts, health care facilities, and schools were successfully completed. All of this happened in spite of unrelenting attacks from insurgents and attempts to kill construction workers.

But even with many successes, mostly unreported and thus unknown, the odds of achieving what was originally hoped for were slight. From the beginning, because Iraq was a collapsed state, few options for legitimate authority were available for consideration. It was impossible to make lasting improvements in services and win the confidence of the people when the previous government and its service delivery structures had pretty much been demolished by the war and postwar looting.

And from the beginning—not months or years later—nasty historic ethnic and historic grievances exploded into the open.

Polite Warnings

While serving as senior counselor for International Civil Society at the U.S. Agency for International Development (USAID), I had been involved in developing new initiatives for third world development. Part of that effort involved an evaluation of the effectiveness of U.S. programs that were targeted to Islamic countries in Asia, Africa, and the Middle East.

At one point we had a secret high-level meeting in Cairo sponsored by the State Department; it brought together U.S. officials from over sixty countries with substantial Islamic populations. Included among the presenters were leading intellectuals from the Muslim world. I vividly recall their sober-minded assessments of what was happening inside Islam. They quietly pleaded with us to appreciate that there wasn't a whole lot that America could do about this struggle, except to align itself with reform movements.

They politely warned that America often played into the hands of those who wanted to use anti-Americanism to advance extreme attitudes. Distrust of the United States and the West has always provided convenient rallying cries for our opposition in the region, and Iraq was no exception. Collectively, they seemed to be saying that while the Middle East needed more American-style democracy, the American government itself was probably not in the best position to directly advance it.

Democracy was not something that could be simply parachuted in. Quite the contrary, it was a way of life that could come only from the people who would be called upon to practice it. To become a democracy, a nation needed a liberal constitution at the top and a civic culture at the bottom that, through experience and time, imparted to individuals democratic habits and skills.

The former would be drawn up on paper and put in place through elites operating at the top; the latter required all of the value-shaping institutions, especially culture and religion, cooperating to produce democratic citizens.

A Time for Seriousness

Neither I nor my civilian colleagues were all that caught up in the great debate over weapons of mass destruction (WMDs); I just assumed that those issues were serious and that the best experts in the world with comprehensive knowledge of military reality on the ground in Iraq were sorting through them.

Those of us in the civilian planning group had a different perspective, and it was fairly uniform. We were committed on humanitarian and moral grounds to removing one of the great tyrants of all time, and were somewhat dismayed as that moral argument was lost. Today, it is hard to even remember the bipartisan resolutions that passed the Congress in the 1990s declaring Iraq under Saddam to be one of the world's great tyrannies, and calling for regime change largely on humanitarian grounds.

The evidence would later emerge that senior civilian and military war planners recognized that the only argument that would supply justification for regime change was the imminent security threat represented by Saddam; and in a post-9/11 world of terrorism, WMDs in the hands of a dictator was clearly the most compelling concern.

The failure of American intelligence agencies to know the facts about Saddam's arsenal would emerge as the biggest controversy of the war.

From time to time, remarks surfaced indicating that the decision to liberate Iraq had been made shortly after 9/11, and that the current debates were really academic, having mostly to do with leveraging support from the international community for the mostly American operation. In any event, the liberation of Iraq was going to happen. The momentum was moving powerfully in that direction by the time I joined General Garner's team.

We believed with equal fervor that if the United States was going to take this action, whatever its justification, it really had to be serious. We had to do the job well, leaving little to chance. It was with that intensity that everyone pursued their assignment. We all wanted it to succeed, and expected that we would be given whatever resources or tools the job required to produce a satisfactory outcome.

Phase IV

Immediately prior to the war, postwar reconstruction planning was occurring around three core functions, which were called "Phase IV" under the military's strategic plan. That term, Phase IV, would become shorthand for all of the deficiencies that existed in the coalition's effort to win the peace after the war. Phase IV was about putting the country back together, "winning hearts and minds," effectively transitioning Iraq to a new government and providing sufficient security to maintain order in the turbulent aftermath of war.

This phase to which we were assigned, Phase IV, would become synonymous with failure. No one doubted that the military victory would come with relative ease. The debate that started well before the first bombing mission was "do you have a plan to win the peace?" That was the most pointed question coming from the journalists and congressional panels scrutinizing postwar planning. No one questioned America's capacity to swiftly prevail militarily. The debate was about our mission—"Phase IV."

The three pillars of Phase IV were humanitarian affairs, reconstruction, and civil administration. Civil administration was basically the plan to take over and run the government on a transitional basis until qualified Iraqis could be found and appointed. Leading the civil administration planning effort was Mike Mobbs, senior policy advisor working under Doug Feith, undersecretary of defense for policy. Chris Milligan, from USAID, where I served, introduced me to Mike, who in turn arranged for me to meet Ron Adams, a retired general who served as Jay Garner's deputy.

The sports stadium at the Olympic village, with its prominent billboard-sized images of Saddam. Uday, who managed everything in Iraq having to do with sports, made sure that activity was used to glorify Saddam and his regime.

Garner's team was searching for people with backgrounds in development and humanitarian affairs, and who knew the players in Washington whom they would need to coordinate with. I quickly reviewed my experience with Arab world policy, particularly the parts focusing on civil society and democratization. Some of my writings on civil society had made their way into Arab and Muslim hands. One book on civil society had been translated into Arabic and was being circulated among civil society intellectuals in the Middle East.

Though I had substantive background on development and civil society policy and had a long history of working with senior officials on both sides of the aisle and with both Democrat and Republican administrations, I made it clear that I had served earlier as an appointee in the Bush administration. I had no idea at the time whether that would help or hurt. I hadn't met Jay Garner yet, but Ron said he thought that having a sense of the president's perspective, his mode of operation and decision-making, and his stake in the outcome would be a positive thing.

I was encouraged by that perspective. By 2006, the accusation surfaced that the Coalition Provisional Authority was crawling with inexperienced and naive staff who were there because of political ties. But from my first day at the Pentagon to the day I arrived in Baghdad, I knew only a couple of officials who had any meaningful connection to the president and the White House.

Jay Garner assembled an exceptional team of highly skilled and nonpartisan officials. In fact, I often drew the opposite conclusion—that the mission was carried out by people who had loyalties mostly to their own agencies back home, without appreciating the gravity of the consequences of failure for the sitting president.

But whatever a person's background or actual loyalty, everyone on the team was unified in wanting the mission to succeed. They wanted success for the sake of the Iraqi people, success for the Middle East, and success for their own country. Periodically I observed that, depending upon how this turned out, the president would be permanently affected. Success or failure on a mission so risky and so potentially controversial would likely seal his fate in history. It didn't take much training or insight to see that. Whatever one might have thought about him personally, the president deserved nothing less than the best effort.

When I met Garner, that sentiment was expressed even more strongly. He said they wanted some people who weren't partisan but who did have "political sensitivity" and knew a little about the commander in chief and how the White House liked to do business. A month or so later, I came to appreciate how important that comment was. I had the clear sense that some of the senior people planning the postwar occupation might have had agendas that weren't entirely consistent with the president's. Ironically, these were the president's most senior appointees operating at the commanding heights of the Pentagon.

The Ramp to War

It took a while to discern just how complicated the political realities were around the president. The decision to liberate Iraq involved a confluence of factors and actors that rarely occurs. Some, like Donald Rumsfeld, were less gung-ho about achieving regime change by military means but appeared willing to do it on the condition that it didn't disrupt his larger agenda, which was military transformation. Of all those who disdained the notion of nation building during the early years of the administration, Rumsfeld was probably the chief critic.

Paradoxically, Rumsfeld had returned to government service after decades in the private sector, promising to bring the military into the twenty-first century, which for him meant proving its capacity for swift and decisive military operations. Such a strategy for the military capitalized on America's unmatched technological superiority and thus its unprecedented capacity to advance its interests. That strictly circumscribed view of the military was combined with a well-publicized disinterest in "nation building."

The Rumsfeld argument prevailed during the 2000 campaign and throughout the first phase of the administration, with frequent references to the folly of nation building. With this view of the military serving as background, it was not surprising that the operation would be launched with as few troops as possible, and little attention would be paid to the requirement for adequate "boots on the ground" following the liberation. That just wasn't what Rumsfeld had in mind for the American military.

Other more powerful networks operating just below Rumsfeld, in Vice President Cheney's policy staff, and stretching through a web of think tanks and military strategy circles, pursued the far more ambitious agenda of transforming the Middle East. These would become popularly known as the neo-conservatives, or "neo-cons." If Rumsfeld's principle consideration was the use of the modern military in dealing decisively with security threats, the priority of the neo-cons was more political. They wanted decisive action to reshuffle the deck of status quo power in the Middle East.

For a few, just settling an old score with Saddam (the failure to take him out in 1991) might have been enough of a factor. The point is, there were many agendas, some in conflict and some in confluence, but all driving toward the same decision. Months into the operation, it became clear to me how badly served the president was by some of the advice he had been given.

The personnel who would be assembled to carry out Phase IV—humanitarian affairs, reconstruction, and civil administration—were a highly diverse group who were not tied into any of the power blocks at the top. They were "implementers." Once in Baghdad, there were no more than five persons who had direct ties back to the Bush White House. A few would eventually trickle in by late summer 2003, but for the first month or two, they represented a very small percentage of the group. The overwhelming majority of people who served were there because they had expertise to contribute. For most of the operation, and certainly during the early stages, the senior officials were all experienced. They were career diplomats, senior administrators, and policy experts. All of them, career and political, were exceptionally qualified and driven by the hope that the outcome would be successful.

Conflict and Chasms

No president, Democrat or Republican, should be expected to turn over an operation as delicate and consequential as replacing a dictatorial regime to nameless career bureaucrats. President Bush was more likely to get honest feedback from people who cared about the stakes for him, and who saw how Iraq and his presidency were tied together. Those stakes could not have been higher. I often doubted how much honest feedback he was really getting from the people who had their own stake in defining reality to him.

Two weeks after arriving in Baghdad, as things appeared more and more out of control, I met with Dan Senor, who at the time was working for White House Strategic Communications (he later became Ambassador Bremer's senior spokesman). We agreed that I should apprise Karl Rove of the grim situation.

I emailed Rove and told him that the environment we inherited in Baghdad represented a Herculean undertaking, that it would likely emerge as the biggest issue in the presidency, possibly affecting his prospects in 2004 and his legacy. I stated that no one in Baghdad seemed to be thinking much about the stakes for the president; everyone was fighting over their own little rice bowl.

It soon became obvious that the divide between the State Department and the Pentagon was akin to the Grand Canyon. There was little doubt why senior officials at the Department of Defense and the White House managed to place complete operational control for both the war and the postwar reconstruction firmly in the hands of the Pentagon, even though the experience and expertise for Phase IV operations were likely to be found mostly at the State Department and USAID.

Here I am at a soccer match in the VIP stand with Iraqi sports celebrities. Sporting events were one of the few activities that allowed people to overlook ethnic and sectarian differences.

From the beginning there were conflicting loyalties and confused reporting systems between the military and civilian operations and even within those columns—for example, between ORHA and USAID. The Pentagon people reported loyally back to Rumsfeld and Cheney. The USAID staff was instructed to stake out their own operation within ORHA, apparently in order to keep their more traditional nonpolitical humanitarian activity somewhat at a distance from what was a political-military operation.

The USAID people could barely contain their dismay that control over the entire postwar mission had not been handed to them. The State Department personnel could often be heard defending Colin Powell and his more skeptical view of the mission. Those detailed from other agencies were caught in the middle while trying to defend their home agencies' stake in the programs and funding. Later, to complicate things even further, each Iraqi ministry to which senior advisors were assigned would be given a batch of Iraqi exiles, sent to us via yet another agency created by the Pentagon in the lead-up to the war called the Iraqi Reconstruction and Development Council (IRDC).

At times, the whole operation felt like a home construction project in which a general contractor had been hired to build the house, had engaged multiple subcontractors to carry out some of the same task working off of a vague blueprint, and then disappeared.

Many ministry teams had staff from four or five different agencies or entities, all separately hired. There was the senior minister advisor of

ORHA with one or two staff. Assigned to his team were members of Army Civil Affairs teams, who reported back to their own command. In addition, there were USAID staff, who reported back to their system; some IRDC staff; and probably some local indigenous staff who were tapped from the Iraqi ministries.

Most reported back to their command structures, which in many cases operated under their own direction. This was especially true of Army Civil Affairs. In my case, there wasn't a single person hired directly by me. All of them came to me from somewhere else. I had no choice but to operate more like an orchestra maestro than a CEO; I could only try my best to inspire them to perform off a common symphonic score.

In my email to Rove, I suggested that he not accept this information from me alone, but that he send someone from the West Wing who would be the eyes and ears of the president, someone who would open a direct pipeline back to the White House. Two weeks into the operation, I came to sincerely doubt that the president would get regular reliable reports, so committed was everyone to putting the best face on reality.

I just assumed that, like all of his predecessors, this president would want to penetrate through the "fog of war" and get the more reliable reports from the front line. My faculty advisor in graduate school at Harvard was presidential historian Richard Neustadt, who maintained that on highly consequential policy decisions, most presidents really "drilled down" through the layers to get truthful information. Shortly after my email to Rove, Kristen Silverberg, who was a senior staffer under Chief of Staff Andy Card, arrived. I always assumed that she was that "front line" person.

THERE WAS ALSO A HUGE CHASM in our understanding of the Middle East. During the liberation of Iraq as well as the postwar reconstruction, I heard frequent references to the parallels to Europe and Japan. Occasionally there was a hint that the Bush administration would take the same tactics to the Middle East that President Reagan took to the Soviet Union, the chief symbol of which was the tearing down of the Berlin Wall. This would be the new bold and decisive global leadership offered by a hawkish Republican president.

The parallel is very problematic, as we discovered soon enough.

Even a casual knowledge of the Middle East would suggest that while military intervention may be justified, the circumstances in this case, including the politics and culture of the region, were very different. In fact, there were almost no similarities. Those reasons were not sufficient alone to decide against military action, but they should have shaped the assessment of how difficult it would be.

Those differences should have been considered in our planning and produced a tough realism in approach. The United States would be trying to take democracy to a people who had never practiced it, and in the heart of a region that had not been modernized, was tormented by sectarian factions and ancient ethnic hatreds, and would probably see the American presence on their soil through the prism of Western colonialism and Christian crusades.

I was never really settled in my thinking regarding whether Islam was a religion that would foster democracy as we understand it. But it was fairly obvious that the soil we would be cultivating in that region would be much less fertile than almost anywhere in the world. If this experiment in transplanting democracy into the heart of the Muslim Middle East was to have a chance, extraordinary attention would have to be given to creating the right conditions.

Democracy in that part of the world would neither be self-generating from within nor likely to respond to simply being parachuted in. There was no deterministic logic to encourage the belief that it would be easily grafted in, given the nation's history. Moreover, our role as Americans in that nation's future, because of our different culture and our history in that region, would be decidedly limited for a variety of reasons that are fairly obvious.

It was pretty much a sure thing that we would be seen both as liberators and invaders at the same time. The idea that great numbers of Muslims would be sanguine about the long presence of a military representing a Western (and nominally Christian) superpower—with its own history of acting out of self-interest in the region—seemed close to zero. That part of the world's suspicions toward America's interests in oil, in Israel, and in regional power run very deep at all levels of society. Very few take it at face value that the United States might be interested in bringing freedom and dignity to Arabs and Muslims. That is simply not the way they see it.

How America pursues its objectives—its assumptions and methodologies—often surfaces as an issue as well. For reasons of our own self-perceptions of goodness, we often just assume that our methods will be understood by Arabs. I often remarked that while many Iraqis were interested in some aspects of the "American way," they had a hard time with the American way of advancing it. It is extremely difficult for the average American to see America through the eyes of the average Arab or Muslim.

My impression again and again while passing through the villages and provinces of Iraq was that, just one thin layer below our superficially friendly conversations, we Americans are very different from Iraqis. It was easy to feel like an alien. This was a long way from home. We wanted to help the Iraqis, but there were so many reminders that what had to be done perhaps couldn't be done by us for the simple reason, paradoxically, that we were Americans and the world's sole superpower.

At least in the rural areas, time had stood still pretty much for millennia, and the gaps created by the combined factors of distance, language, religion, and culture often seemed unbridgeable. In many respects it was true that Iraqis desired what all human beings desire, which is to be treated with dignity and to have better opportunities for their families. But their way of life and ours could not have been more different. The Iraqis were communal while we practiced an almost extreme form of individualism.

To them the tribe and family were the ultimate forms of authority; for us, the individual self is king. They preferred order, while we lean toward rather excessive cultural freedoms. They wanted religion to dominate society and to some extent the state. Even devout believers in America see the daily functions of church and state as different spheres. Whatever new order was about to be created could be developed only by the Iraqis themselves. Many of our own grand schemes for modernizing, professionalizing, and secularizing their systems of government would largely be discarded.

At times, I obsessed over these issues; I feared that sobering facts were being rolled over in the optimistic mood and resolve to act that accompanied the accelerating momentum toward war. There was far too little time to resolve all of these complex issues. Plus, there was also a palpable sense that criticism and doubt were not welcome, even if one's intent was to improve the likely effectiveness of the operation.

Even with our minds buzzing with various scenarios and eventualities, none of us at the time could begin to imagine some of the realities that would follow: the chaos and looting, the uncontained insurgency, near civil war conditions with tens of thousands of Iraqis killed or kidnapped, and new symbols of American moral failure like Abu Ghraib and Guantanamo Bay, which would haunt so many and bruise our international reputation.

Neither could we at that early stage give names to the cast of villains that would emerge, like the thuggish bandit Muqtada al-Sadr and the disgraced and discredited Iraqi exile Ahmed Chalabi. Rarely did the thought occur to us that colleagues might be routinely shot at, some injured and killed, or that each of us would come home with stories of narrow escapes. I couldn't have prepared myself at the time for the sense of loss I would feel later upon learning that my good friend and great Iraqi patriot Ahmed al-Samarrai had been kidnapped. None of that seemed conceivable at the time, even for those of us who were prone to ask questions and ponder the imponderable.

"A Giant Ship Cutting Through a Thick and Treacherous Sea"

Much debate has centered on whether the American troops were cheered as liberators. To some extent they were, but there were also immediate signs of ambivalence and even resentment toward America. At least for the Shia south, America had a history of not being trustworthy.

That said, there were genuine signs of euphoria among Iraqis in many towns as the American military moved north in April 2003. Much of that euphoria would disappear by midsummer. Even the Iraqis had to be surprised by the sudden rush to the surface of attitudes and forces that were antithetical to democracy.

It didn't take months or years for ugly divisions to surface in Iraq, as some seem to suggest. From the first days after arriving in Baghdad, it was clear that Iraq threatened to splinter along ethnic and sectarian lines considering all the ancient hatreds. This was the land of the Sunnis, Shia, and Kurds, and a wider and worrisome gathering Islamic radicalism. There were already reports from the first day we ventured into downtown Baghdad of armed militia organizing to take over government buildings and functions. If there was a reason for the rapid rise of sectarian militia, it was because of our own lack of commitment to offering security for Iraqi facilities. Our weakness became a palpable source of empowerment to the sectarians.

When Iraqis were given an opportunity to elect delegates to the newly created Iraqi National Assembly in December 2005, their first response was to vote on the basis of their own ethnic or sectarian identities. A national unity slate comprising a coalition of nonsectarian parties led by former Prime Minister Ayad Allawi garnered 8 percent. The Shiites, who constitute 60 percent of the populace, wasted no time in taking power and forming an ethnically conscious majority.

Viewed in retrospect, this immediate balkanization made political instability inevitable. If Iraq was on its way to democracy, it would have severe birth pains. Within months of the invasion, Iraq was suddenly in the middle of an insurgency that showed no signs of abating, and insurgencies of this kind often take ten years to run their course, according to experts.

The Iraq we entered was a country destroyed by Saddam to a far greater degree than had been reported. Saddam's crimes of humanity against the people of his country are well documented, but the suffering was compounded by deliberate neglect in governing them. His use of basic supplies such as water and electricity to manipulate and control his people left his country with an aging infrastructure that had not been properly maintained and once-rich farmland now barren, the lush marshlands in southern Iraq having been drained and its soil left brittle and covered with fine silt from the heat and wind.

Few in Washington ever comprehended just how broken Iraq was, not even now.

Expectations were eventually lowered. The idea that the classical notion of warfare, involving conventional military operations, had any relevance to reality in Iraq became abandoned by events on the ground. The earlier boisterous language was understood to be a profound mismatch for reality. The best possible outcome for the United States became avoiding a catastrophic meltdown into internal civil war that could spill over into surrounding countries. Many wondered what honorable options existed for an exit.

Life in the Jungle

The year 2006 was the lowest in a long series of low points. Iraq was caught in the grip of escalating sectarian violence, with political parties, militia, and even old neighborhoods being organized and armed according to religious identity. By mid-2006, the insurgency increasingly metastasized into sectarian warfare between Sunnis and Shia, creating powerful movement toward an irreversibly balkanized nation.

Once peaceful neighborhoods were being gripped with Sunni-Shiite bloodletting. According to the United Nations, upwards of a hundred Iraqis were dying each day due to vengeance killings, with victims blindfolded, tortured, and then shot, execution style. Attacks on the American military doubled, rising from four hundred to eight hundred a week. Basic services such as electricity were barely existent. By overwhelming majorities, both Sunnis and Shiites (91 percent and 74 percent, respectively) wanted the Iraqi government to ask the U.S. military to leave, believing that the American military's presence was provoking, rather than preventing, violence.

One of Uday's bombed palaces. Uday had three palaces all located in close proximity to the main Republican Palace used by Saddam Hussein. All were targets in the bombing campaign.

Tens of thousands of residents from mixed Sunni-Shia neighborhoods fled for safety, creating new partitions along ethnic and sectarian lines. And a new problem was created: refugees. Hundreds of thousands were forced from their homes. Grim reports told of a massive middle class exodus, including professors, doctors, and senior technocrats from the government. Jordan became home to upwards of a million Iraqis who fled the violence.

A Defense Intelligence Agency report in the fall of 2006 described weak governance and no agreement on a national compact as factors driving toward national chaos. Unchecked violence and an atmosphere of fear contributed to a hardening sectarianism.

Violence became increasingly grisly. According to one press report, the killing of seventeen Sunnis was followed immediately by the killing of twenty-seven Shia. On a single night in October, Iraqi police found sixty bodies dumped across Baghdad, all victims of sectarian bloodletting. Recovering the corpses that had been dumped during the night became a daily ritual. Bodies, often found bound and with evidence of such torture as electric drill holes to the body and head, would be rounded up and delivered to hospitals and morgues. Many had been beheaded.

Just how many Iraqi civilians were killed from the war and its aftermath is not known; the Iraq Health Ministry and the Supreme Council for the Islam Revolution placed the number of 150,000. A British medical journal placed the number at 655,000, although that figure was widely disputed.

Reconciliation, which might have been an achievable goal early on, was increasingly cast aside in favor of survival. For those who remained behind in previously mixed neighborhoods, an elaborate set of rituals arose around the need to avoid being killed for one's ethnicity. According to reports, people were changing their identity cards just to survive or were carrying multiple cards. Some Sunnis were even reported to have changed the ring tones on their cell phones from Sunni religious tunes to Shia. Other Sunnis carried cassette tapes of Shia music that they played loudly in their cars as they approached checkpoints. Some hung ornaments from Shia shrines or even pictures of Muqtada al-Sadr on their windshields.

There were no safe places—not homes, mosques, or even military or police bases.

Not even hospitals. There were cases of wounded Sunnis being dragged from their hospital beds and killed. More people with gunshot wounds were treated in their homes, and women avoided hospitals for delivering newborns. One Sunni said, "we would prefer to die than to go to the hospitals."

Very strange things happen when fear takes over and society accelerates toward fracturing and disintegration. Most of the governmental authority becomes irrelevant, and centuries-old tribal traditions based upon honor and respect take over. Legitimate authority gives way to ancient practices of vengeance and domination. When credibility flows from the barrel of a gun and a willingness to punish one's enemies, even gentle Bedouin ways revert to brutality. Sheiks form little fiefdoms to protect their people, meting out severe forms of justice in order to maintain credibility in the eyes of their community.

Violence begets violence. As one sheik described the anarchy, "these days, life is a jungle. A rabbit doesn't survive in a jungle. Only a lion does." Another said, "it is necessary to take a strong stand, so that such killings will not be repeated, and so we can take our revenge." Such is the false logic of the cycle of violence.

Many of the ministries were overtaken by operatives from the Mahdi Army, the radical Shiite militia. It is impossible to tell whether a person is a government official or a member of a militia, or both. By day, they are government officials working at the Ministry of Health or Interior. By night, they are loyal operatives in the antigovernment militia.

There was little security or order, and there seemed to be no political means to establish it. The existing government was beholden to the very radical elements it is called upon to control, and thus has neither the capacity nor the will to impose order.

Iraq has been compared to many things, including America's own Wild West. But nobody in the Wild West was confused over whose side the sheriff and his deputies were on. In Iraq the streets were ruled by gunmen and gangs. The police stopped few cars for fear of being shot. They worked mostly for paychecks. Many were sympathetic to the forces that were our enemy, either out of tacit alignment or for personal survival. Many just seemed to have surrendered to the chaos and were trying to survive by playing it safe.

Hope for a rapid build-down of American forces in Iraq hinged entirely upon plans to quickly train and "stand up" Iraqi police and military forces. But that hope fell short early on for a variety of reasons; not least was the conflicted loyalties of Iraqi servicemen.

Much of the discussion about training security forces during the early years took place independent of an equally important discussion of building civic and political institutions. Training personnel is of limited value in a country in which national institutions have weak legitimacy and the loyalties of many are toward ethnic or party militia. Many of the ministries in the fragile coalition government had been infiltrated by extremist factions, and political parties developed their own militia.

Even the occasional attempt at introducing levity into the lives of Iraqis failed, with satire ending in tragedy. Walid Hassan, a Shiite, made a career out of helping war-weary Iraqis to laugh; he used his weekly television show to caricature politicians and to poke fun at poor security, gas lines, and electricity blackouts. Hassan seemed resigned to his own inevitable death; he sold his car for $5,000 and used it to buy a piece of land for his family. He said, "If tomorrow comes and I die, at least I'll give a house to my kids." The tomorrow he feared came on November 19, 2006, when he was gunned down in a Sunni neighborhood.

Perhaps the surest sign of Iraqi resignation to reality came in their response to Saddam Hussein's guilty verdict. Many Iraqis had hoped that Saddam's trial would provide the ultimate global platform to establish once and for all the dictator's many crimes against humanity. With a successful trial, the monster of Baghdad would finally receive justice, presumably sentenced to death by hanging, and the Iraqi people would experience a sense of closure.

The trial never garnered serious international attention. Saddam's guilty verdict was announced on November 5, 2006, by an Iraqi court with little credibility or international standing. Amnesty International described the trial as "a shabby affair, marred by serious flaws." By that time, most Iraqis paid little notice. Their energies were sapped by the daily struggle just to survive; their hope of a new nation was dashed. A few stopped to participate in celebratory gunfire. Victims issued solemn statements. Some devout Muslims participated in special prayers. But for the most part, the event came and passed with little notice.

AT HOME, AMERICA WAS IN THE GRIP of deep division and despair, with majorities concluding that the entire enterprise was a mistake. Many ask how this might have been prevented. What went wrong? And what can be done? The central question that will always dog the debate about Iraq is whether or not the insurgency could have been prevented during the early months of postwar operations.

Also arriving in the news in late 2006 was a report indicating that Iraq was, along with Haiti, among the most corrupt countries on Earth. Out of respect or a need to maintain a hopeful outlook, little was ever said about the lack of capacity Iraqis displayed from the beginning to run their own country. From my experience, Iraqi ineptitude and lack of initiative were major factors in the New Iraq's failure to launch. Although there were fine exceptions, many Iraqis were lacking the desire or ability to lead, even years into the operation.

In the summer of 2006, I received an email message from a colleague in the Green Zone: "The Iraqis have never worked themselves into a mindset of taking charge of their own lives—they are still stuck in the Saddam-era model that has them complaining and begging until somebody does something for them, but renders them incapable of taking action on their own. The minister of Displacement and Migration is so afraid of making a decision that we cannot even get him to issue us a letter requesting equipment and furniture that USAID is giving away for free, no strings attached."

The email concluded, "I don't think our presence here is doing any good at all." The State Department official added that he spent most of his time meeting with desperate and scared Iraqis who simply wanted help in getting out of the country.

The most tragic unfolding was watching the idea of being "an Iraqi" just disappear and become replaced with ethnic and sectarian identities. For decades, Sunnis and Shiites lived side by side in the same neighborhoods, attending the same schools, often intermarrying. Their look, dress, and speech were pretty much the same. It was considered rude to ask about a person's sect.

By mid-2006, the focus of discussion was on which option was the least undesirable. "Staying the course" was no longer considered viable. All military options emphasized a build-down and eventual withdrawal, not staying the course. Even talk of the need for a strongman emerging to re-impose order through martial law no longer seemed far-fetched.

By the fall of 2006, many concluded that America was heading for an embarrassing setback on the scale of Vietnam. Politicians readily admitted that there were no answers to the dilemma. The strongest justification for continuing military presence in Iraq was simply that conditions would be far worse if the United States withdrew. But defeating a foe or carrying out police functions in the streets had long since ceased to be viable. When asked how effective his unit was in quelling violence, one solider replied, "It feels like we are just driving around waiting to get blown up." He added: we were trained to destroy the enemy, not "to push along a country." In other words, he was saying that peace and security are functions of legitimate political authority and underlying social order, neither of which existed in Iraq.

Sabrina Tavernise described an American military movement in downtown Baghdad this way: "When Americans move through Iraq, they do so like a giant ship cutting through a thick and treacherous sea. They move slowly, displacing the harsh reality on both sides, carving out a trough of safety around them. But after they pass, reality closes back in, in all its sucking, swirling fury." [1]

That sucking, swirling fury was the tormented reality of a world without laws or rules, run by criminals, opportunistic clerics, corrupt politicians, and omnipresent armed gangs often doubling as police officers. With a conventional military operating in the midst of insurgency and anarchy, order is at best momentary and mostly imaginary, always followed immediately by an ominous atmosphere of bone-chilling distrust and lawlessness.

The real debate in the fall of 2006 was whether or not Iraq was experiencing a genuine civil war. From the standpoint of those who served in Iraq, the reality was worse than civil war. Civil war, according to one email circulating out of the Green Zone, "would be a step up." The image of civil war conveys major military forces arrayed against each other. What Iraq was experiencing was total anarchy, with literally hundreds of armed groups with little purpose in mind except vengeance.

New York Times columnist Thomas Friedman, an early backer of the war, captured it well in late November 2006: "This country is so broken it can't even have a proper civil war. There are so many groups vying for power that nobody is even remotely in control of the entire country anymore. The carnage escalates while we stand by and watch." [2] Friedman argued that the only choice was to either get out and leave them to their own fate, or "re-invade" and do the job right this time.

Misunderstanding the Requirements for Success

Could we have "done it right" the first time? The answer is probably no. It is unlikely that the U.S. Congress would have authorized invading Iraq if the condition for doing so was committing three times the levels of force, and committing to spend upwards of a trillion dollars over ten years building institutions and doing whatever it took to cultivate democracy from scratch.

The only logical conclusion, with the benefit of hindsight, is that the invasion might not have been carried out if the facts on the ground had been fully assessed. Former Navy Secretary John Lehman said it well: "There was a total misunderstanding of the requirements for success." Whether it was misunderstanding or willful indifference will be debated for the next century.

Iraq has already been through many chapters since the liberation in early 2003. My story is about the earliest phases, the immediate postwar environment, where I maintain the die was cast. Through the 2005–06 period, Iraq suffered a devastating insurgency and bloody ethnic score-settling, as detailed above.

Starting with the president's decision in 2007 to introduce a "surge" in Iraq, yet another chapter has been written. The outlook is suddenly more optimistic.

Whatever the outcome, as of this writing America is in its sixth year of operation in Iraq, longer than either World War I, World War II, the Korean War, or our own civil war. Many of the factors leading to the length and difficulty of the conflict were determined during the phase in which I served, which I attempt to detail in the pages ahead.

Chapter 1

Prepping for Deployment
The Search for Direction

Jay Garner had a very impressive resume. The tough-talking three-star general had served two tours in Vietnam, led two air defense units in Germany, helped to develop the Patriot missile system, commanded the U.S. Army Space and Strategic Defense Command, and retired as assistant vice chief of staff.

Perhaps more importantly, Garner had also led Operation Provide Comfort after the 1991 Gulf War. In that role, he secured the Kurdish areas in Iraq. Consequently, he was a true hero to the Kurds.

At five feet seven inches, the general is a barrel-chested guy who looks like he did a lot of bodybuilding in his youth. I never saw the man wearing suits. He wore dress shirts, usually white and always unbuttoned at the neck. Well into his sixties, he walked in that "chest first" gait of a natural leader, one who bursts into a room knowing he is in charge or will soon take it. He could cut in on conversations or break away from them without seeming rude. In appearance and voice, he was gruff. But Garner, a native Floridian, always exuded a "Southern Gentleman" essence; you could not doubt his core goodness and decency. Like few people I've ever met, he projected an air of hope about people. This was especially helpful as displayed toward the Iraqis. They needed to see that someone carried hope for them. They had to know that someone believed that, if given the chance, they would do the right and honorable thing.

As a new member of General Garner's ORHA team, I reported at the Pentagon early Monday morning, March 10, 2003. I knew that I wanted this mission. But I also faced a normal degree of internal conflict about it.

Of course, my reasons for signing up were solely related to the post-invasion reconstruction and humanitarian purposes (consistent with the limiting scope of ORHA's name). The decision to go to war was almost irrelevant to the ORHA task. Nevertheless, I had thrown myself into extensive research on the reasons for the war. I saw the removal of Saddam Hussein as an act of justice; he towered among the tyrants of history and was a one-man human rights shredder. Although the act of removing a regime is tricky under international law and had to be reserved for the most extreme cases, I was convinced that if moral and legal grounds did not exist in the case of Saddam, surely no such justification exists (or had ever existed) anywhere.

To say I had a peculiar upbringing is to understate the facts. I was raised in the seriously pacifist subculture of the Mennonites, one of the so-called "historic peace churches." And the Amish effect in Lancaster County had also, I'm sure, influenced my thinking. But I had never been a devoted pacifist. Nor had I advocated it for national policy. At a very early point in my life, during the Cold War period, I moved decisively toward the just war theory. It became clear to me that military deterrence was the only thing standing between peace and horror.

Even with my background, I always admired people who served in the military. I was never a critic of the military. They were the people who were responsible for maintaining the peace. For as long as I remembered having an opinion on the subject, I had a morally realistic view of the need both to have military power on hand in order to maintain the peace and to be willing to occasionally use it. But for me, using the sword was always the option of last resort—always.

I was what you might call a reluctant hawk. I was equally unimpressed with those who tilted toward militarism and those whose views of peace struck me as naive. As a just war proponent, I saw the world as a tough, conflict-riddled place where choices are often between two evils. Much of this issue really comes down to how one thinks about the human condition.

In many cases, inaction is the most unjust and violent choice, a fact that even the Iraq war critics are quick to admit in cases like Rwanda or Sudan. As those cases illustrate, more people die on a given day in the world from a lack of adequate military and police protection than die from military aggression. So, using the military to remove Saddam never gave me moral qualms. This was probably one of those rare examples of where it was the only solution, or so it seemed at the time.

As I entered the strange new world of the Pentagon, I encountered numerous paradigm-shattering realities. One was that, contrary to popular perception, the military is often the most reluctant to use its might. The simple reason is that they know a lot about the horrors of war. The military also learned from the Vietnam experience how quickly they, and not the politicians, can take the blame for an unpopular war. Often, the pressure to move toward war comes from the political sector, not the military. Career military men and women know more than anyone about the things that can go wrong when a mission is flawed.[1]

The people on my team were not caught up in military issues; that just wasn't our expertise. At every step of the planning, we were guided by humanitarian ideals; we were focused on setting captives free from one of the world's worst butchers. I agreed when Paul Wolfowitz referred to the evil of Hitler and the moral necessity of confrontation. He passionately made the case that the civilized world waited too long in confronting the evil of Nazism, and that wait had doomed millions to their deaths and caused a world war. I too saw the elimination of Hitler as an act of kindness to the human race. And, with or without weapons of mass destruction (WMDs), I believed that Saddam was clearly a menace that sooner or later had to be dealt with.

From the time when I first began working with the Garner team, I had remained at USAID. But as an invasion appeared more certain, General Garner worked hard and fast to secure the team of civilians that would go with him into Iraq. On March 13, he asked for a decision. Would I go to Iraq?

From a family perspective, this was as big a decision as any I had ever made. Naturally, I called Sheryl, my wife. I knew I was being thrown into a dangerous situation, but just how dangerous would be determined by decisions made by others, not me. In simple fact, the danger level could not be predicted; it would depend on conditions following the almost-certain war.

How much protection would we really have? To what degree would the violent elements of Saddam's regime have been swept away? What would happen to all of those Ba'ath party loyalists who owed all of their wealth, status, and power to a single man? Just how happy and friendly would the Iraqi people be with Americans taking over? It all came down to the fact that I could not make a decision about going into Iraq based on those questions. My reasons would have to transcend the element of danger. I knew that I felt both a duty to my country and a deep desire to help see America and the mission succeed.

Sheryl had to process the decision with even less information. For her, it boiled down to the fact that I was going to be sent into the most volatile region in the world. After talking it through with Sheryl and our children, I told General Garner that I would go to Iraq.

Pentagon Days

As I and others signed up, the whole venture began to find great traction. Momentum began to build; the morning meetings at the Pentagon were filled with electricity. You could feel an acceleration toward invasion. We all kept closely tuned to what was being said out of the White House and to developments in the Middle East.

Circling the table for those days of planning were General Garner; his deputies Ron Adams and Jerry Bates; Mike Mobbs; Barbara Bodine, a retired diplomat who had been assigned to the team by the State Department; and a variety of military personnel representing intelligence and logistical issues. Every day the group grew in size and stature. This was turning into a very impressive group, filled with people who spoke knowledgeably about what lay ahead. From our main meeting room, you could see into other rooms where specialists crawled on hands and knees poring over military maps.

One day a British general, assigned to the operation, told a story of some Iraqi soldiers who had rushed across the border and tried to surrender to the invading force. They were told, he said laughing, "to go back and return in a couple of weeks." That little moment captured the prevailing idea that Iraq was ripe for the taking, and resistance would collapse. The focus in most of the meetings was on military operations, which few doubted would quickly overwhelm inferior Iraqi forces. No one ever doubted that the military operation would be a cakewalk.

Occasionally, we were reminded that we were being sent in to handle the hard part—winning the postwar peace. But the optimism ran so high that no one seemed too concerned about what would follow. If Iraqis wanted their liberation as we expected, they would probably turn on Saddam quickly and transfer their loyalties to their liberators. They would, of course, quickly sign up to build a new nation. Any doubts were expressed quietly in side conversations.

Although confidence was high inside the Pentagon, the international debate raged louder as the United States moved closer to D-day. The number of Americans protesting the looming war in communities across America seemed to grow day by day. That number included people from my home

It didn't take long after arriving to conclude that our light-skinned GMC Suburbans were hardly a match for the reality of the streets. Civilians were required to travel with "force protection." Most of our guards were highly proficient retired special operations officers who came to Iraq under contract to provide personnel security.

community, many of whom shared my war-resisting roots. I knew some personally; I was sure they would have a few things to say to me directly once they learned about my involvement.

As I came and went from the Pentagon, large groups of war protestors stood gathered at the entrance beating peace drums. Naturally, that sight took me back to the flood of images from the Vietnam era. As I daily walked past the protests, I wondered if the country could, in time, turn against this foreign venture as it did the Vietnam War. Could I personally end up having a cloud hanging over my head? Would my family feel a twinge of embarrassment when the subject might come up years later?

Like my ORHA colleagues, I was prepared to act on faith. For all practical purposes, I was now a military man. Military people always move out on faith. Significant action is not possible without faith in many people and systems, unseen and unknown. I accepted that.

The departure date was surely growing close. I was being pulled into a swirling vortex of planning for postwar reconstruction, all the while rushing to straighten out personal affairs so I could deploy when the order came. In addition, we were all involved in nonstop planning meetings from 7 a.m. until late at night. Soon, we would all be shipped to Fort Myers and Fort Meade for technical training in antiterrorism and self-defense, including training in the use of nuclear-biological-chemical (NBC) protection gear, and detection and evasion of booby traps and land mines.

While the senior civilians at the Pentagon were focused on the big issues, the mid-level army staff that organized the training of the civilians seemed to embrace a different perspective of what might lay ahead. In their presence, we would descend from the planning stratosphere of big ideas for rebuilding Iraq to the hard reality of gearing up in army boots and protection gear for our landing in Baghdad. It represented a cold dose of reality.

We were told to assume that in its desperation, the departing regime would do anything possible to harm or embarrass the United States. They might load the city with booby traps; they may even reserve a few WMDs for our arrival. Anything was possible with Saddam, and it generated great concern for those in our "force protection," the term for keeping American personnel safe and alive.

We were trained in the use of 9mm handguns. That was, of course, a very dramatic leap from the world of laptops, organizational charts, and Power-Point presentations. The assumption that we civilians would always be well removed from harm's way pretty much evaporated at that moment. It was a little detail that I did not pass along to my family until much later.

At this point, it was pretty clear that our operation would be embedded in the military's. The fact that we had to prove proficient in using the 9mm before leaving Fort Meade conveyed rather crisply and without much subtlety that we would likely end up in threatening environments.

We would not be allowed to depart without five mandatory shots: tetanus, malaria, smallpox, anthrax, and TB. We were prepared for a wide spectrum of dangers from chemical agents to mosquito-borne disease. And they educated us about a range of illnesses generated by fatigue, poor sanitation, and the suffocating heat that would envelop us night and day.

Naturally, with this kind of preparation, I wondered what my first day on the job would be like in downtown Baghdad. It would certainly be a far cry from my daily routine in Washington. After the physical, I was directed to a small room in the crowded basement office at the Pentagon to meet with military lawyers. They assisted me in writing a basic will and giving my wife power of attorney. Writing a will certainly brought a clear perspective to the mission.

Five days of checklists seemed overwhelming. I had the distinct impression that this phase of the operation was thought through last and was being patched together hastily. Given the hot climate and difficult environment of Baghdad, we were told to pack lots of casual clothes such as Dockers slacks and polo shirts. Even though we would be senior government officials conducting official business, we were not asked to pack business wear. I packed one blazer and one pair of dress slacks in the hope that we would have some occasion to dress up, if for no other reason than out of respect for the Iraqi people. I knew they were a proud people, and I thought they might take offense from our casual appearance.

We were issued all kinds of regular army gear, including a helmet, boots, three sets of regular army shirts and pants, overcoats, and Kevlar vests. I couldn't really imagine using this stuff. I was, after all, a civilian. But the helmet and Kevlar vest turned out to be the most prized property in Iraq; I would wear them every time I went out.

We were finally informed that we would be living at a hotel in Kuwait City. Any further information on our location was classified. The last thing that anyone wanted was for our headquarters to become the target of missile attacks from the north or terrorist operations. What if Saddam organized a shadow movement of assassins and infiltrators just to inflict havoc on the operation?

The team continued to take shape. But six days before deployment, we had a grand total of five people for civil administration sitting around a small table in the basement of the Pentagon. Bob Woodward and others have revealed the severe limitations of the team. For whatever reason, Garner was simply not given the people he needed. I later learned of the wrangling all across the administration over the structure and staffing of ORHA.

President Bush had issued an executive order that essentially commanded department heads across the entire U.S. government to lend qualified staff to the operation. Many balked, either because their agencies were already overextended or out of a concern for personnel safety. Apparently even a presidential decree could not trump bureaucratic prerogatives.

Initially, the staff positions would be funded out of already strapped budgets at places like USAID. No new money would be appropriated for another six months. We all felt like we were assembling the vehicle while driving it.

By week's end, the daily meetings at the Pentagon ballooned into standing room only. Officers from the various services marched through the meeting rooms giving brisk reports on the timing of military operations. The atmosphere was charged with calm and composed intensity. Colonel Dennis DeGraff and the other officers responsible for the logistics of the operation were under especially intense pressure. But they were completely professional and unflappable. Had the room become engulfed in flames, I'm sure they would have directed people into escape in that same clear, low-key voice of assured authority. One officer mumbled "blessed are the calm," describing the capability of the military that is so impressive. For the most part, all staffing was marked by that characteristic. Crises tend to bring that out in people. Frankly, I was proud of this group.

Finally and thankfully, the staffing pace picked up. From day to day, the Garner team continued to swell. What started as five quickly became eight, then twelve. Something had apparently broken free in the interagency support for our mission. Very qualified people, like retired ambassadors and senior policy analysts, were joining the team. These professionals displayed a "can-do" spirit, and I noticed their speech patterns were very direct and brief. They were not given to quarreling, second-guessing, or wasting time. They were the kind of people you wanted nearby in a dangerous place.

Strangely, very few of these people lasted very long. The working environment became very political. Several never made it to Baghdad at all; two went home shortly after arriving in Kuwait City, and the rest ended up having fairly short stays in Iraq. Many of these people who came together at the Pentagon and later in Kuwait City would be long forgotten within months of arrival in Iraq.

Only a few from the original group served for an extended time. In fact, at a small Pentagon event commemorating the end of the Coalition Provisional Authority (CPA) and Ambassador Bremer's return on June 28, 2004, Secretary of Defense Donald Rumsfeld referred to the team as though it had continued intact from the beginning. He was apparently unaware that no one from that original group was even in the room except me (and maybe one or two others). Most of the original group did not serve for more than a couple months.

Army logistics was responsible for sorting out and providing the supply requirements (from vehicles to cell phones). But it was hard to determine supply and logistics needs for a mission that might be over shortly after the war was concluded. Every aspect of planning was tied back to core assumptions about the missions—how long we would be there and the scale of our operation.

Days before deployment, we were all asked to write memos about our concepts of operations, de-Ba'athification, and forms of communication for reaching and educating the Iraqi people. Surely, I thought, these things had already been worked out. Why was our group, days from leaving, being asked to develop detailed operational plans? Was this simply a case of one hand not knowing what the other was doing, or was it possible that this type of planning had simply not been done?

Of course, most of us in the room were policy planners by training and experience. So, we charged into the assignment. I had designed many organizations and government programs; I could define the scopes and parameters of work. Let the imagination run, we were told. But, still, it seemed strange to engage in such an exercise in the bowels of the biggest government agency and biggest war planning machine on planet Earth. Was it really the case that senior policy people in the Office of the Secretary of Defense (OSD) either believed that this planning was not needed, or that the details would be worked out following the war?

I remember asking, "Haven't these matters already been addressed?" The deputy secretary for policy, Doug Feith, ran a very secretive operation. Most of us had met him only once or twice. I later learned that many of the plans from Feith's office were considered very "close hold." That was true in part because they—the Pentagon people—didn't trust the diverse group that Jay Garner had assembled under ORHA, and in part because the plans were never fully developed at the level of operational detail. The thought and planning that had gone into the big questions of politics and governance were little more than broad concept papers. An operational plan for postwar civil administration simply did not exist.

I and others expected that at some point the Defense Intelligence Agency would bring us detailed printouts of what was known about Iraqi ministries and government functions. I assumed they would give us assessments under various possible scenarios after the government was decapitated. That never happened. Most of us assumed that we would step into a model similar to that of architects and general contractors who had worked through the plan in detail. We would more or less be the carpenters and finishers. But, except for identifying some of the big humanitarian problems that might logically emerge—like health, food, water, and sanitation—there simply was no comprehensive plan for reorganizing and managing civil administration.

We later discovered that the lack of planning was because people in high places simply did not believe they would be necessary. Jay Garner was told repeatedly to plan for a "short stay, light touch." He was given an organization (ORHA); a mission to enter Iraq after the war, fix a few humanitarian problems, and organize a quick transition to Iraqi control; and then . . . leave.

Of course, during those days, General Garner was quickly assessing the staggering dimensions of the mission. The old military tactician was caught between the hard realities of postwar reconstruction and an administration that was primarily focused on invasion. According to Bob Woodward, when Garner presented postwar plans to Secretary Rumsfeld, "Garner could see that his mind was on the upcoming invasion, not the aftermath. Garner found himself waking up at 2 a.m., dictating to-do lists. He realized he had been given an impossible task but the military man's can-do attitude prevailed over doubt." [2]

To be fair, it is true that no one had a template for militarily replacing a Middle East dictator in a country with a long history of ethnic strife, religious divisions, and no democratic experience. It had never been attempted before. There is no such thing as a perfect plan that can be rolled off the shelf for every contingency.

But, at the same time, the premise of the invasion and postwar reconstruction was deeply flawed. The casual attitude about postwar realities, the enfeebling lack of sufficient troops or resources, and the idea of just handing it all off to "the Iraqis" all grew out of defective assumptions. For example, no one seemed to realize that Iraq had no towering figures who would compare to South Africa's Nelson Mandela, who possessed moral and political gravitas and could emerge to unify a nation that had a known history of deadly sectarian division. The closest thing to a template might have been the British experience in establishing the new Iraqi nation following the collapse of the Ottoman Empire. Of course, that result was not very encouraging.

All of these major risks and uncertainties—postwar looting, dealing with the remnants of the Saddam regime, the need for adequate resources and security—were knowable prior to the invasion. They were inherent in the decision to launch the military operation and in fact had been laid out by planners at the State Department. With all of the evidence, pro and con, placed on the table, surely the president had to know the historical dimensions of this high-stakes gamble. I am convinced he did know, at least in broad strokes.

In simple fact, the ORHA team had to be prepared for anything that came. Most of us could not imagine Iraq being governable after three decades of dictatorship. My own focus on the planks and principles of civil society convinced me of the absolute necessity for restoring the community-level institutions and cultural support systems. If we were going to liberate the Iraqi people, we needed to put in place conditions for sustaining that liberty. To simply get rid of Saddam and leave the rest to chance made little sense.[3]

As a team, we tried to think through arriving in Baghdad and taking over all official governmental functions. How much of the previous government would still be functioning? Would the workforce be intact and responsive when we showed up? Would the populace be eager to move forward? Would the government structures still be standing?

Of course, we knew that a plan would have to be developed for preserving governance; in short, we would have to keep some government officials and get rid of others. As we would eventually discover, this issue would probably be the most critical to success. It was the backdrop for everything. We were taking over a country that had been under the ruthless domination of a dictatorial regime. Presumably, everyone who had been charged with high-level responsibilities under Saddam's Ba'athist regime would be unfit to serve.

Pentagon discussions on this issue went quickly to the liberation of Germany from the Nazis. Of course, people would have to be replaced. But how deep do you go? What do you do with these deposed regime loyalists? The issue of replacing senior Ba'ath party officials and Saddam loyalists would continually percolate and never really be resolved. It was just impossible to know with certainty who should go and who should stay.

Doing it right would require a huge system to evaluate, case by case, tens of thousands of Ba'athists, and we weren't planning huge systems for anything. One presentation proposed contracting a major firm to screen the entire workforce of the Iraqi government! How would that even be possible in a country in which millions served? How long would it take? What would it cost and who would pay?

Speaking of expenses, at the time there was no special appropriation for a postwar administration. Whenever the subject came up, everyone just assumed that we would use existing Iraqi resources, perhaps oil revenues or recovered gold or currency reserves.

Fort Meade

As war and our pending deployment became more certain, we were bussed to Fort Meade for further training and outfitting. Those days became a blur of army gear, antiterrorism training, cultural education, medical procedures, and other pre-deployment checklists.

Time ran out before I could get my dog tag, which was somewhat bothersome; having one would certainly improve chances of survival in the event of an "incident." I had promised my family that I would do everything to get home safely. Obviously, I owed them that. Beyond my own desire to live, they deserved my best effort in ensuring that their father and husband returned home safely.

During the Fort Meade training, we were told that we would be responsible for things like management of garbage and utilities, emergency shelters and food rations for displaced people, clearing roadways, and security patrols. Someone mentioned that we would "restore newspapers." It really sounded like the kind of emergency relief operation you could expect after a bad storm swept through town. It didn't sound at all like nation building. In fact, not once did any Fort Meade briefing (or in any other in that month and a half of preparation) convey that we would be responsible for managing all the core functions of a nation. We were encouraged to believe that much of the existing government would be in a functioning state and that Iraqi technocrats could fairly quickly resume operations. Less clear was what would replace the actual regime of Saddam Hussein once he was taken out.

Broader responsibilities for governance—justice and law enforcement, energy production and distribution, immigration, labor, commerce, foreign affairs, education, culture, and women's affairs—increasingly became part of the discussion in our meetings. We would also need to be an interim law-enforcing agency during a transition into full constitutional government in Iraq. We would need commercial law, penal law, and labor law to replace the arbitrary law that existed under Saddam.

Yet, at no point prior to our arrival in Iraq was the term "occupation" ever used. It was just assumed that we would help, or advise, the Iraqis in restoring these essential functions. The predominant impression was that we would fix a few things and then hand everything over, and this would happen very quickly.

The senior advisors would be assigned to reorganize twenty-one (out of twenty-four) ministries of the national government in Baghdad. Bruce Moore and Buck Walters would serve as the regional coordinators for ORHA. But "we will not actually run things." I interpreted this vague and confusing direction to mean that we would advise and help build foundations for a new government system. It was all plausible if the positive scenario would just unfold as hoped.

For example, we were certain that public servants, the police, and the army would return to work and that the monies to pay them would come from the $1.6 billion in frozen Iraqi assets. The apparent policy wanted public servants and police to stay in place. Of course, we would soon learn that a major policy battle was raging over "de-Ba'athification" (what to do with those who served in Saddam's government). We were told that an attempt would be made to use the Iraqi army for reconstruction. This was the first time that this contentious issue surfaced. Reconstruction would be a very labor-intensive business, and the idled Iraqi army would be ideal for that.

Understanding Iraq

At Fort Meade, we were given intense briefings on the historical, social, and political landscape of Iraq. It brought to mind my work back at USAID: I had sorted through the issues that so divided the Middle East; those same issues suddenly made their way to center stage in and following the 9/11 terrorist attacks.

Iraq, as the briefings explained, was made up of Kurds, Sunnis, and Shia. Of course, most Americans knew only two words about Iraq: Saddam Hussein. And, yes, he was the most dominant feature of the land. Saddam stood ruthlessly at the helm of Iraq, but in reality he was also the lid that kept the internal divisions from coming to a boil.

We learned that Iraq was a nation of 23 million, roughly the size and population of California. It was staggering to think that our little group of several dozen people would be airlifted into Baghdad to help run a nation the size and population and California.

Ethnically, Iraq is about 80 percent Arab, 15 to 20 percent Kurd, and maybe 5 percent Assyrians. Most live in the middle of the country and along the two great rivers, the Tigris and the Euphrates, which had sustained life there since the beginning. Except for maybe 3 percent of the Iraqis who identify themselves as Christian, Iraq is Muslim. Of the 95 percent who are Muslims, about 60 to 65 percent are Shia and the rest Sunni.

Views of downtown Baghdad from across the Tigris River.

I had attended many conferences sponsored by the State Department and think tanks on the state of Islam and the growing tensions due to the increasing Islamic radicalization. A genuine extremist movement was emerging. The most violent extremists, as we all know now, were signing up for terrorism. But it had not been that long since Iraq had been viewed as a country of moderate Islam with higher-than-average education. Many believed that in Iraq, unlike Egypt and Saudi Arabia, Islam might even emerge as a force for democratization. The fact that Saddam had suppressed open conflict might actually have set the stage for a new era.

All Muslims trace their religion back to Muhammad in 610 AD, but that common origin did little to produce a common view of religion or a host of social, cultural, and governance issues. A vast chasm divides typical American attitudes from Islamic perspectives on God, pluralism, tolerance, personal responsibility, and many other issues. Perhaps the most significant difference is the enormous implications spawned by one of the simplest words in our vocabulary—freedom.

As Islam was discussed, we received our first introduction to that grossly underestimated cultural divide between Iraq and America. In fact, our countries have very little in common. That fundamental reality explains many of the miscalculations that followed.

And, of course, great chasms also exist among the various ethnic and religious factions in Iraq. Overwhelming majorities of Iraqis held in common a longing to be rid of Saddam. But that may be where the similarities stopped. The depth of the conflict of visions within the Iraqi people would quickly become apparent. Americans are often quick to project our own idealism and goodwill on the rest of the world while considering reports of irreconcilable differences as unduly pessimistic. After all, that is the kind of optimism that Americans routinely bring to their own divisions and problems.

We just assume that people everywhere want what we want. To the degree that the American people are even familiar with Iraq's internal divisions, we tend to view them through the same lens as we might view, say, Puerto Rican or Chinese communities in any American city. Although often volatile and raucous, they are generally homogenous. Leading up to the war in Iraq, too little attention was given to the reality that, in a country presumably united by religion, the hardliners in one religious faction viewed the other group as heretics and worthy of death.

Neither was sufficient attention given to the consequence of the Sunni minority having ruled over the Shiite majority for thirty years. Under Saddam, the Sunnis seized much of the nation's wealth and violently suppressed the Shiite majority in the south as well as the Kurdish minority in the north. Those scars are profoundly deep and difficult.

We also received a very helpful introduction to various nuances of Iraqi culture. For example, we were told the Iraqis had a completely different concept of time. They did not relate to clocks the way we did. I remembered this later, as so many Iraqis ran hours late for meetings. In fact, they called attention to our own preoccupation with time with a line that, I'm sure, they had used for many decades: "they have the watches, we have the time." Translation: the Americans (like the British and others) will be here for a while and then be gone; be patient, we will frustrate and exhaust them, and we will have our country to ourselves.

We were also warned that their sense of individual responsibility was severely limited, due partly to culture and partly to dictatorship. In America, the sun rises and sets on the individual; that carries strengths and weaknesses. Among the strengths is a clearer sense of individual rights and responsibilities. We were also briefed on the way Iraqis identify with the group. Everything the individual does relates in some way to deeply ingrained communal practices and beliefs.

Near the end of our Fort Meade training, General Garner addressed the group. As a good commander, General Garner wanted the group to be prepared for the worst. He said that the "first ten days will be as chaotic as hell." That was an easy prediction to make, except that he might have said the first ten months. Or the first three years. Or that establishing order might take an indefinite period of time. But "ten days" stuck with me. It certainly implied that, after a short period of time, chaos would be replaced with order. Like everyone on the team, Garner was hoping that the full might of the American military would establish order and authority so that we could move in to do our job.

Garner appeared tough and unapproachable. But he was bright, decisive, and big hearted. He cared deeply about his people and what they signed up for. It sounded strange for a general to say "you're gonna bond like you've never bonded in your life." We would be "making history," and that was a high privilege.

Home

After the Fort Meade training, I headed home. I talked to each family member separately and together, sharing many of my inner thoughts about the road ahead. The backdrop for our conversation was the palpable sense of dread and fear in the country over the reality of terrorism and now war. Naturally, many feared that an invasion of Iraq would produce an immediate retaliatory response by Islamic terrorists. The president's Homeland Security advisor, Tom Ridge, was making regular television appearances, dispensing practical advice on commonsense remedies about food, water, and medical supplies. He also generated some ridicule in his comments about duct tape. But this was uncharted territory. Never before had ordinary Americans had their lives disrupted with this kind of information.

Throughout the post-9/11 period, I had communicated as much and as clearly as possible with my family. One of my emails read: "We are entering a period of uncertainty with no clear understanding of where events are taking us. There are real dangers of increased terrorism during this time. We must think very clearly and have our wits about us; not be overcome by fear nor be oblivious to the dangers. Fear is a natural physical reaction; a logical response to perceived danger. It prepares you to take preventive action in order to keep yourself safe. But a paralyzing fear is the enemy."

The deep springs of faith informed and fed my attitude and, of course, my communication. One of my email messages to my family reminded them: "Fear, for persons of faith, is an act of disbelief because it assumes that God is not sufficient as our protector. Whatever our fate, whether we live or die, our mission is to be faithful."

We had a wonderful weekend together. And then it was time to leave. When I kissed our youngest, Margaret, good-bye, a lump filled my throat. What were the chances that I was leaving for the last time? Unlikely, of course. But the chance was sufficient to reprioritize everything. That is why those good-byes are always seared in the mind; every little detail is vividly remembered—the color of my children's eyes, the speech inflections, the precise outlines of their profiles. Maybe I will be killed, brought home seriously disabled, or perhaps become a hostage. What would it be like to settle back into normal living? What will I see and experience there, and how will it change me?

ON MARCH 18, THE PRESIDENT WARNED SADDAM of imminent military action. He offered a plan that would prevent military invasion: Saddam and his two sons must leave the country within forty-eight hours. With this ultimatum, it was now clear that the only one who could prevent a war was Saddam himself.

The following day, when the warning had expired without any response, the president announced the early stages of military action. Bombs fell on Baghdad on March 20. The war was on. And I would soon be there.

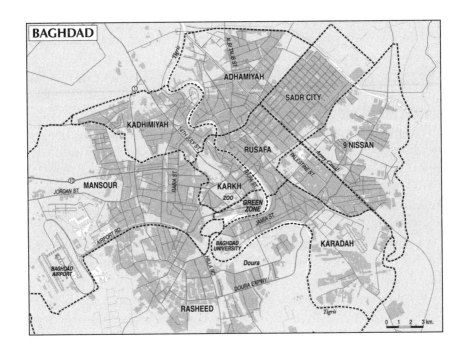

BAGHDAD

ADHAMIYAH

SADR CITY

KADHIMIYAH

RUSAFA

9 NISSAN

MANSOUR

JORDAN ST.

KARKH

ZOO

GREEN ZONE

PALESTINE ST.

Army Canal

14TH JULY ST.

RABIA ST.

RAHL ST.

JAMIA ST.

BAGHDAD UNIVERSITY

Doura

KARADAH

BAGHDAD AIRPORT

AIRPORT RD.

HILLA RD.

DOURA EXPWY.

RASHEED

Tigris

ALBI TALIB ST.

Tigris

0 1 2 3 km.

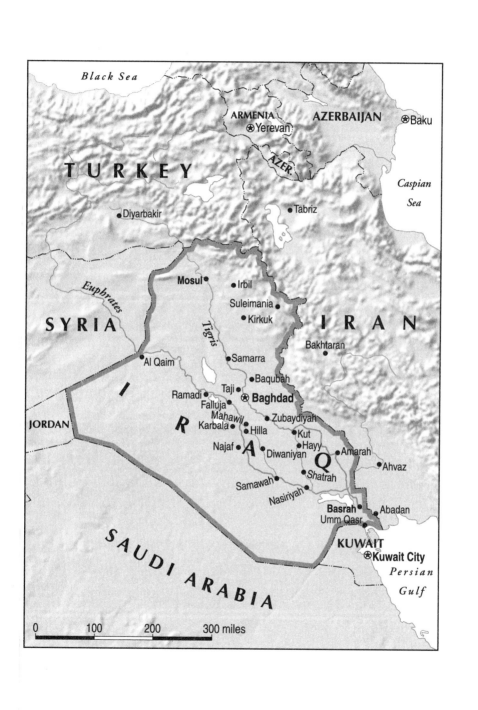

Black Sea

ARMENIA   AZERBAIJAN   ⊗Baku
⊗Yerevan

T U R K E Y   Caspian
                                            Sea
AZER.

•Diyarbakir   •Tabriz

                    Euphrates   Mosul•   •Irbil
                                         Suleimania
S Y R I A   Tigris   •Kirkuk   I R A N

                        •Samarra   Bakhtaran•

          •Al Qaim
                              •Baqubah
     I   Taji•
              Ramadi•   ⊗ Baghdad
              Falluja•
JORDAN   Mahawil•   •Zubaydiyah
          R   Karbala• •Hilla
          Najaf•   •Kut
               A   •Hayy
                   Diwaniyan   Q   •Amarah
                                      •Ahvaz
                        •Shatrah
          Samawah•

               Nasiriyah•
                           Basrah• •Abadan
                           Umm Qasr

                        KUWAIT
S A U D I   A R A B I A   ⊗Kuwait City
                            Persian
                             Gulf

0   100   200   300 miles

Chapter 2

Camping Out in Kuwait
Expecting "Brief Stay, Light Touch"

WE HAD ALL SAID OUR GOOD-BYES. Our planning work at the Pentagon and training at Forte Meade was behind us. We cleared out of our space and loaded up our documents and gear. We were off to Kuwait City.

Several weeks earlier, General Garner had sent a team into the region to find a temporary home and office for the group. With little time to plan and after reviewing the limited options, he decided that the only practical solution was leasing a large portion of the Kuwait Hilton. It would serve as our home for the next six weeks. The lovely, well-equipped, world-class property sits on the banks of the Arabian Sea. Aside from the facility itself, our location was the best possible; Kuwait City is reasonably secure and within easy traveling distance to Baghdad.

We took over an entire waterfront section of two-story villas, each with comfortable bedrooms and balconies facing the beach. The downstairs parlor in each villa was converted to office space. Very quickly, the computers, desks, and other office equipment that had been hastily purchased or leased on the local market filled the area. The walls were covered from end to end with maps, diagrams, and organizational charts.

Effectively, we turned a large resort hotel into a campus. In fact, the grounds resembled a university campus with broad walkways winding through large open spaces of rich, rolling, lushly irrigated grass. At almost any time, you could see small groups of four or five staff members in deep discussion across the lawns and in the Hilton's own Starbucks.

Staying at the Kuwait City Hilton made perfect sense on practical grounds because little else was available and we had no idea how quickly we would need to pack and move north to Baghdad. But it was also known to

The Kuwait Towers, a prominent part of the skyline of Kuwait City.

be one of the playpens for the Middle East's tycoons and privileged political class. It would not be the last time we worried about the symbolism of our accommodations; our next headquarters would be Saddam Hussein's opulent palace on the banks of the Tigris River.

But looks were deceiving; the war was under way just north of us. In fact, on March 26, two missiles hit the Kuwait City area. Jay Garner's deputy Ron Adams issued a stern warning about our need to keep biochemical protection masks with us at all times; this wasn't a joke, he insisted. "You have been issued the equipment and trained in its use for a reason," he barked.

He was right. The next day, the sirens blared again at 11 p.m. warning us of a Scud-missile attack. This time we all promptly jumped into our chemical suits. Not knowing what else to do while I waited out the attack, I dropped into bed and fell sound asleep. I woke up wearing the full chemical suit . . . and saw the chemical mask lying beside me!

On March 29, we were told that a low-flying missile had hit in the area and we needed to be cautious. At 5 p.m. sirens blared again and we hurried to the bomb shelter. Later, we learned that the Iraqi missile launcher was destroyed by one of our F-16s. As a civilian, I had never had such clear personal reason to be so thankful for the protection afforded by our military.

The recurring missile attacks certainly raised questions among our team members; why were missiles from southern Iraq getting through to Kuwait? The Iraqi army had reportedly retreated north or was disinterested in fighting. At one point there were media reports of our military facing surprising resistance, and then another of the troops getting bogged down in a sandstorm. We couldn't help wondering whether the liberation of Iraq might be tougher than anticipated. Were there miscalculations?

In an email to Sheryl, I wrote: "the word incongruous comes to mind when I try to describe the combination of living in luxury yet having to respond to air raid sirens on a fairly regular basis, which means keeping gas masks and body suit (we were trained to jump into them in a minute or less) close at hand in case a missile actually got through. Only two did, one striking a downtown Kuwait mall and the other dropped harmlessly into the sea."

The missiles were Silkworms and were launched from Iraq. We were protected by American patriot antimissile defense systems, one of the most efficient air defense systems ever devised (General Garner helped to develop it).

Because of the possible danger from local Shiite radicals, we were required to travel in convoys on the few occasions we went out in Kuwait. At that time in Kuwait, large majorities of local Arabs actually liked Americans, thanks to the fact that America saved Kuwait as a nation in 1991 when it expelled Saddam's occupying army. Nevertheless, we were warned that even this island of friendliness had a small underground minority of radicals whose loyalties were to Islam or Arab nationalism and who really did hate us.

It was also incongruous that we were living in the Kuwait Hilton's quite wonderful housing, enjoying its food and services, on our way to the extreme austerity of Baghdad. For the first two weeks in Iraq we would eat MREs (meals ready to eat), sleep on cots in sleeping bags, and clean ourselves with towels and bottled water. The Hilton's restaurant represented an almost absurd preparation for Iraq. The multiple buffets of exquisitely prepared meals and mountains of artfully presented desserts would compare to the best of London and New York.

Though the place was luxurious, the workload at the Hilton was anything but a breeze. We all knew the reality of the situation, and it took almost no time after arriving to jump into the most intense pace and heavy workload. Dozens of urgent tasks remained to be finished, and we all knew we could be thrust into Baghdad at any time. We had to be ready to move quickly, and yet we did not feel even close to being ready to deploy.

Most of us worked seven days a week, partly because of the workload and partly because our normal weekend practices did not match up with those of the Arab culture. Sunday, our Sabbath, was just another workday in the Middle East, so we considered it a "reduced workday," which really meant only slightly fewer hours. Friday, a normal workday for us, marked the beginning of the Muslim "Gathering Day" (Sabbath). Out of deference to the local culture, we at least declared Fridays as non-meeting days.

For the weeks I was in Kuwait City, my family knew only that I was in an undisclosed place in the Persian Gulf. Secrecy was vital; we did not want to become an inviting target for Saddam Hussein's bombing campaign. Although the potential fury of his present-day military strength was, at that time, unknown, the fact remained that he had invaded Kuwait City in 1991.

At that time, he used poor jobless males from Iraqi towns and villages as cannon fodder. Not surprisingly, Kuwait was as eager as any Arab city to get rid of Saddam, yet there was also great trepidation about what might happen next. Memories were very fresh among the Kuwaitis of their encounter with the full wrath of Saddam in 1991. He had invaded, occupied, and then raped and pillaged the entire city on his way out following Operation Desert Storm. All of Kuwait City was in a state of alert. The streets and highways were mostly empty.

Early into our stay at the Kuwait Hilton, word leaked out about our location because reporters were staying in the same location trying to cover the war. Almost overnight we came under heavy security. Concrete barriers lined the entrance to the hotel, and Kuwaiti and American patrol boats policed the ocean side of the facility.

Most of our time in Kuwait City was spent fine-tuning plans to reopen and operate the ministries. To test operational proficiency, there were daily "rock drills," the term for a type of reconstruction "war-gaming" that prepared everyone for quick adaptation in an uncertain environment. We would also need to formulate plans to coordinate the national ministries with the regional structure that existed. There was the real risk that regional administration would be completely cut off from national planning and reconstruction operations. Reconstruction programming would have to be integrated with a sophisticated effort to involve local citizens in identifying needs and local governance teams.

As the weeks passed, more and more diagrams appeared on the walls of the Kuwait City villas where we worked. As one planner put it, "If you can't flow chart it, it ain't going to work." While that might have been true from

The Kuwait City Hilton, our home for six weeks.

a planning standpoint, we would learn soon enough that flow charts were of minor utility in the seat-of-the-pants, invent-as-you-go environment of Baghdad. We had no way of knowing this at the time, but as we were drawing up extensive plans to restore services and jump-start ministries, the entire administrative structure that existed under Saddam was pretty well being destroyed by the war and the looting that followed.

The logistics planning in Kuwait City did not anticipate a long stay. The image encouraged at ORHA headquarters was one of getting into the country, getting things back in shape, and then just going home. We would "work our way out of a job" quickly, we were assured.

The Garner Team

The time in Kuwait offered a rare opportunity to get to know the other team members. Perhaps it was the sea breezes, the isolation of the property, our remoteness from home, or all these factors. But the occasional work slowdowns offered some time to get to know my American civilian colleagues better, including their personal attitudes and political views.

Many have said or implied that the ORHA group comprised incompetent or partisan members. That was anything but true of Garner's team. As a senior staff member who was onboard at the beginning and at the end, I never saw that. The people who signed up for the mission—including former ambassadors, PhDs, college presidents and professors, senior government officials, and career specialists—were exceptional in every dimension. They all reflected very impressive credentials and backgrounds in various reconstruction specialties. The senior advisors who went into Kuwait and on into Baghdad weren't particularly caught up in the military or political issues. Most signed up because they really wanted to help create a better life for the Iraqi people. They were some of the sharpest and most idealistic people I ever met. They saw it as an exceedingly serious and morally justified humanitarian mission.

Many of the postwar critiques miss a central point: that group was conscientious, competent, and dedicated, and reflected a wide range of views about the war and even about the administration (despite comments to the contrary, very few had any ties to the GOP or the White House). But, more than any other characteristic, the civilian staff believed that if their government was going to bring about regime change, nothing could be left to chance. *It had to be done right.* They were deeply committed to the need for plans and resources that would match the postwar challenge. That's why they signed up.

Many on the team quietly voiced concerns about the timing of the invasion and the resulting international divisions. These were sophisticated and experienced people; they knew enough about international politics to know that those conditions could spell isolation and global polarization for the United States, hurting our own chances of success in dozens of consequential ways.

I frequently heard skeptical comments, especially from State Department types, about the difficulty of transplanting an American-style Jeffersonian democracy onto Iraqi soil. But no one seemed opposed to taking Saddam out. Most on the team were humanitarians and idealists who believed there was a time and place for the United States to remove murderous dictators for the sake of humanity, hopefully with the world's support and cooperation.

For many team members, the idea of removing Saddam was not tied to a grand ideological vision like Pax Americana or remaking the Middle East to suit American interests, or anything like that. It was just a basic feeling that justice had to be done. Again and again, as we shared personal reflections on the operation, the consensus favored taking out a tyrant and giving 24 million Iraqis their freedom. That seemed noble and morally justified.

Whatever their political views or private misgivings, everyone who signed on was committed to doing the best job possible. They were all adults; even those who had misgivings about the president recognized that it was his job alone to make the decisions. Those decisions were tough ones; and once they were made, everyone in the U.S. government carried a responsibility to support the commander in chief. More than anything, everyone wanted the project to succeed. This was the most daring and consequential mission of at least a generation and possibly a century, given that it was being executed in the heart of the turbulent Middle East. It could change the balance of power for generations to come.

That was the bottom line: We wanted America to succeed, for the sake of the Iraqi people, for the sake of the region, for the sake of our own country's reputation, and (at least, for some of us) for the sake of the president. People were very aware of the enormous risk involved. The risk of failure, at least in general terms, was painfully obvious to all from the beginning. The fallout from a failure to establish a stable government would reverberate in that region and around the world for generations to come.

Facing the Intelligence Problem

Each of us exerted nearly superhuman effort trying to make it work, and we just took it for granted that we would be given the tools we needed to do the job. In time, however, as the civilian team discovered just how poorly the whole operation was funded and supported, many began to doubt if the government was actually serious about the effort. For some, it became a true crisis of faith. Why are we doing this, they would privately murmur, if our country is not serious? How could our government take on such a consequential mission and fall so far short of the requirements on the ground in so many areas?

Those reservations aside, the disposition of the team was (most of the time) quite confident. You heard lots of chatter about reorganization plans and "concepts of operations." We started turning out enough paper to fill filing cabinets. The legal specialists worked on plans to replace Saddam's dictatorial law with legal reforms covering labor, commerce, and penal laws. Another expert on commerce wrote what appeared to be a book-length treatise on promoting economic growth.

But while it was impressive professional work, it lacked a sense of connection to reality in Iraq. I was struck again and again by how little we knew about Iraqi ministries and the realities of the country's basic infrastructure.

I asked repeatedly for some intelligence on the inner workings of the Iraqi ministries. It never came, and I had to conclude it didn't exist. In simple fact: to do the postwar job well, we needed to know much more than we did. Although little was known by the general public during Saddam's reign, most scholars, technicians, and authorities assumed that the intelligence services of the world's sole superpower must be busy penetrating the inner workings of the Iraqi government and collecting essential information. It never occurred to me that our intelligence services might not even have the significant and requisite information on the inner workings of Iraq prior to our arrival.

Of course, now it is clearly known (as government investigations have revealed) that a range of deficiencies in America's intelligence and foreign policy operations in the Middle East were exposed by 9/11 and the aftermath. For decades of the Cold War, foreign policy careers were not made by Middle East appointments. That was undoubtedly true for intelligence services as well. At the time of the Iraqi invasion, we had far too few policy experts and Arab language specialists. That was a weakness of the U.S. government dating back decades and through numerous administrations. The Middle East just never got the attention that the Soviet Union and the Eastern Bloc received during the Cold War.

Whatever information the intelligence services did have, they didn't share with us. I always suspected they had embarrassingly little information. Worse than being thin on facts, we detected that the Central Intelligence Agency (CIA) had its own agenda. Old vendettas among competing U.S. agencies were magnified by the invasion of Iraq. It was remarkable to me how many Iraqis referred to the divisions of the U.S. government as though they belonged to separate countries. Some factions had the backing of the defense department, others the CIA. And the CIA rarely conveyed the sense that they were on the same team.

HAVING RECEIVED NEXT TO NO GUIDANCE from the policy operation at the Pentagon and even less from intelligence services, we were pretty much left with having to create something from nothing. Most turned to writing extensive memos on what interim government operations would look like, more or less imagining what we would confront once arriving. The longer we sat in Kuwait City, the more it began to feel like a graduate school exercise at the Kennedy School of Government, where I had done graduate training. Much of the writing was done to satisfy Washington's insatiable need for paper and reporting, which was usually used to give the mid-level managers back home a sense of connection to the historic mission that was taking shape, and the opportunity to brief their superiors. I do not recall any of those dissertations ever being used or even mentioned after we arrived in Iraq.

Throughout the course of our time in Kuwait City, the phrase used most frequently to capture our growing collective anxiety was "winning the war, losing the peace." What if the military won the war handily, as everyone expected, and we would preside over a failure to secure national recovery and stability? There simply was no way of knowing what would happen on the ground in Iraq once the "shock and awe" bombing campaign was over, and the governance of that country became America's responsibility. The least we could do was carry very cautious and conservative assumptions in with us, and prepare for medium- to worst-case scenarios to play out.

The description that made its way into our circles from the State Department was the now famous "Pottery Barn rules" offered by then Secretary of State Colin Powell: "you break it, you own it." Were we prepared to own it? Obviously, that was a policy question that had to be sorted out well above us, but no question was more loaded with ramifications for what we would be called upon to do.

Meeting Our First Iraqis

In addition to getting to know my American colleagues better, evenings also gave opportunity to meet new people who were finding their way to ORHA headquarters from the Iraqi world. With warm ocean breezes and the sight of the sun setting over the Arabian Sea, many conversations turned to the Iraqi perspective on the future. These interesting and diverse people all held in common a deep visceral hatred for Saddam and his ruthless reign. Many traveled a great distance and at great personal sacrifice just hoping to join our team. They couldn't believe that the liberation they had only dreamed of for many years was actually unfolding before their eyes. Here they were sitting down and having dinner with the team that would move in after Saddam's henchmen were moved out.

The conversations were often heartrending. Tamara, an Iraqi exile, told how families under Saddam had been threatened or saw relatives killed. Tamara described how Saddam maintained control over his officials by threatening their families. For example, anyone fleeing Iraq would immediately lose family members to imprisonment or death. Tamara described the horrid treatment of women by Saddam and his sons. The reports from these Iraqis emphasized over and over that human life counted for nothing under

These images, taken by a colleague of mine, show two views of Camp Bucca, the U.S. Military's largest detainee camp. It sits near Umm Qasr, a port city in southern Iraq separated from the border of Kuwait by a small inlet.

Saddam and the Ba'ath party. Unsurprisingly, many Iraqis were psychologically traumatized. Tamara told us of a woman who had merely waved to the troops as they moved north; she was later found hanged.

It was logical to assume that many Iraqis would view and trust us as their liberators. But Tamara told us in sobering and tragic detail why so many Iraqis felt betrayed by Americans. Our military was directly blamed for the failure to remove Saddam in 1991, and that failure had resulted in a Shiite slaughter. Her words carried a blast of reality, a warning that many will distrust us.

I also met Ammar Shawkat, who barely survived an encounter with Saddam's hatchet men in the early 1990s. Ammar had a deep passion for the children of Iraq. He wept when I probed into why I should put him on my team. Solidly honest and straightforward, he would become my right-hand man. In that role, he helped design a variety of projects and programs to reorganize the Ministry of Youth and Sport and the Olympic Committee.

Ammar was extremely capable and also very suspicious of other Iraqis. As a thoroughly Westernized (from living in exile in Germany) and fervently secular man, he represented one minority of Iraqis who really did believe in the need for a nonsectarian state. Ammar was that most rare Muslim, believing that state and religion had to be separated for the sake of both. He was deeply suspicious that many Iraqi exiles would return carrying their own Islamic agenda. Later, he repeatedly got in trouble by confronting fellow Muslims, including members of our own American team, about the need for a secular state. Their disdain for his secular ideas was so great that many tried to have him removed. For me, those clashes with Ammar became an early and clear signal that American-style "secular" government would not work in Iraq.

This early experience also raised another serious question: how could so diverse a group of Iraqis work through their differences? Would they develop the spirit of trust and compromise that we take for granted in our own society, or would they continue to be suspicious and distrustful? Would they always resort to sectarian fighting? I did not sense great interest by Iraqis in what we would call the foundational liberal principles of democracy; they seemed to have little capacity for tolerance and compromise. In this and other conversations with Iraqis, I and others saw that vast panorama of truth and mythology. No one doubted that the atrocities under Saddam were tragically real and pervasive. They were, after all, widely documented. But there was clearly another dimension to consider.

The Iraqi community, terrorized and traumatized for so long by Saddam, was the source of seemingly endless stories, most of them very real, some the products of imagination, and others simply distorted by the embellishment that naturally accommodates the rumor mill. The Iraqi culture was a "whisper down the lane" environment where little information could be verified. Did they actually believe all the stories, or were we Americans being played with?

Some of the stories sounded so outlandish that they started to raise doubts. I thought some had to be tall tales or the kinds of distortions that take root naturally among exiles. The storytelling was circular; every report of an atrocity was presented as part of a case to justify Saddam's removal. And since Saddam was such a monster, whatever one imagined him doing, he must have done.

One story floating around the Iraqi community was that Saddam had constructed a massive underground tunnel system that was so extensive and sophisticated that he could disappear there and never be found. The tunnel was likened to the subway in Washington, DC, and it belonged entirely to Saddam and his family. The underground structure was, reportedly, built with such devious ingenuity that it might be impossible to find, and it had sufficient supplies to sustain its occupants for a long time. As it turned out, Saddam was found hiding in a far less auspicious hole. An underground system of tunnels was never found.

This was the kind of unreliable information that would enter the public debate back home unfiltered, producing credibility problems in too many cases. Of course, a major part of the story that emerged after the war was that much of the information coming from the exiles had been distorted (especially intelligence reports on WMDs).

AMONG THE IRAQI EXILES WHOM WE MET was journalist Kanan Makiya, who wrote the book *Republic of Fear* (one of the more authoritative books on Saddam and his regime which helped build support for the war). Unlike the other Iraqi exiles I met who were mostly consumed by a hatred for Saddam and could think of little else, Makiya seemed preoccupied with the future that was now unfolding. He was deeply concerned about the possibility of ethnic and religious factions spinning out of control; he clearly wanted us to take all precautions.

Makiya was particularly concerned about religion and how Iraqis would play the sectarian card. He worried about what the Shiites might do after taking their place as the true majority; would they deal fairly with the Sunnis? How difficult might that become in establishing an Iraqi state? "Shiite theology," he said, "does not go well with the state." He strongly urged that religious and nationalist parties be contained. He also expressed the hope that Iraqis would want to be Iraqis and not Arab nationalists.

At that point, we were suddenly called away to another meeting. I had hoped to ask him if he addressed this concern with senior officials in Washington. Later, in a published interview, he reported that he asked the president whether he knew about the Sunnis and the Shia. According to Makiya, the president asked: "who are they?"

Internal Conflicts

As we worked in Kuwait City, internal divisions and conflicts began to surface. Clearly, in order to be effective, ORHA would need to integrate military and civilian elements into one effective unit. But people serving in it had inherent conflicts of command. We worked for ORHA, but who exactly ORHA reported to was a bit confusing.

To start the process of sorting it all out, daily meetings were convened to process through operational issues. When and how would ORHA take over? Army Civil Affairs would be aligned with ministry teams but would also take the lead where ORHA staff was lacking (this would be true for most of Iraq outside of Baghdad and two small regional offices during the first several months). Army Civil Affairs would follow ORHA's leadership when possible; it would function quasi-independently when required.

It became clear that the Pentagon would lead not only the military actions but the post-military civilian operation as well. It made perfect sense for the chain of command to be made clear. In retrospect, given the strained and dangerous environment and the confused chain of command that was put in place, I often wondered whether the Pentagon Civil Affairs should not have done it all themselves. At least, they should probably have led for a few months or until security had been completely established.

Later in Baghdad, a great deal of time and energy would be devoted to "de-conflicting" the military and civilian command systems. I also occasionally wondered why ORHA even existed; it was another organizational layer and, therefore, another opportunity for conflict. In many respects it was a hybrid organization that was no match for the larger, stronger, and more essential army. That would all change.

So it made a certain amount of sense for Secretary Rumsfeld to be given authority over the operation, given that the chief backers of the war were at the Department of Defense (DoD) and Vice President Cheney's office. The secretary of defense's office harbored deep distrust of the CIA and the State Department. They believed all along that careerists from those agencies would try to scuttle the operation. The historical record was clear; during the Vietnam War, the CIA showed its independence by directly challenging decisions and information coming from the Pentagon.

But Rumsfeld's leadership also raised an irony. Of all the senior officials, Rumsfeld had neither the interest in nation building nor the institutional resources to carry it out. At no point during the early months was there a sign that the Pentagon had any significant interest in, or patience for, post-conflict nation building. As the name ORHA implied, postwar planning was focused on repairing services and treating humanitarian conditions in the hope of a quick withdrawal.

What the Pentagon lacked in interest it also lacked in expertise. The fact is that most of the proficiency in post-conflict stabilization, management of humanitarian affairs, and a host of other nation-building fields—from democratization to crafting constitutions—simply did not come from the military. That kind of expertise was located at the State Department and USAID. Rumsfeld had shut down the one institution on the subject at the Army War College, apparently hoping to eliminate it from the Pentagon's portfolio.

All of that was moot, however, because DoD senior officials believed that Iraq would be liberated without need of a huge postwar occupation complex and without extensive planning. There would be no need for a broader team of experts who could handle the complex task of postwar stabilization, recovery, and, yes, nation building. The Iraqis could sort these things out on their own. The message often repeated had been "brief stay, light touch."

The Defense Department's reach for control of the operation was a major reason for the intense infighting in Washington. USAID and the State Department were reduced to minor roles as the war drew closer. Funds were diverted to DoD; the army was assigned a variety of tasks such as housing and reconstruction, irrigation, oil, electricity, and transportation; and ORHA, the vehicle for organizing the restoration of government services, was created under Secretary Rumsfeld's immediate command.

Other pieces of the postwar project had already been contracted out to Beltway firms, like the Iraqi Media Network (IMN) project. Incidentally, the entire IMN project was managed as a contract, outside of the direct line of ORHA control. I caught a fascinating peek into the messiness of these kinds of operations; on Sunday, March 23, I went into Kuwait City with Mike Furlong and his Arab interpreter. Mike was operating under a Pentagon contract to set up communications services in Iraq immediately after the war, one of the early operations that completely flopped.

In order to get a lot of equipment into the country quickly, he needed to get airport and customs clearance to fly in his own C-130 airplanes. I watched into the wee hours of the morning as Mike huddled around a table sipping tea in a room full of Arabs, working his deals. The entire scene felt like a shadowy rogue operation. None of these operations was carried out under the actual supervision of ORHA (of course, in wartime, they rarely are). That would soon change when Dan Senor, then Margaret Tutweiler, would attempt to assert some control over their daily activities.

Occupation or "Brief Stay, Light Touch?"

I do not recall a single conversation that used the language of nation building, or offered any signal that we Americans would be rebuilding Iraq from the bottom up. Every issue carried a "brief stay, light touch" assumption and feel. In other words, we should do enough planning to address immediate problems, but remember that we won't be there for long.

The early stages of the operation frequently revealed the inherent uncertainty of the mission. Would it be a swift liberation—in and out—as the language usually suggested? Or would Iraq's long-term success require something closer to occupation? In that case, the language we used in describing our purposes would need to clearly and confidently express authority and seriousness.

At one point, someone used the phrase "minimize displacement." It was a curious phrase that described, however unintentionally, a strategic postwar doctrine coming out of the Pentagon. It captured well the working assumption—widely embraced back in DC at the time—that the operation would be swift, successful, clean, and minimally disruptive. Presumably, it would leave much of the previous infrastructure, both physical and human, in place. The idea suggested the image of a relay race; we would take the baton from one group of Iraqis, carry it a certain distance, and hand it off to another group of Iraqis. Before long, of course, the whole track meet would be over.

The basic character of postwar Iraq kept appearing and then shifting into other shapes and patterns. Mixed signals flowed from Washington. Some projected "brief stay, light touch." Others suggested a postwar pattern closer to occupation or nation building.

But the very existence of a debate on these issues tended to create a tension between two opposite visions: "brief stay, light touch" and occupation. It became downright schizophrenic. The bottom line implication of this was essentially a "nation building on the cheap" kind of reality. Increasingly, it felt like Washington wanted us to do it, but do so without commensurate authorization or funding.

For example, there was a debate over what the postwar operation would actually call people like me who would "take charge of the government." This seemingly innocent issue was actually hotly debated back in Washington at the highest levels at the Pentagon and the National Security Council (NSC). The original twenty-four officials, who would serve as replacements for Saddam's departing government ministers, would be for all practical purposes "interim ministers." Clearly, it seemed, each of us would be the one person in decision-making authority for that government ministry.

Yes, there would be Iraqis in the vicinity, and we would engage them as best we could. But as a practical matter, we would be in charge. It was really that simple. Once we arrived in Iraq, the Iraqi people themselves began to refer to us with such honorific titles as "Mr. Minister" or "His Excellency." They wanted us to take charge and couldn't understand our hesitancy to do so, especially after the looting decimated much of Baghdad. At least in the early going, we were the only ones they actually trusted.

But to actually call us interim ministers would make the U.S. government sound like an occupying power. We were informed at one point that Secretary Rumsfeld suggested that we be called "senior liaisons." That title carried the implication of facilitating communications between two or more parties. It would certainly reassure anyone concerned about the appearance of heavy-handedness or the arbitrary use of power. A senior liaison was not himself an authority; he would only represent one authority to another. Jay Garner settled on "senior advisor."

There was only one problem. Who would we be liaising to? In my particular case, I would be assigned to take over all of the functions that had been carried out by Saddam's eldest son, Uday. We certainly had to assume that both he and his entire upper tier of lieutenants would be gone. I could not imagine anyone from Uday's operation exercising authority in the next phase. Nor could I imagine anyone serving as liaison between them and someone in the Pentagon.[1]

Policy people from the OSD ultimately settled on "senior ministry advisors." The term at least had the advantage of suggesting that we Americans might have advice to give and that the Iraqis might need some direction rather than merely sitting across the table and exchanging equally valid opinions. But it wasn't better by much; it was still devoid of authority. The title implied that we were there only to offer insight and whatever guidance the new Iraqi administration may request.

Of course, the real crux of the problem was: what if the forces that moved into the vacuum created by Saddam's removal had their own agenda and momentum, such as the very real possibility of trying to establish an Islamic theocracy? After America invested so much blood and treasure, would we just advise, smile for the cameras, and move on?

In short, there was no team and no structure to advise. We were it. In fairly short order, we would discover that there was only one power with the resources and resolve to establish order, and that was the U.S. government. There would be no remaining Iraqi authority left in place to liaise with or even advise. Every last vestige of the previous government—Saddam Hussein and all of his henchmen, his secret police and military generals, and his Ba'ath party thugs—would all be captured, dead, or gone.

So, of course, the U.S. objective was regime change. The very idea that some responsible element would be in place waiting to quickly rise to the occasion was naive, and somewhat ironic in light of what was known and often repeated about Saddam's dictatorship. The case against Saddam was that he was a violent dictator who ruled with an iron fist over every square inch of Iraq and killed anyone who had the slightest doubt about him. Why would any of these people want to work with us (or us with them)? Additionally, there were no venerable leaders who had survived in obscurity or prison who could be brought back and put in authority (like a Nelson Mandela). There was simply no one who could—by virtue of his moral authority, gravitas, and esteem in the eyes of his countrymen—lead Iraq.

As we would increasingly learn after arriving in Baghdad, this myopic view that some new order could just spring out of Iraq's tormented condition was supplied from the beginning by the Iraqi exile community. Selling the idea of "regime change on the cheap" helped make the case for the war. Many Iraqi exiles promoted the idea because they imagined themselves running the country, and they were encouraged in this belief by very senior people in the Department of Defense.

It was rather remarkable to consider that a power as large and dominant as America was prepared to undertake the controversy of liberating Iraq but then suddenly become squeamish about exercising power once there. If there was a reason for that, it was the fear among senior officials of even greater fallout in the international community than what had already occurred.

The widely held hope across the American government was that many international allies who had a problem with the war might have a change of opinion once it was over. They hoped that those nations would step forward to help reconstruct Iraq. Establishing martial law or ruthlessly suppressing the looting might have sent the wrong message. As one official told me, "We don't want the Russians and the French accusing us of being just like Saddam." As it turned out, a variety of factors kept them away, including the postwar chaos. The net result was that the failure to secure broader international support before the war began produced additional crippling vulnerabilities in the postwar period.

Squeamishness was clearly not what the Iraqis themselves wanted. As they saw it, if they deserved to be delivered from tyranny, then they also deserved a new system of rule of law. And that was possible only if the United States took decisive action to bring it about. The Iraqis wanted freedom from fear. They were a brutalized and traumatized people. They bore severe psychological pains from the Saddam years, and paranoia was for them an understandable outlook.

The biggest factor of all in their continued fear during the early months had to be the fact that Saddam and his two sons were still unaccounted for. They knew all too well what the old regime was capable of. They also knew from their own history what would happen if we failed to establish order because of a fear of appearing like an occupying power. They knew something about dictatorships and where they came from: chaos and lawlessness. The Iraqis were well aware of this.

Venturing North

Several from our ORHA team managed to get included on one or two day trips out to the Iraqi countryside, effectively making scouting missions. On April 1, Mike Gfoeller from the State Department arrived back from Umm Qasr, the southern port city of Iraq that had already been liberated as the army moved north. His report was sobering. He described conditions that were far worse than we had anticipated: no government, no police, no civil administration. People roamed in a dazed state. Even the dogs, he said, were gaunt and appeared to be lost in a state of confusion.

This is a ruin near Umm Qasr, an area known to be a hotbed of persistent rocket attacks by militants, as photographed by a colleague who visited the area.

Gfoeller said that the only security and public order that existed were being offered by our army. There was no functioning local authority and, he reported, government offices were badly looted. This report, coming from southern rural Iraq, was a foreboding sign of things to come. The news media was already covering the massive looting in Baghdad with pictures of pickup trucks and donkey carts brimming with looted property, teenagers scurrying away from sites carrying as much on their backs as they could manage, and army personnel passively looking on. Of course, the army wasn't sent to Iraq to prevent looting.

Gfoeller, who was an experienced Arab hand, was concerned that we would be too soft in our approach to restoring the government. Such an approach would be interpreted by the Iraqis as weakness. It will not work, he predicted. "People have been brutalized under Saddam. Now, they need to feel like they are not only free but safe." As much as most Iraqis welcomed the removal of Saddam, most could not shake the paranoia about a return to power by "Ba'athist Butchers," perhaps even by Saddam himself, or the rise of reprisals among the people.

The looting, more than anything else, encouraged the view that Americans were not serious about establishing a new nation. To this day, most people assume that the looting was confined to Baghdad. Reports were never compiled on the full scale of looting. But it happened from one end of the country to the other. The cost of the looting must have run into the tens of billions.

The coalition forces represented the only existing law and order and civil administration presence. Obviously, the coalition forces were badly overstretched. The looting problem was one of the issues raised again and again by every team assembled to study and plan the liberation. And it was unfolding before our eyes.

It was also becoming apparent in early April that many Iraqis whose assistance we would need were containing their enthusiasm. For one, the Shiites were far less welcoming of the Americans than hoped. Their reluctance was due to the slaughter that occurred in 1991 following America's refusal to support the Shiite uprising in the south that we had encouraged them to start. We were also starting to wrestle with the complications generated by lingering fears of Saddam and the remnants of the Ba'ath party. Many who worked in the government wanted to continue to serve but were fearful that—with Saddam and his tyrants still at large and Ba'ath party informants crawling all over the place—information on their collaboration with us would be passed along. Many Iraqis just refused to believe that their ordeal was over until they had convincing proof that Saddam as well as his two sons were dead.

Departure Time: Baghdad Falls

More and more of the daily reports included information on plans for moving north, along with discussions of the operating environment that existed in Baghdad.

We were once again briefed on the potential dangers—how to detect and avoid land mines and booby traps, starting with the obvious practical advice that we all stay on hard surfaces and avoid suspicious objects on the ground. We were warned to be very careful when navigating our way through vacated buildings; sympathizers from the deposed regime might have booby-trapped the place on their way out.

On April 4, we learned of the fall of Baghdad. We stood in semicircles around the TV, spellbound by the same images that the rest of the world was witnessing. We watched that strange combination of (1) jubilation at the site of Saddam's statue being dragged down by an American tank and (2) the pictures of nonstop looting that seemed to signify out-of-control lawlessness.

The following Sunday, April 6, at 1 p.m., we were told to go to the tennis courts for an "all hands meeting." We assumed this would be a pep rally before departure. It increasingly appeared that it was Garner's turn to lead. The cameras were pointing more and more in his direction. He arrived at the meeting with his deputies in one of the GMC Suburbans. The gathering was mostly ceremonial, designed to boost morale and solidarity. There was a broad sense that our planning work was finished and we could take real pride in our efforts. Whatever lay ahead, we were as ready as we could be under the circumstances.

The brief meeting ended with a sketchy report about an advance team being sent north to scope out the situation and make arrangements for our relocation to Baghdad. How exactly would this transition from Kuwait City to Baghdad be carried out? The plan was a phased movement into Iraq. The "early entry command group" or "Advon" (for advance) would go in first and appraise the situation. Then, an "initial main" advance team would enter with a team of engineers, establish headquarters and secure the perimeters, maybe make some initial contact with Iraqi leaders, then begin to work on supply, logistics, and housing needs for the larger civilian team that would soon follow.

On April 7, the army hosted a large festive poolside dinner party at the Hilton. There was a great feeling of solidarity. Word from home, however, offered a different perspective. We were hearing from reliable sources that Washington was in a state of near paralysis over decision making.

By the second week of April, tension was building inside and outside ORHA with the spotlight increasingly turning on our leader and team. The headquarters was crawling with skeptical media trying to figure out who we were and what our plans were. Frequently, stories would make their way into the press based upon overheard conversations at dining tables in the Hilton restaurant.

Where was the civilian team that was needed to organize the postwar project? everyone was asking. Weeks had now passed and we were still sipping Starbucks at the Hilton because, according to Garner, CENTCOM was worried about inserting civilians into a dangerous environment. More and more media reports were making their way out of Baghdad, describing a city in bad shape. *Washington Post* reporters Peter Slevin and Vernon Loeb reported that "the Pentagon ignored lessons from a decade of peacekeeping operations in Haiti, Somalia, the Balkans, and Afghanistan. It also badly underestimated the potential for looting and lawlessness after the collapse of the Iraqi government, lacking forces capable of securing the streets of Baghdad in the transition from combat to postwar reconstruction." [2]

One report indicated that services were basically nonexistent, with electric power at 40 percent of pre-war levels. CNN was reporting that Baghdad's health system was breaking down, raising the specter of major health and safety issues. The media also repeatedly showed the mountains of trash that had accumulated during the war. I didn't know it at the time, but the monumental task of cleaning up Baghdad's trash following the war would have my name written on it.

On April 9, our discussions accelerated on how to bring about a gradual "rolling transfer of power" from (what was called at the time) an "Interim Coalition Administration" to an Interim Iraqi Authority (IIA). It was obvious that our imminent departure was provoking a debate about the need to quickly facilitate Iraqi authority once arriving. We would put in place a temporary authority to cover basic governmental functions, relying on the Iraqi technocrats who were willing and able to help.

We knew our departure north could happen any day. By April 15, the United Nations (UN) was reporting that southern Iraq was declared "permissive," or safe enough to enter. On April 17, the move north was discussed pretty widely across the compound, with heavy overtones about danger. Simon Elvy, a member of the British foreign service, suggested that we take a group picture because we "might not all come home alive."

For a brief moment Simon's candor prompted talk about families and how likely it was that someone would lose their life. This talk became fairly common, although very quietly in conversations involving two or three. No one showed the slightest hesitation to move forward, and no one wanted to undermine general morale.

The pace of talk about deployment north to Baghdad picked up daily. On April 18, there was much discussion about the growing urgency to get to Baghdad. The Iraqis were asking questions about their future and showing signs of restlessness. But while the south was secure, Baghdad was still dangerous.

Should we deploy partially north, say to Basra? Or should we deploy to the Baghdad airport, camp out in tents, and wait for conditions in Baghdad to improve? At one point we were shown a hand-sketched description of an office complex set up in a tent city. I was starting to imagine occupying an office. Would we have Iraqis come to us there, or would we go out and meet them?

At this stage, the remaining dangers in Iraq were being presented in the daily intelligence briefings as a few diehards who didn't actually welcome us, all of which would quickly disappear as Iraqis got about the business of enjoying their freedoms. Clearly the fall of Baghdad, almost two weeks old now, did not result in favorable conditions for building a new order. The mind raced trying to imagine what it would be like to establish a government under those circumstances.

Naturally, we were more eager than anyone on Earth to hear how American personnel were being received (following the military operation) in the towns and cities on the way north. It seemed that senior advisors would be traveling by ground in convoys and would need to plan for trouble along the way. From reports we had received, anticipating trouble meant preparing for the possibility of being stopped by bandits or attacked by rocket-propelled grenades (RPGs).

On April 20, Garner took his first trip to Baghdad in order to at least make a showing to the media and the Iraqi people, and to get a sense of what things looked like there. The murmuring around the Kuwait Hilton was that there was a lot of remaining danger. Much of it was not being reported in the media, in large part because the media was still embedded with the military as it continued northward. What was coming through the media was a constant drumbeat about the absence of civilian administrators in Baghdad. We sensed that a collision of sorts was approaching that forced a tradeoff between our safety and simply getting to Baghdad to confront the increasingly urgent conditions.

We were reminded again and again that "force protection" was the most important priority. And, at that stage, it was simply not possible to move the civilian group safely to Baghdad or keep them safe once there. With one stray mortar, hundreds could be lost. The greatest debacle would have been if Saddam or his henchmen held a chemical or biological weapon and waited until we were all in place to release it.

I was beginning to comprehend the risk. The first senior ministry advisor for health, who was traveling with Garner, went to visit a hospital to assess the state of health care. His vehicle was shot at three times. That was our first hint that the large fleet of three-seated Suburbans, purchased for the civilians, would be sitting ducks. They were "thin-skinned" SUVs purchased right off of a new car lot in Kuwait City with no alterations made.

These stories of trouble in Baghdad would continue right to the moment of our deployment. One USAID vehicle was shot at. Another Suburban was totaled while traveling at high speeds to avert roadside attacks.

The reports I found most worrisome had to do with crowds of kids gathering along highways, slowing down and in some cases stopping vehicles,

A sign at the border crossing warns those on the ground that they are about to enter Iraq.

then surrounding them so that they could not resume forward movement, breaking windows, and stealing equipment and supplies off of roof racks. The description sounded like ordinary street thugs. One soldier traveling with a civilian convoy had his pistol stolen right out of his holster when he stopped and attempted to befriend a crowd of kids. Another had a hand grenade stolen from his ammunition pack while he was holding a machine gun in his hand. Weren't the crowds supposed to be standing by the roadside in orderly rows cheering us on?

Back in Washington, when the question came up of how Americans would be greeted upon their arrival, the response was always that the Iraqis had suffered a lot under Saddam; they would likely be friendly, grateful, and accommodating.

APRIL 20 WAS EASTER SUNDAY and someone organized a nondenominational sunrise service on the beach. This was not a meeting that we wanted to widely advertise in that predominantly Muslim country. Nearly two hundred people showed up and participated in joyful ecumenical singing. I think it gave them a sense of normalcy and connection to home. It would be one of the unusual religious experiences in a Muslim land, the birthplace of all major world religions, including my own. It was one of those experiences where the mind could not help but drift in the direction of asking whether the three major religions of the world that originated in the lands around us would ever live in peace, and would our actions hasten that day.

All senior advisors were told to be ready. Baghdad might not be safe, and our headquarters would not be operational, but it was time to go.

Chapter 3

Wheels Up to Baghdad
To Fix a Broken Country

THERE HAD BEEN MUCH DISCUSSION over the prior weeks about where we civilians would be housed inside Iraq. Obviously, we would need a secure location, with adequate office space and services. For those and other reasons, we couldn't simply check into the most convenient local hotel in downtown Baghdad.[1]

Baghdad International Airport (BIAP) was briefly considered as a temporary site; if the violence had not subsided in downtown Baghdad, perhaps we could erect tents in an encampment on the grounds and possibly use airport facilities for offices. BIAP was about a twenty-minute drive out of Baghdad, and was the site of some of the heaviest fighting during the war. Many of the fields around the airport had been used by the Iraqi military for quartering troops, training, and equipment storage.

That plan was also rejected because providing the necessary security would tie down too much of the army. Plus, even if the 82nd Airborne would secure the entire perimeter of the airport, the tents would be too vulnerable to mortar attack. If attacks starting coming, we would all be sitting ducks and would then have to find another place. So why not turn to that more secure location first?

From the beginning, the army civil engineers had their eye on Saddam's presidential palace. It was conveniently located at the center of power in downtown Baghdad and inside the safety of what became known later as the Green Zone. It had many obvious advantages over other options. And it had one significant disadvantage: appearance. Not missing an opportunity to introduce more jargon, someone asked, "What's the optic lay-down?" In other words, what would our taking over Saddam's palace look like to America and the world? What would the Iraqis think about that? How could liberators not appear to be occupiers if we moved into Saddam's offices and residence?

It was Garner's decision to use the palace, and even though it generated some heat back home, it was a sound judgment. After considering everything, it was the only complex that afforded safe, practical quarters for the team of bureaucrats who would stream into Baghdad. Bremer's team, although initially voicing an interest in moving the headquarters after arriving, quickly changed their minds when they saw conditions.

Destination Baghdad

On April 22, the decision was announced that senior advisors would be flown by C-130 to Baghdad airport that coming Thursday. Army logistics decided, based upon stories of resistance and violence, to abandon land travel to Baghdad. What a media fiasco it would have been if several members of the civilian team were injured or killed on the way in. Flying by military aircraft would be faster and safer.

That Thursday, perhaps the most memorable day for all of us, eighteen senior advisors were loaded into a bus and taken out to the military base in Kuwait City for departure. We had our first introduction to the long delays and many snafus that would accompany our travel in Iraq. Incredibly, the flight for this group of senior officials and diplomats had not been arranged. The one aircraft that was available for us was diverted at the last minute to transport a general. We sat at the airport for three hours.

Finally, the C-130, notorious for loud rattles and violent shaking, rumbled and vibrated its way down the runway. We lifted off. With the wheels up, we were leaving behind the cozy existence and relative safety of Kuwait City. Next stop, Baghdad.

FOUR HOURS LATER, THE SOUND OF SCREECHING TIRES meant we had arrived in Baghdad. The first aircraft load of senior civilians coming in to rebuild a country was on the ground. As we taxied, I looked around the C-130 and studied the faces. All expressions carried the same uncertainty about what might be awaiting.

Baghdad International Airport had been the site of major military action. But a small section had been secured and opened up for U.S. military and ORHA travel. They were still cleaning up and moving in porta-johns and other temporary facilities for the army at the outskirts of the large airport complex. The terminal was filthy, littered with piles of discarded

MREs and water bottles. The soldiers looked like they had gone for weeks without bathing.

We waited for another two hours. The headquarters at the Republican Palace, responsible for sending armored vehicles for our transportation, was not notified that we were arriving. Repeated attempts to make radio or phone contact failed.

The major media in Washington and around the world had been getting more aggressive each day, asking where the civilian managers for post-military Iraq were. Well, here we were, and our first day involved five to six hours of sitting and waiting. Were these delays just isolated cases or symptomatic of larger weaknesses?

While we waited at BIAP, we listened to stories from the army personnel who had been there during the previous week. The place was abuzz with talk of dramatic events. Several leading "deck of cards" figures had been brought through there, as was a skid containing hundreds of millions of dollars of seized currency.

Finally heavy transport and artillery vehicles arrived to carry us to the palace, but only half as many as were needed. Obviously, there were too few people available to transport us, and they were somewhat overwhelmed by the circumstances. The logistics folks at the palace told us they had not heard that we were coming. We piled as many as possible into civilian vehicles and put the rest in heavy armament vehicles. We all wondered if this transportation fiasco represented an emerging pattern.

The road to downtown Baghdad was littered with bombed out cars and military equipment. Much of it had just been pushed halfway off the road onto the shoulder. Very few vehicles traveled the highways. Those that did seemed to speed by nervously. News coverage was still reporting gunfire between vehicles and coalition forces, as well as along the Tigris and Euphrates rivers.

The first impression of Iraq was the pervasiveness of Saddam's presence. The entire country seemed like a monument to his ego. At short intervals all along the road, we saw large imposing statues of Saddam in various uniforms and poses. Many of them had been shot up and damaged, first by our troops, then by the Iraqis. In fact, the Iraqis had gone on a spree of trying to tear down the remaining images of Saddam. It was obvious that the Iraqis hated Saddam, but we couldn't help wondering if they could function without him.

WE ARRIVED AT THE PRESIDENTIAL COMPOUND as night was falling. The first sight I had of Saddam's palace, the place we would convert to our headquarters, was like a trip into a world ordered entirely around one person: Saddam. Looking down on us were four 40-foot busts of the dictator across the roof of the building: a young, muscular, handsome Saddam looking like a young Arab prince. It certainly felt strange to be unloading our bags at the place where Saddam and his elite loyalists had recently resided. Though the building was not bombed, it had suffered concussion damage from 2,000-pound bombs that had hit the power-generating station next door and Uday's palace a short distance away.

This meant that our new home had no windows, no electricity, no running water, and limited communication links to the outside world. All of these services had to be created. We would need a couple of mobile military power generators to produce electricity until a more adequate power plant could be constructed. For the first few days, those generators illuminated the central part of the palace. But we had to use flashlights to find our way out to our living quarters.

Phone service in Iraq was destroyed. The only telecommunication possible for us would be through the Thuraya satellite phones that we brought with us. And they worked only outside the building, and only if you were facing the satellite to which they were linked. Cell phone services would not begin to arrive until weeks later. After repeated tries, I was able to make contact with home. I felt like I had landed on the moon. The lack of connectivity in Iraq would prove to be one of the biggest impediments to contact with the Iraqi people for the first month we were there.

The sun was sinking behind a large grove of palm trees and the palace was growing dark as we off-loaded our duffle bags. We would need to set up our living quarters in the palace before the building became completely dark. So we climbed to the second floor and started our search for a bedroom. It was pretty much a matter of just finding a suitable room, helping yourself to it, and making it livable.

The living quarters of the presidential palace had hundreds of bedrooms with baths and showers, although they weren't working. Its dozens of kitchens reeked of rotting food. The bedrooms were strewn with blankets and bedspreads and clothes from the previous occupants. Some of the quarters looked like they might have been a permanent home to their residents; they were still filled with belongings and household goods. Of course, much of the palace would soon be cleaned and reorganized for the massive bureaucracy that would move in and use the space under established rules.

After setting up cots for four in one of the bedrooms,[2] we walked and probed for some time that night with flashlights and candles. The palace was massive—two main floors and a basement under portions of the building. It was indescribably eerie to explore by flashlight, knowing that just weeks before Saddam and his minions had been roaming those same halls. My mind searched for comparisons for our surreal exploration; the best I could do was to imagine intruders making their way by flashlight through the White House at night.

Arriving so soon after Saddam's downfall represented a unique opportunity to explore the mostly empty palace and sprawling grounds. Some of my colleagues, who had arrived a day or two earlier, showed us around Saddam's hideaways and office. They pointed out where large supplies of cash had been found.

The Palace

Saddam had built so many palaces for himself during his thirty-year reign that just counting them was difficult. One estimate placed the total at eighty. And they were found in every corner of the country. Many were small in relative terms and used only for brief stays or summer vacations.

The ORHA team stayed at the largest and most garishly opulent of Saddam's palaces, the Republican Presidential Palace, located in the heart of the international zone on the banks of the Tigris River.

Saddam's fascination with palaces began as soon as he consolidated power in the 1960s, at a time when healthy oil revenues allowed him to spend money on both himself and the people. In a way that makes sense only in a dictatorship, Saddam went on a palace building binge in the 1990s when the country was suffering from sanctions and plunging steadily into economic dysfunction.

The palace had been hit in the 1991 American bombing campaign. Large portions of the structure lay in ruins. In true Saddam fashion, not only did he quickly repair the old structure but he also launched a massive renovation, tripling the palace's size and adding large colonnaded wings to form a semicircle on either end. And, as if that was not a sufficient statement to the world, he erected four twenty-foot-high bronze shoulder and head busts of himself wearing a warrior's headdress. It was impossible to approach the building from any angle without being overwhelmed with the quadruplicate presence of the brooding Arab dictator, casting a defiantly martial gaze out over all of Baghdad.

It's hard to say how often or for how long Saddam stayed at the Republican Palace; he was always on the move in order to avoid danger, which is partly why so many palaces were built in the first place. Each was lavishly supplied and staffed, and each prepared exquisite meals 365 days a year for Saddam and his traveling companions in the event he chose to show up.

The precise function of the presidential palace under Saddam was not clear. He had offices there. He stood there periodically as judge and jury of personal enemies in the so-called interrogation room. It appeared that he met regularly with his military generals in the large dining room.

From appearances, the Republican Presidential Palace might have been designed mostly for ceremonial activity and entertainment; the palace had hundreds of bedrooms for his guests. It radiated a sense of royal decadence and ostentatious vanity. There was a ballroom that approached the size of a football field on one end. In the middle of the palace was a dining room with a huge V-shaped table half the size of a basketball court. After the invasion, the dining room was converted into a mess hall that would serve millions of meals.

In the middle of the complex was a rotunda with ceiling windows curving across the turquoise dome. It was only slightly smaller than the U.S. Capitol's rotunda. When we arrived, the rotunda featured a huge mural of Saddam, much like the murals in the U.S. Capitol dome. In the mural, he is handing a brick to a common laborer. Shortly after arriving, the army draped over the mural a large blue tarp, enabling Iraqis to pass through the rotunda without offense.

The construction of the palace consumed a lot of sandstone and marble for its thick walls and long, wide hallways. The palace was a two-story beige structure, encircled by a steel fence fifteen feet high, with a main guarded gate at the front entrance and other smaller guard stations on both ends in the rear. Around the back of the palace were large gardens and palm groves with walkways. Just beyond the palace grounds and running along the Tigris River was a concrete floodwall with a well-paved road on the top, undoubtedly used for security. The flat riverbanks were covered with demolished antiaircraft guns and military equipment. During the early months, we felt relatively free and safe during daylight hours jogging along the path.

The Green Zone was filled with odd remnants of the Saddam regime. In addition to the presidential palace, there were several other large complexes.

From the upper floors of any building, one could see what was left of the headquarters of the Ba'ath party headquarters, a five-story Council of Ministries building and a large international conference center that resembled a large shopping mall. Except for the convention center, most of the major buildings were reduced to fragile shells by the bombing.

In each, some sections had completely collapsed. Many still-standing exterior walls were bulging outward from interior explosions. Many walls were pulverized from mortar attacks. Several buildings were completely flattened from top to bottom, lying on the ground like a layer cake. The grounds contained many bomb cavities some twenty feet across and fifteen feet deep.

A short ride from the palace was the Baghdad Zoo, where lions once belonging to Uday were now being kept. On the way to the zoo was the tomb of the unknown soldier. The massive concrete structure, with gently sloping drive ramps up to the top, resembled a parking garage more than a memorial. Just beyond the memorial were the parade grounds, with a quarter-mile asphalt strip the width of a six-lane freeway. At each end were massive sets of crossed sabers, raised approximately a hundred feet into the sky and held in place at the bottom by a fist and muscular forearm rumored to be shaped after Saddam's own. Sprawled awkwardly around the base of the sabers were thousands of helmets, collected apparently from the dead bodies of Iranian solders.

At the midway point of the parade grounds was a concrete viewing stand where Saddam would gather his Ba'ath party and military elite to witness the display of his goose-stepping Republican Guard, interspersed with tanks, armored trucks, and antiaircraft equipment. At the center and top was a podium where Saddam would stand and fire his rifle in celebration of his defiance of anything or anyone who would dare resist his power.

At the opposite end of the Green Zone was the Al Rasheed Hotel. It was clear from the design of the hotel that it had long been the gathering place for high-society elites. The downstairs had high ceilings, ornate furnishings, and a large lounge that would match that of Western hotels. It was owned and controlled by the state so that strict surveillance could be maintained on the few foreign visitors and journalists who ventured to Baghdad. And the tall, square-windowed hotel was haunted by stories of Wild West–style parties hosted by Uday. This was the site of many Iraqi wedding parties where Uday surveyed the social landscape for a young beauty, even the bride herself. Many ended up taken to his palace, raped, and beaten or killed.

The Oasis

The Green Zone was a self-contained city within a city, fully walled around the perimeter, with massive gates and stone archways with its own elite security. Entering it was like driving into a massive amusement park. In addition to all of the official buildings, this space contained thousands of elite military and government officials under Saddam. It was basically an oasis for Saddam's enriched elite.

The residents had their own schools and a hospital that boasted the best care available in the Arab world. In the years leading up to the invasion, the infant malnutrition rate in Iraq steadily climbed. But there was no awareness of the harsh daily realities encountered by ordinary Iraqis here, where the privileged and padded few raised their children in a small utopia.

Saddam did not want those who came physically close to him to mingle with the Iraqi population; they might become compromised and turn on him. His survival depended upon heaping more and more privileges on a decadent and corrupt class surrounding him. For them, Iraq truly was the glory of the Arab world.

The residential sections of the Green Zone were organized much like an American subdivision. Along the main drag were entire sections of high-rise luxury apartments, which were reportedly home to senior Ba'ath party officials and military commanders. Clearly, the occupants had put up a fight here before being killed or disappearing. Many of the high-rise buildings were pockmarked from mortar attacks. Others had the sprayed markings of .50-caliber machine-gun fire over entire sections.

Turning off the main road was like entering any gated community. Just beyond the major boulevards were narrower streets curving through neighborhood after neighborhood of luxury homes and villas.

The villas were set back off the roads and slightly obscured by date palms and various imported and carefully watered trees. Grass was a symbol of privilege, and this was the greenest section of the Green Zone. Many homes had small lakes in the rear, all linked together and fed by a well-flowing stream of water with large exotic fish. Resting on the banks were little rowboats and paddleboats. Circling the finer homes were hedges and low stone walls. Most featured nice patios with balconies overhead, looking out over rich landscaping dotted by a variety of imported plants.

On many occasions as I traveled through these neighborhoods, now occupied by American military and contractors, I wondered where these elite lieutenants in Saddam's regime had gone. What are they now doing?

Transformation

By the time we arrived, the palace was a dark, cavernous place of mostly empty rooms stacked with bedroom furniture and wide halls filled with the echoes of distant conversations and clopping shoes. Once the place was made suitable for living and working, it looked much like a college campus townhouse, with beds, shelves, and furniture scavenged from parents and yard sales.

Slowly the palace was transformed into the offices, meeting place, and mess hall for the massive occupying force. By midsummer most of the hundreds of bedrooms would be converted to offices, with door plaques indicating rooms that were government ministry headquarters. The palace was now the national government of Iraq, and we were in charge of it.

Getting adequate phone service and computer lines took months, but by midsummer the palace was crawling end to end with miles of power cables snaking along, crossing, and intersecting on the marble floors and secured in place by duct tape.

The furniture was a very strange hodgepodge of what could be rounded up from Saddam's storage facilities along with the cheapest K-mart–style laminated desks with stapled particleboard drawers. Accompanying each desk was a short swivel office chair with plastic rollers.

The palace had been cut off from Iraq's electrical grid, which wasn't really functioning anyway. Large generators supplied limited power. Before air conditioning arrived in midsummer, someone made the decision to purchase hundreds of cheap aluminum and plastic fans. Before long most of them broke, often with the motor shaft and nuts of the fan blade coming undone and causing the blade to wobble and vibrate across the floor before dying altogether. Soon, little clusters of discarded fans, broken swivel chairs resting off balance or on their sides, and other broken furniture began accumulating in the rooms and halls.

Intermingled with the new and cheap was the old and gaudy. Saddam's furniture included ornately carved armchairs and loveseats with curved gold leaf wooden legs and high backs. They sloped awkwardly and uncomfortably backward, and their soft cushions were covered with crushed velvet fabrics. The tables were big and husky with heavy-duty legs but cheap veneer surfaces.

Our very ordinary cuisine was catered by Kelly, Brown and Root, subsidiary of the giant defense contractor Halliburton. Every meal featured an excellent salad bar but otherwise was fattening fare of high-calorie meat and mashed potatoes and gravy accompanied by severely steamed peas. What the menu lacked in quality it more than made up for in quantity. Had it not been for intense heat and exhausting physical exertion, many would have left the battlefield bulkier than when they arrived.

For sleeping quarters, hundreds of house trailers were moved onto the grounds behind the palace and around the surrounding palaces. Perhaps the largest symbols of occupation were those white trailers. Satellite photos of the palace taken before we arrived and five months later displayed a Green Zone completely converted to occupation use, with what appears like thousands of little matchboxes all over the grounds within several blocks of the palace.

The comfortable but spartan trailers were about thirty feet long with a small entrance, a single bath and shower the size of a small closet, and bedrooms on either end. Each bedroom was about ten by ten with two single beds each. This was a far cry from the Kuwait Hilton.

As the months wore on and conditions deteriorated, the trailers became heavily sandbagged, with some trailers completely hidden inside a sandbag fortress, with a tiny opening at the door.

Small Comforts

Behind the palace was a large Olympic-size swimming pool with a water fountain at one end and a twenty-five-foot-high concrete diving board that would become famous in press reports as a place of parties and fraternization. Around the pool were patches of dry, parched grass shaded by date palms.

The pool area resembled the scene of a large country club with its own guesthouse and open patio at one end. When we first arrived, the pool was like a stagnant pond: murky water with pads of green algae on top. Within weeks, the army had the pool drained and restored to its original blue lining and supplied with fresh water.

Before long it was surrounded by chaise lounges and became the site of loud pool parties, with water fights and high-dive competitions. A typical afternoon combined the familiar scenes of home and symbols of war. Next to stacks of machine guns and desert-colored combat boots were soccer balls, Frisbees, and headsets. The female soldiers seemed to enjoy being surrounded by admiring males, who outnumbered them by ten to one.

The pool became the symbol of occupation. That was truly unfortunate and unfair because it was one of the few comforts available for hardworking service men and women. I was always encouraged by the sights and sounds

An abandoned Olympic swimming pool. The entire compound around the presidential palace featured exquisite and well maintained facilities, but all were abandoned at the onset of the war.

of soldiers laughing in that sad country. For the few troops who had access to the palace, it was a place to cool off and regain some equilibrium.

The army understandably tries to offer troops stationed abroad some basic comforts. What private company would do anything less for personnel serving for long periods of time away from home under hazardous conditions? I knew of no one who spent more than a short afternoon break at that pool.

Crawling along the front of the palace were light armored Humvees equipped with .50-caliber machine guns, operated by soldiers who appeared to be in their teens. Convoys would form there to accompany us to our destination in downtown Baghdad. Soldiers could be seen there in small circles smoking, checking maps, and making small talk. I had remembered the palace and surrounding Green Zone as a fairly casual place. We came and went, occasionally driving ourselves into the safer neighborhoods in surrounding Baghdad for a night out at a restaurant.

When I returned later in 2003, that same area gave a different impression. Now the place had a certain chill to it. I saw truckload after truckload of ten-foot T-walls of reinforced concrete, which increasingly lined major entranceways and trailer areas. Their purpose was to prevent collateral damage from car bomb blasts. There were layer upon layer of army checkpoints with winding mazes of concrete barriers, razor wire, and hand-painted signs warning that the driver was entering a kill zone. Accentuating the state of security were M1 Abrams tanks visibly posted at the major intersections even within the Green Zone.

At that point, security had become a part of nearly every conversation. The absence of sufficient numbers of convoys was a constant drain on the morale of senior ministry advisors and their staff. Policy required that we travel in our Suburbans with a lead and rear vehicle, preferably with heavy guns. After months of frustration, CPA turned to contracting out security. The standard private security detail was a big, burly ex–navy SEAL with twenty years' experience in special operations. Eventually, upward of twenty thousand private security personnel would be operating in Iraq at any given time; they were professional tough guys who worked under their own rules of engagement. The private security details were welcome additions, but they were yet another parallel universe operating within CPA.

A large parking lot had been carved into a patch of rocky banks and abandoned trash across the street. It was covered with fresh highway stone and contained row upon row of dusty Suburban SUVs. Just beyond the parking lot was a large concrete pad cleared for helicopter operations. The constant takeoffs and landings of Blackhawks and large transport helicopters created unrelenting background noise.

Looking out the office window, you could see the helicopters rising and descending, slowly sweeping across the palace area at low altitude, whipping a haze of dust. The dust was a constant companion. Occasionally sandstorms blew through; the dust was so fine that it looked like smog. It lay suspended just above the ground before settling down and seeping through every tiny crack in cars, buildings, and nasal passages. Everything from the sidewalks, to the grass and roses, to the lamp stands lining the curved driveway would be covered.

First Night in the Palace

Our first night was an introduction to just how difficult sleep would be. My roommates were great guys, but three of the four snored. And the night silence was frequently broken by the bursts of machine-gun fire, sometimes followed by returned fire. Periodically the thunderous sound of heavier artillery rattled the window frames and broken glass and echoed off the sandstone walls of the palace. The stillness of the night was also interrupted by the roar of diesel engines and steel tracks as tanks rumbled through the street in front of the palace. It sounded much like the rumble and roar of an approaching train.

The sound of gunfire in the background reminded me of the opening day of buck hunting in my native Pennsylvania. In this case, however, those pulling the triggers would kill us if given the chance. Fortunately, the thick walls of the palace provided serious protection. In the coming months, bullets did fire through windows and mortars did hit the palace. I was relieved that Garner chose this place. Miraculously, personal injuries were mostly prevented.

Bedtime Stories in the Presidential Palace

Night after night for the first few weeks, we would all make our way by flashlight to our second-floor bedrooms and huddle around a small coffee table to eat MREs and talk. Basic services such as electricity remained so poor that there was little else you could do late at night.

For the first three days, we could only "shower" with water from small plastic water bottles. Finally, a trailer with six temporary showers arrived for the entire group. Because there was no special shower space for the women and because most of the staff were men, one hour was set aside for women to enter and shower.

The room we converted to our bedroom was pitch black after sundown, except for the soft gleam of candlelight flickering from a circle of sofa chairs. We had to squint to fix our MRE meals. MREs were about all we ate during the first two weeks until the military contractor, Kelly, Brown and Root (KBR), was able to set up operations and bring food in from Kuwait and Jordan. Except for the coffee, dry Danish pastries, and bananas we received in the morning, MREs would be our food.

The evening chatter over MREs and candlelight with our colleagues would become an unforgettable nightly ritual. The social life on the second-floor corridor was the closest thing to bonding that happened there on the war front. Each of us would tell the day's war stories and give our assessment of how things were going.

One of the most fascinating experiences of Iraq was the people we met there. It is said that the war front attracts a certain type of person—the adventurer and risk taker. Iraq attracted a variety of men in midlife who had weathered all kinds of exotic missions and encounters with danger, like my good friend Terry Sullivan, who had won the Purple Heart as a navy SEAL and walked with a limp. Terry was a survivor and an unflappable problem solver, and one couldn't have asked for a better roommate.

One evening, Terry and I joined a couple of male colleagues for a cigar on the balcony of the presidential palace. We stood talking, overlooking the large expanse of gardens that Saddam had built. Joining us was the army engineer I had met in Kuwait City who had been responsible for finding our real estate. He was pleased with the decision to occupy the palace.

A typical late-night scene on the balcony of the presidential palace, with my good friend Terry Sullivan on the left and an unknown individual on the right.

He described the very first night when he arrived at the palace. Lions, which had been released from Uday's personal zoo during the conflict, were roaming around the palm trees and fruit orchards just beyond us. Local Iraqis who had slipped into the palace compound turned it into an opportunity to do some hunting. He also described investigating the palace after arriving, including finding rooms and vaults that had been used to store cash.

Not surprisingly, our late night conversations carried some private hushed grumbling about services, security, and the lack of basic support. Open complaining was rarely heard; everyone knew that grumbling had a contagious effect, and we owed it to our mission to keep a positive outlook.

The conduct of my colleagues under such challenging conditions was truly remarkable, and something I will never forget. There were occasional harsh exchanges as difficult issues were raised, and an occasional power struggle was openly aired in a meeting. But, amazingly, I never saw exchanges that were truly out of line.

The candor and grumbling were confined to private group settings, mostly small circles of four or five. It was natural to have doubts about the level of resources and planning we saw around us. We all felt like whoever planned the operation simply did not give much thought to what would be needed to restore services and re-create a government.

The Baghdad Zoo, where Uday's lions were transferred from his palace after the war. One of the early international news stories was the outpouring of concern worldwide for the welfare of the animals.

According to a July 27, 2003, article in the *Sunday Times* (London), an executioner to Uday revealed how he helped drag two 19-year-old students—romantic rivals of Uday's for a woman's affections—into a cage at Uday's palace to be devoured by his lions. "I saw the head of the first student literally come off his body with the first bite," he told the *Times*. "By the time they were finished there was little left but for the bones and bits and pieces of unwanted flesh."

The postwar period was without question the most pivotal to producing the desired outcome, but the conversations late at night revealed the pervasive lack of resources and support. Inadequate security generally, and too little military support for the ministries in particular, were especially crippling. We never had enough convoys to get around during the day, and travel without them was very dangerous.

At the three-week mark, the palace windows were still broken out. As a result, the heat, mosquitoes, and heavy dust made sleeping very difficult. When we woke up, a film of fine brown dust covered everything, including our bed linens and clothing. Our mouths and noses were dry from having inhaled it all night long. The first thing I did in the morning was to gulp down water and snort the dust out of my nose.

Rats crawled through the food that had not been cleaned out of Saddam's many kitchens. Not far from the palace were pools of contaminated water. The large pool behind the palace was half full of brownish green water. With all of the filth and rot around us, we quickly recalled the Fort Meade warnings about malaria and other diseases.

The mosquitoes probably posed the greatest concern. In our morning meetings, we would look around the room and see faces covered with large red mosquito bites. That provided some comic relief. We finally managed to purchase mosquito nets and rig them up over our beds—just as they are used in the third world. At one point in the early weeks, all four of my roommates became sick. Fortunately, they quickly recovered.

Soon, we began seeing groups of Iraqis who had been hired to clean and repair the palace. Day by day their numbers grew. They filed through in long lines and appeared trained to be strictly obedient to their foreman. They would show up in the morning, do their scrubbing, and then march back in a single line to their buses and leave. Later, the local Iraqis started making their way into other support services, working as interpreters and transportation aides. As the price of working for us, many of them encountered threats and violence. The price for us was that some were allegedly informants and became potential dangers to us.

Every night and every morning at our 7 a.m. staff roundtables, we heard very dramatic stories of danger, difficulty, and treachery, and some of true heroism. Gary Voegler, who was handling the oil ministry, described how a meeting he was holding with Iraqi oil ministry workers was disrupted by loud booing. It turned out that one of the oil ministry employees, who had been invited to play a management part in the newly organized ministry, was a former Ba'athist and Saddam backer. The anti-Ba'athist group made it clear that they would not allow the meeting to continue under the circumstances.

Instead, the dissident group turned to a quiet, soft-spoken colleague whom they trusted. They raised him up on their shoulders, symbolizing their trust in him and his leadership. As Voegler soon learned, he was the man who protected the refinery from looting following the war. At considerable danger to himself, he hid the fire trucks and slept at the refinery to protect the equipment and facility from looters.

Some stories, like that one, inspired; most carried the heartbreak of a destroyed country. Senior advisors frequently encountered heartrending stories of Iraqis whose lives steadily disintegrated following the war. One advisor reported that one of his workers borrowed a car and drove for three hours in order to meet him. The man, who had seven children and a pregnant wife in need of medical services, simply had no money to care for them. The young Iraqi father just sat there and sobbed.

Many stories told of Iraqis wanting to know where their next paycheck would be coming from. We heard of questions shouted in anger: "How do we get back to work?" "Where do we go to get paid?" One Iraqi advisor told us, "If you don't fix that problem, Saddam will be elected in your first election." Iraqi friends began telling us about a very well-organized movement coming together to undermine us. We could almost feel the earth shifting around us.

THE DRIFT OF OUR DAILY "SHOP TALK" would flow from one ORHA colleague talking about visiting a prison where large-scale torture had occurred under Saddam. Another would tell of visiting Saddam's ministry of defense, where he collected thousands of valuable documents.

Many comments from Iraqis reflected admiration of General Garner, but also the concern that he was being too "nice" and was too slow to establish order. He was making mistakes. For example, according to some reports, he was too quick to appoint only those recommended by senior advisors.

That template, developed back in Washington, was failing. Some of my colleagues described how their ministries were rapidly becoming war zones in themselves. The health ministry, in particular, became the battlefield for a tug of war between hostile groups that were fighting each other to take it over. This was the first report we had received of Shia power groups emerging and asserting themselves. Almost immediately, the language was sectarian.

This wasn't a case of "Iraqis" stepping forward to take over. These were Shia militia taking physical custody of the ministry building.

One of my most unforgettable memories into downtown Baghdad was when my convoy passed one of the many large busts of Saddam that were still standing. Two boys, appearing about fourteen, had climbed up on one of the large stone statues of Saddam. With hammers and small chisels, they were chipping away at the head of Saddam. As we slowly passed, they each turned in our direction, smiled brightly, and spontaneously gave us a thumbs-up. It was one of the high points of my experience and symbolized the hopeful side of what we were doing. I came there to help the youth, and if the sentiment expressed by those two boys was shared by other youth, perhaps Iraq had a future.

THE GREEN ZONE WAS SOMETHING OF A PARADISE—a verdant mixture of gardens, ponds, streams, ornamental bridges, and private villas. It is somewhat similar to the National Mall in Washington. But it was also a place of poverty and squatters. In the early days in the Green Zone, we had opportunities to wander around the grounds and through the palaces and government buildings that filled several square miles along the Tigris. Everywhere, we could see signs of a regime and its military that put up one last fight and then fled, defeated. Behind the presidential palace, lining the banks of the Tigris, were antiaircraft guns, unexploded ordnance, and crates of unspent .50-caliber bullets. I saw wrecked and bombed vehicles and a disabled presidential helicopter. All of the troops' quarters along the river displayed gaudy pro-Saddam slogans and pictures painted in garish reds and greens.

Saddam's abandoned helicopter.

Presumably they stood in the hope of appearing like devoted followers of the strongman whose palace they were protecting.

Spread all over the grounds within blocks of the palaces, I saw dozens of items left behind by Iraqi soldiers. Around the barracks were green Iraqi army shirts bearing the Republic Guard or Elite Republican Guard insignia, mingled with discarded chemical masks. There were black berets, army helmets, weight-bearing straps, and ammo packs. Scattered across the troop barracks were small care packages filled with basic toiletries and dog tags with their owners' names engraved in Arabic. Obviously, many of the soldiers just left their items behind and fled.

On occasion I accompanied an army friend, responsible for document recovery, to explore some of the government buildings that were bombed. On one such visit, we went through the badly bombed Council of Ministries building. Four holes in the roof, approximately three feet wide, revealed where bombs had penetrated and then exploded inside the building. The entire structure appeared swollen by the blast. Two-foot-wide concrete pillars, with inch-thick steel rebar, were blasted in half like wooden sticks. Ceilings hung down and floors were piled high with fallen panels, dust, and mangled trash.

We visited what was left of Tarik Aziz's office and found correspondence he'd had with U.S. officials. The contents of his library, now blown across little mountains of blasted and burned office supplies, included books on American politicians like Newt Gingrich and George Herbert Walker Bush.

During those early days in the Green Zone, I also had many opportunities to talk to Iraqis and Americans who had been involved in (or close to) the taking of the grounds. I had conversations with some of the brave American soldiers who helped liberate Baghdad and were among the first to arrive. Many of these soldiers, accustomed to fighting and moving forward, were now taking up stationary posts around the Green Zone maintaining security and directing traffic.

A Very Strange Place

One soldier named Jeff, who told me he was nineteen but looked more like sixteen, went into some detail about his liberation-period job of removing bodies from the path of oncoming military vehicles. He properly disposed of body parts and buried the dead as best he could according to Muslim traditions. He took this responsibility very seriously and worried that, in the haste and pressure of war, he might not have done it properly in every case.

It was impossible to miss the images of Saddam, "strongman and defender of the nation," everywhere we turned. One could not travel a single city block or visit an office building without encountering prominent displays of the image of Saddam.

Jeff put a brave face on what he saw and projected a fairly cavalier tone as he described his experience, but his eyes told a different story. In addition to appearing tired and gaunt, he looked like a boy who had lost his innocence the wrong way. Perhaps he would wake up some day after returning home and look back on it with different feelings. I wondered how his life would turn out in ten or fifteen years when he had to make sense out of those grisly scenes.

Most of our late night chatter sessions were about the remaining violence. There were even growing daily reports of trouble around the palace. We could hear regular AK-47 gunfire from across the Tigris, and even some from within the Green Zone. Shots were fired from just beyond the palace in the direction of the main gate. One tough-talking State Department colleague described having to travel in a civilian vehicle through a congested area without a convoy because security support was not available. They did so with guns loaded, cocked, and pointed outward. Baghdad was generally a mess, and our failure to confront it effectively was having real consequences for Iraq's political future.

One day in late April, four people traveling in a mixed group of soldiers and civilians were involved in a remarkable incident. According to the report, when the convoy got stuck in traffic, one person was shot. When the rest of the group bailed out of their vehicles, three more were shot at. And when the American soldiers killed the shooter, some of the Iraqi locals dismembered him. This was an act of vengeance being carried out against the shooter, whom they believed to be a Ba'athist.

What a strange place: some Iraqis were so hostile to us that they would try to kill us; others were so supportive of what we were trying to do that they

This ammunition used in marksmanship training before the war had been stashed at a youth training center.

would dismember a fellow Iraqi's corpse to display their rage at his conduct. This was a culture in which at least some lived by an "eye for an eye" ethic. When any of us stood in these open and crowded places, we wondered, *what if a significant number of the Iraqi people shifted from appreciation for us to opposing our presence?*

What percentage did that gunman represent? we wondered. We were told that 1 percent of Iraqis were dangerous fanatics and that they will always be around; "They will not go away and will probably pose a danger forever." We were also informed that there were sufficient guns in Iraq to fully supply several standing armies. Although Saddam restricted the availability of guns during his reign, among the destructive actions he took at the time of his regime's collapse was to allow senior Ba'ath party members to store large stashes of weapons and ammunition in their homes. We even found at least one stash in a youth training center. He also emptied the prisons of common criminals. The combined threat of stashes of weapons and ammunition and armed Ba'athist common criminals crawling all over Baghdad was sobering.

Though none of us on the civilian team offered opinions about troop requirements before the war, after the first couple of weeks in Baghdad, most of us concluded that we had about a third of the troop strength that was necessary. The troops were spread far too thin. Whenever soldiers were moved from one assignment to another in response to an urgent need, they just created a new gap.

Apparently the stories from the street matched the intelligence reports that were beginning to trickle into the palace; significant hostility remained. The danger was underscored when a U.S. staff member ventured just beyond the compound into an area that had not been swept and raked for mines and was injured by a booby trap.

That incident prompted Jay Garner's deputy Jerry Bates to call a meeting on the second day, April 25. He must have just been given a security briefing because he sternly made his way through a long series of demands about protecting ourselves. According to him, the environment in and around Baghdad was still "hot," meaning that although our military had established basic control, a lot of insecurity remained. There was a lot of shooting across the city, he said, some of it celebratory and some of it aimed at us. And, he told us, there were paramilitary elements and many Ba'athist Special Forces still lurking around looking for trouble. Obviously, not all of them had been killed or had fled the city.

It quickly became apparent that tough new ground rules would be implemented for our movements about the compound and beyond. The bottom line, Bates said, was that people are still being shot at and consequently "no one goes anywhere without coordination with the ops [operations] center.

"You can't," he forcefully declared, "roll on your own. No free agents. No primadonnas. Force protection is key." These blunt orders were delivered in that staccato rhythm so typical of military men. We knew he had to be in possession of sobering information.

I heard the term "force protection" used frequently, and I deeply admired and appreciated the military concern for our safety. Was the war not quite over, or was it continuing into a new phase?

A Broken Country

Services were poor to nonexistent for the first month. We had to get by with porta-johns, temporary shower stalls, MREs, lots of bottled water, and our Thuraya satellite phones. To look in any direction was to see dirt, trash, and choking dust clouds. The atmosphere burned the eyes and dried the throat.

The dry, energy-draining desert heat reached 130 degrees in the afternoon. To stand in the open sun was to feel like you had walked into a furnace. The heat radiated up from the asphalt and penetrated through our thick army boots. In the background were the constant rattle of firefights and the rumble of heavy mortar explosions. Sleep was disrupted by explosions that sounded like the thunder of a summer lightning storm.

Incredibly, none of that seemed to matter to the group; I heard very little complaining about what we had to endure. The very diverse group that served would, by midsummer of 2003, swell into the thousands. But from the beginning, it seemed that what everyone had in common and what everyone wanted, from ORHA short-termers to State Department careerists, was to simply see things work.

When we had arrived in the ancient city of Baghdad, we were all shocked and stunned by what we saw; the damage from the bombing, looting, and burning was catastrophic. Looters had dismantled entire buildings, first clearing out all furnishings, then prying loose the flooring, wiring, and even toilets and window frames. They even carried off electrical gauges and controls.

The two most discouraging revelations during the early weeks in Baghdad were discovering the scale of looting and the condition of the ministry buildings. We received our first images of the looting from TV in Kuwait City. Then we saw it on the streets of Baghdad. Our first intelligence briefing on the state of government buildings, supplies, and equipment was genuinely depressing. We were told that "ministry buildings are mostly gone."

My immediate reaction was that this factor alone would set back recovery by years if not decades. At the time of this writing, three years after the invasion, many government ministries were still operating in temporary locations and lacking adequate office equipment such as desks and computers. Everything was picked clean in most government buildings, including universities, police stations, municipal buildings, and even many hospitals, and there never really was enough money to replace the equipment and materials carried off in the orgy of looting that followed the war.

THE LOOTING WAS HEARTBREAKING and infuriating. As it always does, the looting led to the wider breakdowns of the country. Looking back, it is clear that the looting never really ended; it merely metastasized into sabotage. A single grenade to a pipeline or a rifle shot to an electric power line was all it took to halt forward movement. The cost of the devastation would run into the tens of billions. Iraq was a broken country.

Smoke was still pouring out of the windows of the Ministry of Youth and Sport when I arrived, and the Olympic Committee building lay in ruins. I never was able to find a single senior official from the ministry; they were all hardcore Ba'athists and had apparently disappeared the moment we arrived.

The criminal elements were on a rampage of armed robbery, kidnappings, and car-jackings.

Whatever reconstruction or governing templates might have existed in Washington or Kuwait City were of little value at that point. Many judgments would have to be made on the ground. To borrow a football metaphor, it was now time to "call the audibles," and from my experience Jay Garner (and, later, Paul Bremer) did some excellent quarterbacking under the circumstances.

In the midst of the dangerous and chaotic environment of the postwar period, each of the ministry team leaders struggled against the odds to build a new government and a new life for the Iraqis. In spite of the devastation and dysfunction, we all knew we had a job to do and spent the early weeks working sixteen-hour days, seven days a week. We lived and worked in intense dehydrating heat, fighting for a few hours of sleep at night on cots in mosquito-filled rooms with broken windows. Later we moved, some into tiny trailers and others into large common rooms stacked with back-to-back temporary beds.

FOR THE ENTIRE TWO YEARS THAT I SERVED, there was a near consensus among both my civilian and military colleagues that the postwar operation was woefully lacking adequate security and that most of the early assumptions of senior Pentagon officials were seriously, if not fatally, flawed.

To actually stand in the midst of Baghdad was to be overwhelmed with the incongruity of the oft-repeated mantra of "light touch, brief stay." I heard that phrase used a dozen times back in Kuwait City. These basic operating assumptions were deeply embedded at the Pentagon's policy office, and they were extended over the planning process for regime change of which we were all a part.

But from the moment Baghdad fell, it was apparent that we were going to leave a heavy footprint and stay awhile, not by design but by default. Iraq was a collapsed state, a non-state. It wasn't a matter of giving someone the keys and just handing the vehicle over. There was no vehicle. To leave immediately would have ensured a rapid and inexorable descent into civil war.

It took being there on the ground to appreciate fully that Iraq was practically America's fifty-first state. But there was a huge disconnect. Although it was never stated, the underlying assumption seemed to be that the atmosphere following the liberation would be so filled with joy and the Iraqis so possessed of high ideals that they would coalesce quickly in a spirit of collaboration and goodwill to build a new political order.

That might actually have been realistic under circumstances of stability and order, but not under the ones we encountered following the war. Baghdad was a tense and chaotic place. Although Iraqis were pleased to be rid of Saddam, their general mood was one of apprehension. Iraq was now a society set free from a tyrant but without a legitimate political state, no functioning government, and descending into public disorder due to limited security.

Our mission as civilians was captured and defined in ORHA's name; our job was to quickly address reconstruction needs following the war and attend to any immediate humanitarian concerns such as water, sanitation, and food. We would also start the process of repairing damage and rebuilding the country (especially in such critical sectors as oil). But basically the team was told that after these tasks were completed we would all just go home.

Not for one minute in the aftermath of the liberation was this outlook realistic. All we saw around us upon arriving was lawlessness, looting, and a collapsed state. Yet the original rosy assumptions in Washington remained unchanged for months, long after a major adjustment in course could have made a substantial difference.

The die was cast during the first month or two after our arrival. The disorder we faced, along with our lack of capacity to forcefully confront those conditions, set the stage for the reality the United States has endured since that time. Ambassador Bremer would arrive and face the growing reality that our presence and role was becoming an occupation. But he would still struggle for months to gain adequate security, resources, and personnel from Washington.

It was clear to us that other forces—regime remnants, Ba'ath party people, and corrupt business cronies of the former regime—almost immediately sensed their opportunity. The early weeks in Iraq felt like watching a crash unfolding in slow motion: a collision of pre-war plans and postwar reality on the ground. It was obvious to us that reality would not dawn on Washington for some time. The collective mindset of soaring expectations that preceded the war was not about to be suddenly altered with more sobering assessments from Baghdad. The chaos was mostly dismissed by the secretary of defense as the extravagant exuberance of a people set free.[3]

I had spent my adult life doing analysis and writing extensive reports on complex issues. Yet I found myself incapable of describing what we inherited in Iraq. It wasn't just the chaos, which would become well reported; it was a deep dysfunction on every level. Post-Saddam Iraq was a completely collapsed state and there was no new political or social order waiting in the wings, available to emerge on cue to center stage.

Iraqis look for information shortly after liberation. Their faces reveal a wide range of emotions from jubilation over being rid of Saddam to fear of a new totally uncertain future.

Rarely was there an honest discussion in the lead-up to the war about the likely difficulty of establishing order and authority—the core functions on which everything else depended. Most of us argued repeatedly and forcefully that very strong authority—perhaps even martial law—would need to be exercised in Iraq. According to Jay Garner, he had requested a constabulary and support for policy training but was blocked by National Security Advisor Condoleezza Rice.

While at USAID I had reviewed the state of research on post-conflict stabilization, conflict resolution, and the difficult challenge of transforming institutions that had served totalitarian purposes into peaceful and democratic purposes. In police states, the cancer of totalitarian control and treachery pervades everything. How do you purge the old system and its culture of distrust? Is it enough to simply rush forward toward elections?

The deep fear and distrust inculcated by three decades of dictatorship in a country well known for raw ethnic and sectarian divisions were not going to yield to a new democratic ethos by just putting new people in charge. By liberating Iraq, these complex internal problems of social and political order would pretty much become our responsibility. These risks were known by the experts[4] and were inherent in the decision to liberate Iraq.

In one of the best pieces written about the chasm between pre-war planning and postwar reality, James Fallows wrote in early 2004, "Almost everything, good and bad, that has happened in Iraq since the fall of Saddam Hussein's regime was the subject of extensive pre-war discussion and analysis. This is particularly true of what have proved to be the harshest realities for the United States since the fall of Baghdad: that occupying the country is much more difficult than conquering it; that a breakdown in public order can jeopardize every other goal; that the ambition of patiently nurturing a new democracy is at odds with the desire to turn over control to the Iraqis quickly and get U.S. troops out; that the Sunni center of the country is the main security problem; that with each passing day Americans risk being seen less as liberators and more as occupiers, and targets. All of this, and much more, was laid out in detail and in writing long before the U.S. government made the final decision to attack." [5]

Chapter 4

Civilizations Collide
Seeking Legitimate Authority

WHEN AMERICAN FORCES ARRIVED IN BAGHDAD, two very different cultures collided. The events following liberation cannot be understood without appreciating the enormity of that cultural divide. This was incredibly tough territory for Western liberal democrats, which we all were, whether Republican or Democrat.

For example, America maintains a commitment to "the rule of law." We also strive to be "fair, responsive and transparent." These Western values are, for us, as effortless as inhaling and exhaling; they are part of our secular religion. But how would these highest ideals of governmental practice, informed by Western liberal idealism, be transplanted into the harsh environment of Iraq? The Iraqis were a scared, distrusting people who had been terrorized for decades. Yet we imagined them ready to celebrate their newfound freedoms and immediately take up the challenge of building a democracy.

Even more basically, what did these liberal Western terms even mean in the context of their experience, history, and religious culture? What exactly did "fairness" or "responsiveness" mean in a culture where just finding the right Arabic translation for the word "freedom" was difficult?

Spending six weeks in Kuwait City before launching to Baghdad was very revealing about who we were as Americans. More than anything we prepared ourselves to behave like the nice, sophisticated, and tolerant Americans that we were—an outlook that was strongly encouraged by the breezy assumptions from Washington about our mission. As we thought about the task ahead in Baghdad, we were brimming with our own sense of goodness, which we assumed would carry a certain power in itself. We would arrive, reach out, and help a populace eager for what we had to offer.

"Reaching out, helping, and advising" were the phrases (and attitude) that dominated postwar planning—that is how our mission sounded. We were the helpers, not the rulers. And that is what we would broadcast to the Iraqi people. We would let them know that they are now OK: they were in good hands. We would tell them of our plans to offer "stability, predictability and continuity of essential government services."

After all, we were Americans, and noble ideals and the highest standards of professionalism flowed naturally for all of us. It would become obvious to all just how serious we Americans were about running things well, about insisting on the best way of doing things and settling for nothing less. We had all experienced the most advanced administrative structures that democratic societies have built, and believed without hesitation that there was a superior way of running things that everyone could quickly comprehend and embrace. We also believed that everyone was thoroughly rational and appreciated the life of the mind and of reasoned debate.

Yet beneath it all, none of this seemed to add up.

I kept asking myself how it would even be possible for us to move into a city devastated first by dictatorship, then bombing and war, and finally the chaos of postwar looting and regime collapse, and just be helpers. How could we assume that the same Western concepts of idealism and competence were waiting just below the surface in a country that had been so devastated by all those factors? And how would any of this be possible, even with full Iraqi cooperation, without our establishing and firmly exercising authority, giving direction, and guaranteeing safety? Those are the most basic requirements of public order anywhere. Would high-minded Iraqi career civil servants just show up and say "yes, that's a good idea; let's do it that way"? Would everyone look around the boardroom table and nod in pleasant agreement?

THE IRAQIS WERE A WOUNDED PEOPLE and needed to be treated with compassion. Jay Garner's strong tendency was to treat them with care, but some of us felt like we lost the game during the early period because we were so concerned about acting nice. We often acted as though we were a visiting Rotary Club, chattering endlessly about our big ideas for democratic and professional government. Increasingly, it seemed that we were not being responsible as the occupying authority, confronting problems directly and forcefully where necessary.

For example, many of Ambassador Bremer's critics treat him as though he arrived eager to be the American viceroy, the twentieth-century Douglas

MacArthur who would spend years presiding over a thorough remaking of Iraq's society and government. The reality is, America was a reluctant occupier. We became an occupier because the circumstances allowed nothing less.

Behaving like a Rotary Club can be reassuring to the watching world— everyone is so civil, cooperative, and eager to extend goodwill and trust. Except we were in charge, and these attributes did not exist in great supply in the context around us. Niceness was not a remedy for the ratcheting upward of violence in the streets. And it was never the answer to dealing with the often cagey Iraqis.

The only respect I ever generated came from confronting troublemakers directly and toughly—firing them and handing them over for investigation or indictment. In one case, I fired an American Iraqi who had proven subversive to American purposes; it took me seven hours of wrangling with lawyers and senior CPA staff to get it done. He was put on a plane for home. The story of that buzzed widely throughout the other Iraqis. A few hated me for it, but most knew that he was sabotaging our policies and purposes. They knew I did the right thing. In fact, I would have appeared silly to have not done exactly what I did.

I strongly disliked the authoritarian culture that tends to predominate in much of the Arab Middle East; I often doubted whether it was compatible with democratic society. I hated even more having to, occasionally and as necessary, adopt their practices. But in so many ways, we had to do so in order to get anything done. It seemed like the only way to get things done was to put real toughness in our eyes and voice when dealing with the Iraqis. It was so clear to me that if we were to ever get to the place where democracy was real, then we all had to stop psychologically projecting our own goodness and reasonableness onto a people who had a significant bent toward ruthlessness in behalf of personal gain.

Lest I be misunderstood, let me be clear that there are many kind and generous Iraqis. But they tended to not be the ones seeking power, position, or privilege. They were the ordinary people whom many of our soldiers and contractors met and befriended; they were the ones just praying earnestly that somehow a better life would be forthcoming. Many of these Iraqis became personal friends and remain close to my heart. Nothing I write here would be particularly controversial to them. They often said the same things. They frequently mentioned, for instance, that many of their fellow Iraqis could not be trusted.

National Governance: In Search of a Legitimate Iraqi Regime

This culture clash formed the matrix of some of the biggest postwar issues. For example, the biggest hot potato of all was the issue of securing interim political authority in Iraq. We all knew that the question of who would actually have political authority was well above our pay grade. At one point in Kuwait City, Garner blurted out: "no one in this room has a vote on how the Interim Iraqi Authority will work." The way it was presented suggested that this issue was the exclusive domain of people well above us, and all of us would be wise to steer clear of it.

Accordingly, it was the least discussed topic by those of us serving on the front lines of reconstruction and humanitarian assistance. But, in fact, we were significant "stakeholders" in that process. We were all deeply affected by interim authority issues; little else could be made to work if the transition to Iraqi rule could not be managed. To the greatest extent possible, transitional authority would need to promote national unity by representing all Iraqis and all social groups.

But few indigenous institutions would be ready to manage the process. Political institutions and civil society, it was fair to assume, would be very weak if not entirely nonexistent. We would need to lean to some extent on returning exiles, but their role could be only brief and transitional in scope, oriented toward securing the path to elections.

Whether our stay was short or long, Iraqi leadership would have to take over at some point. And that leadership would need to be competent and legitimate in the eyes of the people. That would require some form of widely accepted process involving the Iraqi people.

Of course, the country would need a new constitution. What constitution would be recommended for the transitional authority? Perhaps an amended version of the 1970 constitution, or maybe the 1925 constitution put in place by the United Kingdom (UK). A significant minority of Iraqis seemed to believe that a restoration of the monarchy was the way to go. The monarchy option, never seriously considered, represented a compromise between pure representative democracy and the authoritarian government that existed under Saddam. Its appeal was that it would contain the factions.

In any event, it was widely assumed that the constitution should guarantee nondiscrimination among Iraqis, due process of law, property rights, freedom of expression, peaceable assembly, freedom of religion and conscience, and an end to torture.

And, of course, the new government would need new leaders. We caught many facts and impressions that slipped through from the contacts that various people had with Washington, especially the Pentagon. If the Pentagon could have had its way, it would probably have installed a friendly regime, presumably led by their favorite, Ahmed Chalabi. It would certainly have been accompanied by a governing council and cabinet supplied largely by Iraqi exiles and their contacts in Iraq. At that stage there really was no way of knowing whether such a plan would work or not. I address the Iraqi exile dilemma in more detail later.

Other plans for political transition had been developed by the State Department and outside study groups. But they weren't really being considered at that time. I never got the sense that alternative plans were evaluated long before the invasion. The original plan for postwar Iraq was to provide security, bring about a stable environment in Iraq, facilitate functioning civil administration, and reduce the size and scope of the military in society.

The rough outlines for transitional government were pretty straightforward: an Interim Iraqi Authority consisting of a balanced council of high-level Iraqi leaders, quickly established in order to immediately put an Iraqi face on the postwar operation. Among the factions and parties that could be counted on for assistance were the Kurdish Democratic Party (KDP) and the Patriotic Union of Kurdistan (PUK).

At this early stage, the governing council would be divided according to branches of government, with a legislature comprising sixty-five exile members who had "agreed to live in Iraq and stay there." That reference could apply only to the exiles. A "higher judicial council" would draft an interim constitution, or rely on an amended version of the constitution that was in operation before Saddam. The administrative branch would comprise local technocrats working with appointed Iraqi advisors (again presumably returning Iraqi exiles). These Iraqis, working together, would think through how to best earn the support of those inside the country.

From time to time, we caught glimpses into why major details of postwar governance were being overlooked and why Iraqi exiles, so deeply trusted at the time by the Pentagon, were favored to take control. It seemed that the calculation (at least with some at DoD) was to treat Iraq much like Afghanistan—liberate, consolidate power in friendly hands, and move on.

At various times during our stay in Kuwait City, we saw signs that the Pentagon was planning to move onto Iran and possibly Syria, both regarded as equal troublemakers. We needed to "re-cock," as one official visitor from the Pentagon was overheard saying. This kind of talk was always mumbled and half-serious. At first, I thought it was the kind of tough talk that naturally accompanies operations like this (injected to keep the adrenaline going). But when I heard the term used again and again by other people, I realized it was actually a serious idea among those who had a larger vision for the Middle East.

Although that idea seems outlandish now, it was a lot less so in the early post-9/11 climate. The United States had been attacked and was facing a variety of enemies that were armed and dangerous. Some of that danger (especially from Iran) was more "clear and present" than that represented by Iraq. If we were willing to face the fallout from taking one power out, why not attack its heavily armed neighbor? And when you add in the factor that the senior American officials who orchestrated the liberation of Iraq did not operate within conventional foreign policy boundaries, it actually wasn't that far-fetched to imagine.

That idea never found much circulation in the civilian circles, and I seriously doubt that it was ever presented to the president. Whatever shortcomings might have existed in the analysis preceding Iraq, I just couldn't image the president being willing to take that kind of gamble. We all remembered the strong feeling of having the entire free world firmly and emotionally behind America following the terrorist attacks of 9/11. We also knew that the controversy of the Iraq invasion left the world a lot more divided.

Iraq was enough to swallow. As the world's sole superpower, the United States was already viewed with some suspicion in the region. I couldn't imagine the international community tolerating the United States sweeping through the Middle East and Asia, taking out every regime we disliked. If I was wrong, the world environment had changed since 9/11 more than I thought.

Iraq's History

While stationed in Kuwait City, I spent hours researching Iraq's history, especially the experience of the British in the 1920s. In fact, everyone who agreed to serve in ORHA should have been required to read the British-Iraq history. Britain's attempts to create a Westernized democratic order had profound echoes for the U.S. invasion and occupation of Iraq.

I found it particularly compelling that most senior planners seemed to assume that, at some point in the twentieth century, Iraq modernized and, therefore, the Iraqi people were now ready for democracy. That assumption, more than any other, would be severely tested. What was eerie was how each of the stages of difficulty encountered by the United States during the first year paralleled that of the British occupation in the 1920s. The casualties of war at approximately the six-month mark were almost identical.

In the 1920s, the British had 133,000 troops in Iraq. Then as now, the conventional military forces of the British were severely disadvantaged by the stealth guerilla tactics. The enemy was a mysterious element that rarely confronted British forces directly.

Before long, the British felt trapped. Military operations became expensive and lost public support. Much like the American approach, the British realized that they could not occupy the country and expect to achieve peace. So they made a series of attempts to create "councils" of Iraqis to run state affairs. Because they were handpicked by foreigners, these Iraqi rulers failed to gain legitimacy with the Iraqi people. Elections were held in 1924, but under a constitution drawn up to satisfy British concerns. Numerous Iraqis came and went from cabinet positions, but they never really gained the respect or legitimacy of the Iraqi people. Increasingly, the Iraqi rulers were seen as corrupt and isolated, directing most of their energies toward keeping the British happy.

In another striking comparison, attempts by the British to build democracy suffered from a lack of supporting civic institutions. According to William Polk, democracy building failed because of a "lack of developed civic institutions," combined with an imbalance "between the cities and the rural areas, the rich and the poor, the landed and the landless, the literate and the illiterate," all of which "created a sense of frustration and anger." [1]

Loyalties became very confused. The Iraqi security forces increasingly found themselves standing between the British and an unhappy electorate. So they turned to secretly subverting British rule by forming secret societies and mounting coups, most of which failed but did succeed in preventing any government from getting securely established. The first successful coup was in 1958 when a small fledgling faction destroyed the monarchy by killing the king.

One of the most sobering and relevant monographs I discovered was published by the Washington Institute for Near East Studies, a major Washington think tank that features on its advisory board a dozen titans of American foreign policy, ranging from traditionalists to neoconservatives.

"U.S. Policy in Post-Saddam Iraq: Lessons from the British Experience," by Michael Eisenstadt and Eric Mathewson, was published in early 2003, before U.S. military operations commenced in Iraq. It opened by saying that

Here I am attempting to reorganize and open a community center, one of hundreds across Iraq that were part of our civilian reconstruction efforts. The community centers were the only available hub for regenerating civic life and providing programming for youth.

while much had changed in Iraq, "Britain's experience shares certain striking parallels with U.S. involvement in Iraq."

Eisenstadt and Mathewson, while seemingly sympathetic to the invasion, predicted difficulty in balancing America's traditional interest in stability in the region with the broad new goal of democratization, particularly in achieving a broad-based postwar government that incorporated all ethnic and sectarian divisions. It further conveyed the hope that the Coalition Provisional Authority could avoid "retribalization" and minimize the need for a long-term military presence.

Although the British sustained far more casualties in the military operation than the coalition forces did in 2003, they still easily captured and initially subdued Iraq. The British forces, according to this rendering of history, "marched swiftly northward, at first meeting little resistance; the euphoria this created encouraged those in charge in Delhi and London to contemplate an immediate dash to Baghdad."

According to official records, some senior British government officials voiced a concern that caught a familiar reverberation in our own experience: "We must at least consider the possibility of a peace which will not give us the absolute political control of Mesopotamia."

Like the military operation, the civil administration started with relative calm. Initially, according to the report, residents of Baghdad received their liberators with enthusiasm. But such sentiments evaporated quickly and were replaced steadily with a resentment that grew and culminated in the "great Iraqi revolution" against the British in June of 1920.

The British insisted that they came as liberators, not conquerors, and did not plan to impose alien institutions on the Iraqi people. But the difficulty of providing security and order combined with a variety of unpopular economic measures turned the tide of opinion inexorably and stiffly against them.

The 1920 revolt forced the British to redouble their efforts, in particular to more earnestly try to create a system of democratic governance for the Iraqis. But they proved equally inept at that. They tried to create a parliamentary system that would provide some popular representation while preserving a monarchy friendly to British interests. Because the British simply did not believe that the "orientals" were capable of self-rule, they introduced half-measures that were received by the Iraqis as sham democracy. The constitution was drafted by three British advisors from the Iraqi Ministry of Justice, positions that closely resembled those of the CPA eight decades later. It was a Western liberal system of rule of law, not one that reflected Arab or Muslim customs.

Although the Ottomans had ruled Iraq through intermediaries, the requirement for governance was now thrust upon the region, and the British had to make it work. After a short period of relative calm, the British army ran into problems. With hindsight, said the report, "both the state and its military contained deep-seated elements of instability that gradually worked their way to the surface."

The British found themselves stretched far too thin across the vast territory. The result was frequent excesses to control the population with "rumors, constant unrest, and repeated killings." When it was clear that there were too few troops for the task and the "boots on the ground" were expanded fourfold, Iraqis became resentful. It didn't help that the British relied heavily on Sunnis, who had played a key role in governing during the Ottoman period, in a country in which Shiites were the majority. Most of the institutions created by the Brits favored Sunni Arab elites, who were appointed by undemocratic means and mostly chosen based upon their commitment to British colonial interests.

For a while political and social equilibrium was maintained under Faysal Ibn Husayn, who had been picked by the British to build a new Iraqi state. Faysal died at the early age of fifty; following his death, Iraq "degenerated into a series of unseemly struggles for power." In 1936, Iraq experienced the first of many attempted military coups.

The Shiites, the then disfavored group, were severely underrepresented in cabinet positions and the parliament. Because the British-imposed system never overcame the appearance of farce to the Iraqis, there were fifteen military coups from 1936 to 1968. By the time the Ba'athists came to power in 1968, the army had already become one of the most powerful institutions in Iraq, responsible for political repression and crushing ethnic uprisings. Once Iraq was harnessed fully to the Ba'ath agenda under Saddam, little was left of the British attempts to introduce democratic pluralism.

The difficulty then, as now, was that Iraq had never been a unitary country like some of its Arab neighbors whose borders and government had been established and operated for centuries. The Kurdish north had been chaotic and did not view itself as part of a larger Iraq; it hoped to have its own separate state. Central and southern Iraq directed their attention to Iran. The provinces that constituted Iraq, according to the report, "sat there awkwardly together."

Iraqis could never overcome their suspicion that Britain was not entirely interested in indigenous development and rather had its eyes fixed on maintaining its strategic oil interests. The brief period of relative peace that followed British control "soon began to fray, largely because the military paid little attention to the needs and wants of the Iraqi people," and because the British "turned to the tried and true policies and bureaucracy of their civil administration in India." British officers became involved in every aspect of Iraqi life, usually compounding problems by reinforcing doubts that Iraqis would ever gain their independence.

The notion of broad-based political transformation of the region proved to be an elusive and costly objective. The experience throughout the 1920s was one of steady British military retreat under conditions set for them and not favorable to their objectives. In October of 1921, the British and Indian armies had seventeen battalions stationed in Iraq; by 1930, there were none. The only presence was four squadrons of the British Royal Air Force, which regularly resorted to bombing in order to punish uncooperative tribes.

In what could have been taken as a mandate for the aggressive dismissal of Ba'athists later adopted by Ambassador Bremer, the report expressed deep concerns about the military. It predicted that "a massive amount of dismissal and retraining" would be required, and Iraqi civilian control could be established only gradually. It said, "over the past five decades, the greatest threat to the stability of Iraq has always come from small cliques that take control of the military (or paramilitary force) and use it against various elements of the population for their own ends."

Hence, the Eisenstadt and Mathewson report stated, "most of the population will not accept any 'easy' post-Saddam solutions (e.g., interim governments that include or are led by retired, dismissed or 'neutral' army officers who have a measure of persuasive power); such arrangements would come across as preservation of the status quo."

The dilemma for the British as with the CPA was determining just how powerful and independent the new Iraqi army should be allowed to become. An army too weak to maintain order leaves the new nation in a perilous state of insecurity and at risk of failure. But an army strong enough to dominate the political order could easily take its own action against elected rulers, repeating the cycle of the past. As it turned out, the Iraqi forces proved too weak under the British, and Britain was forced to reoccupy the country through the period of World War II.

The report also called for a truth and reconciliation commission, a war crimes tribunal, or both, and predicted that such a step will be "absolutely essential if the regime's victims are to achieve closure." As I have argued elsewhere, the avoidance of this process designed to allow traumatized Iraqis to come to terms with the torture and abuse of Saddam's rule proved costly to social and political stability.

In an ominous warning, the report predicted, "If the United States undertakes long-term military involvement in Iraq, it will likely face challenges similar to those that characterized the British military experience in Iraq during the first half of the twentieth century . . . Whether they liked it or not, the British would be unable to extricate themselves from the responsibilities involved in occupying the regime."

In some respects the report was too optimistic. For one, it predicted that the tribal leadership had lost influence, thanks to Saddam's repressive controls. In reality, the tribal structure of Iraqi society was quickly restored following the liberation, due in part to the coalition's failure to provide security and to immediately create a viable national alternative.

Second, the report suggested that it was a misperception that the Shiites would have little interest in a theocratic republic like their Iranian neighbors and would overwhelmingly opt for a secular and democratic state that balanced regional and sectarian interests. While it turned out to be true that the Shiites had little interest in a repeat of a strongman ruling Iraq out of Baghdad, the interest among Shiite sects for a religious state became apparent almost immediately after Saddam was removed. As it turns out, just about everyone studying Iraq had missed the powerful currents within Islam toward a more muscular religious state.

One of the key "lessons learned" from the British experience was that merely establishing democratic structures does not ensure democratic outcomes. Democracy was discredited under the British for a variety of reasons, including corruption, unmanageable conflict, and tribal allegiances that trump liberal democratic principles. For democracy to ultimately triumph, the report concluded that Iraqis "must create their own institutions of civil society and strengthen basic freedoms, which are essential preconditions for building democracy."

Iraq's Promise

Although Iraq's history is marked by turbulence and instability, it nevertheless boasts a rich cultural legacy. Iraq made major contributions to civilization and to religious history. Most scholars believe that Iraq is the site of the biblical account of man's beginnings in the Garden of Eden. The ancient city of Babylon—"the gateway of the Gods"—was located about fifty miles south of Baghdad. The code of Hammurabi was developed by the king of Babylon in the second century BC.

The belief that the country had unique potential in its land and natural resources has long fueled a sense of hope for Iraq's future. Iraq seemed to have so much potential. Because of its religious history, there were significant possibilities for religious tourism. Some of the holiest Shiite shrines are in Iraq.

It also had enormous agricultural promise. It could grow almost anything. In fact, until the late 1950s Iraq exported food; it was considered the breadbasket of the region. Unlike its neighbors, it was uniquely blessed with two large rivers. It always seemed that, with proper attention, livestock, grain, dates, and fish farming could rebound. Agricultural experts have long believed that Iraq could once again become the breadbasket of the Middle East.

Then, of course, there was the oil supply. If black gold is the ticket to national wealth, Iraq should have had no difficulty building a modern nation. It has one of the world's largest proven oil reserves (second only to Saudi Arabia). And that is counting only the discovered oil. One large pool of untapped oil in the Baghdad area is believed to contain more oil than all of Saudi Arabia.

If Iraq's future prospects were sobering, it had less to do with its economic and cultural potential than with the nation's bleak history in the area of governance. Iraq has a long history of being known for its divisible component parts, not as a whole nation. The most consistent description of Iraq is that it is an artificial and contrived nation, consisting of three main regions and two major branches of Islam. These internal relationships have never been stable. The boundaries of modern-day Iraq are less than a hundred years old.

Iraq's history of being vanquished dates back many centuries. It was overrun by Mongol armies in the thirteenth century. Iraq has also had a long history of internal violence and failed attempts to gain a stable and humane civil order. Modern history began with the aforementioned British occupation following the collapse of the Ottoman Empire.

Saddam Hussein

Playing a minor role in that action was twenty-one-year-old Saddam Hussein. Saddam, who started his career as a low-level functionary in the Ba'ath party, slowly made his way by cunning and treachery to dominance by the late 1970s. Saddam masterfully outmaneuvered rivals and moved ruthlessly and efficiently to gain and consolidate power. The original idea of opening Iraqi society to broad participation was abandoned. Using government patronage, the Ba'ath party steadily extended over the Iraqi workforce.

During the early phases of Saddam's rule, it appeared that he sincerely desired to build a modern nation with an advanced infrastructure through aggressive investments in public works. Expanded oil production made it possible to build highways, bridges, schools, universities, and even museums and theaters. Had Saddam continued along the path of national development through public works, he might well have built one of the more advanced states and modern economies in the Middle East. However, all of that investment came to a halt when Saddam began turning to foreign adventures. Iraq's eight-year war with Iran cost hundreds of billions of dollars and hundreds of thousands of lives.

In the late 1980s, Saddam also began his aggressions against Kurdistan, seeking to rein in the independently minded people. Saddam fomented strife between Kurdish groups and had Iraqi troops, along with Kurdish militia, carry out broad murder and theft against the Kurds. Chemical attacks on the Kurds in Halabja resulted in thousands being gassed to death and nearly a million people displaced.

Saddam Hussein, widely regarded as pathological and paranoid, created a state that killed efficiently. It has been said that Saddam killed more Arabs than anyone in the history of mankind. He was a deeply disturbed figure who rose to power from the lowest rungs of Iraqi society and ruled with a cunning and treachery that may be unmatched. His rise to power was fueled by an ability to align himself with figures more powerful than he was, and then outmaneuver them.

After achieving maximum power, he eliminated anyone with the slightest trace of disloyalty. When he rose to the top of the Ba'ath party in 1968, his first action was to call a party meeting. Casually sitting before them smoking a cigar like a gangster, he had those he perceived to be dissenters sent outside and shot.

He controlled people through terror, often pitting individuals and groups against each other. Always a student of Hitler and Stalin, he built one of the most chilling police states in history. The methods of terror and torture were innumerable and imaginative. After coming to power, he sent his own people to Bulgaria and Eastern Germany to study the most effective methods of defeating political rivals and terrorizing the people. Iraq was the place where some of the most diabolical forms of torture ever devised by humankind were routinely practiced, often on people whose only sin was displaying a capacity for independent thought.

There was also a stunning scale of corruption. When officials had license to kill, they also had the freedom to force people to pay for everything they received. Teachers, artists, and soldiers all had to offer bribes to conduct basic activity.

The aggressive action inside Iraq and with neighbors only intensified the hatreds and increased the number of enemies that Saddam had to contend with. Therefore, he spent much of the rest of his life trying to stay in power by destroying threats, purging his party, and murdering anyone considered a rival. Those he wasn't destroying, he was enriching. The loyalty of tribal chiefs was bought through gifts of land and money.

No one has ever doubted that Saddam was guilty of crimes against humanity. He massacred or drove into exile hundreds of thousands of Kurds in 1983 and 1988. He slaughtered the Shiites and buried them in mass graves.

Saddam also controlled individuals by threatening their families. It was not uncommon for the relatives of a defector to be imprisoned or killed. When officials were sent out of the country on business, their families were required to stay behind to prevent defection.

Mahdi Obeidi, who was a senior advisor to Saddam on Iraq's nuclear program, said, "it is difficult to describe the sense of total fear we lived under. I censored myself at work and at home because I knew my family wasn't safe." He described Saddam and his men as "cordial but chilling, masters of deadly insinuation. With a single glance, they could freeze your blood." According to Obeidi, a common gesture among them was the finger raised and drawn across the throat.[2]

Georges Sada, who served at one point as vice marshal in Saddam's military, has written that Saddam created "a world of extremes, of revenge and hatred, and of incredible cunning and deceit." Above all, Saddam had to keep people believing he was ruthless. He would shoot high-ranking officers on the spot and ordered the imprisonment or torture of officials for the mere suspicion of insubordination. This was a culture of raw fear and blind obedience.

Sada tells the story of a dear friend of his, Dr. Raji al-Tikriti, a physician who had provided him with medical care on numerous occasions. In a weak moment while visiting informally with some other doctors, Dr. Raji made a disparaging comment about Saddam growing up in a poor, uneducated family in Tikrit.

When word of the slight reached Saddam, he invited Dr. Raji to the palace to assist in meeting some kind of medical emergency. After arriving, Dr. Raji was taken to a basement room, where he encountered Saddam and fifty elite guards. While sitting and smoking a Cuban cigar, Saddam ordered his beefy soldiers to stomp him with their hobnailed books. They kicked him and jumped on him until he was crushed to death. Dr. Raji's body was then placed inside a kennel with a pack of starved dogs. They devoured his entire body.[3]

Saddam had used killing and torture for three decades as an instrument of state power. It was necessary, he believed, to keep people in place. Most Iraqis had stories of life under Saddam and were eager to tell them. Many Iraqis we met had relatives who suffered torture or lost their lives at the hands of Saddam and his minions. I found it remarkable that so many Iraqis felt that the simple struggle to avoid torture or death had become a major part of their life stories. Rather than directing mental energies toward building a better society, they were forced to apply them toward avoiding pain or death.

As Iraqis reflected back on the experience of living in fear, they recalled feeling that the most merciful and thus preferred treatment was a sudden,

Scenes from uncovered mass graves in the Hilla area.

painless death. They were fatalistic and dismissive about death; they considered it far better than the thought of being tortured.

Saddam tortured and killed on an industrial scale, much as was done in Nazi Germany. In Hilla, several mass graves were discovered where Saddam deposited some of the hundreds of thousands of Shiites he slaughtered. According to survivors and eyewitnesses, Saddam organized large earth-moving equipment to dig ditches and earthen basins in the side of small quarries. Thousands of Shia were then bussed and shot execution style on site. The operation required great organizational skill and efficiency.

We heard many sickening stories of Saddam's sadism. According to survivors of his 1991 slaughter of Shiites in Hilla, family members were forced to perform sexual acts on each other while relatives watched. Reportedly, indescribable acts of sexual torture were carried out against women. Before shooting them, the soldiers helped themselves to the women in ways beyond the imaginations of civilized people.

Other eyewitnesses testified at Saddam's trial about how bodyguards would watch the women bathe, shooting over their heads. The victims would frequently be abused; some were buried alive.

Given Iraq's enormous potential in people and natural resources, many hoped that, with the removal of Saddam, Iraqis would be set free to pursue the development of an advanced nation with democratic institutions and civil society.

The History of Civil Society in Iraq

We hoped that at least a rudimentary tendency toward democracy was lodged within the Iraqi soul, grounded possibly in a faint memory of the practice of civil society decades before.

The conventional historical view of Iraq held that it had no prior experience with democracy or civic institutions, the foundation stones of democratic government. While it is true that Iraqis never got to exercise full democratic rights, a more careful reading of the history suggests that prior to Saddam there was actually a fairly thriving civil society. Before the Ba'ath party took power in 1968, there was a significant degree of cultural pluralism and civic traditions. Eric Davis has written that during the period of British rule and monarchy, Iraqis "built a rich and varied society of ethnic inclusiveness, artistic freedom and civic involvement."

Davis also noted the existence of a distinguished legal profession dating back to the 1908 establishment of the Baghdad College of Law. There ensued a thriving culture of learning in the form of student and professional associations. In fact, some of the clubs were formed to generate solidarity against the monarchy and British colonialism.

In addition, there was a fairly broad intellectual and artistic culture consisting of artisans and literary organizations. According to Davis, Iraq's literary organizations "influenced the entire Arab world by challenging classical forms of Arabic poetry that had not changed since pre-Islamic times." He adds, "Artists salons, like the Pioneers and the Baghdad Group of the 1950s, made strides in the visual arts, producing the acclaimed Freedom Monument in Baghdad's Liberation Square." Iraqis "of all social classes and ethnicities" read papers and discussed politics.[4]

Until the Ba'athists suppressed all labor groups in the 1980s, independent worker organizations fought for the economic rights of workers and consumers. Even following the monarchy's fall in 1958, the government of Gen. Abdel Karim Kassem promoted a broad nationalism that was inclusive of all ethnic groups and avoided sectarianism. The Kassem government, according to Davis, enacted a variety of social reforms to promote equality and established "state-run museums, film and television programs" in the hope of promoting cultural pluralism. Although those patterns continued for a while following the 1963 assassination of Kassem, civil society was increasingly forced underground. By the time Saddam rose to power, the flourishing street culture of bookstores and small-scale civic associations was being destroyed. Saddam took it upon himself to attempt a rewrite of history, expunging from the record the success of civil society prior to Ba'athist rule.[5]

Also offering a hopeful sign of Iraqi possibilities was the extent to which civil society made a rebound during the 1990s as the Kurds regained some autonomy from Saddam. Those of us who traveled on official trips to the Kurdish cities in the north were surprised by the relatively vibrant media, university life, and range of associations, especially women's groups.

The work of the "Future of Iraq" Project is by now very well known. It was formed in collaboration with the Iraqi exile community and funded by the State Department in the lead-up to the war in order to draw from their diverse talents and prepare for post-Saddam Iraq. The seventeen working groups covered a wide range of economic, infrastructure, and national security issues, but placed a heavy emphasis on recovering a free media, civil society capacity building, and establishing democratic principles and procedures for the new Iraq.

In a widely circulated State Department publication, describing the group's activity, Iraqis were reminded of a time "now more than three decades past" before "Saddam consumed their nation" when their "cultural heritage, their oil wealth, and the education and skills of their people earned Iraq a respected place in both the Arab world and the larger international community."

The working group on civil society, which held its first session in February 2003, reported: "it is natural for Iraq, as the historic cradle of civilization, to have a civil society that respects, protects, and empowers Iraqis to prosper in a democratic government." The clear hope was that the civic activity and broad debate forged within civil society would encourage agreement on democratic principles and practices so that, as one participant put it: "we feel that we are Iraqis before we are Kurds or Shias, or Sunnis, Arabs or Turkmen."[6]

Preparing to Run the Ministries

Most of the planning taking place at the NSC and the Pentagon in Washington looked down on Iraq as if doing a flyover at 30,000 feet. The farther away from realities on the ground, the more the discussion focused on the macro issues, such as establishing transitional governance and dealing with the regional and international fallout from the invasion. It had little to do with the details of postwar rehabilitation.

Those of us in Baghdad did not have that luxury. The core mission of ORHA was, of course, established to preside over postwar reconstruction, which meant ensuring that plans were in place for humanitarian problems and for bringing about an orderly transition in the management of government ministries. So, for us in ORHA, a more practical and immediate question than how the world was reacting to the U.S. invasion was how the Iraqis would react to us. Of course, they would be happy to be free of Saddam, but their perceptions and attitudes would probably be more complicated than that.

Iraqis, after all, were thoroughly a part of the culture and mentality of the Middle East, not Europe or Asia. They too had swallowed the raw propaganda about America and Zionism that was routinely circulated in the Middle East by autocratic rulers, Islamists, and Arab nationalist movements. What's more, the diehards around Saddam, who would lose everything upon our arrival, undoubtedly had a variety of wicked tricks at their disposal for undermining our success and turning the Iraqis against us. We knew that, in addition to the deposed regime elements, it was likely that hardened criminals had been released from the prisons.

Naturally, the first consideration in moving into Baghdad and taking over ministries would be safety. Despite the prevalence of rosy predictions, more realistic assessments were also given. For example, we were told that the environment would be "semi-permissive" at best. Those were issues for the military to confront, but they would affect us deeply—both our safety and our ability to perform our jobs were on the line.

Army Civil Affairs, the wing of the army serving as our partners, would precede us into Iraq, attempting to establish safe conditions. The job of Civil Affairs, one of the most impressive and least appreciated divisions of the U.S. Army, is basically an armed civil administration unit that restores order and services like electricity, water, and sewer and food distribution to communities immediately after a war.

Typically after the army completes its conquest in a given area, it reallo-
cates some combat forces to supply stability needs, and then works with Civil
Affairs to restore normal functioning. They try to establish a semblance of
order and normality and secure whatever local cooperation they can achieve
before the civilian administrators and diplomats arrive.

Those in Civil Affairs came from all walks of life. Many have advanced
degrees and impressive resumes. One Civil Affairs army lieutenant on my
team had two doctorates. My chief of staff was an army major with advanced
degrees who served back home as a church pastor. It was truly an interesting
blend of experience and talent.

In addition to restoring services in the towns and villages of Iraq, a major
objective immediately following the war would be to take the first steps to
draw citizens into the local decision-making process. Civil Affairs personnel
were supposed to reach out in the very confused situation following the war
to civil society, to the extent that it existed. Following them and hopefully
building upon their work would be sizable local governance teams staffed
by USAID contractors who would try to generate input from local citizens
into governance.

In broad strokes, civilian teams under the leadership of USAID's DART
(Disaster Assistance Response Team) were supposed to be ready to go to all
provinces to conduct assessments and then implement plans to build trust
and participation among local residents. The final stage involved some form
of transition to legitimate authority. The stages all made sense; it just seemed
especially optimistic that this degree of civilized conduct would at all be in
the cards.

It was rarely clear who among local Iraqis was worthy of interim leadership and generated broad trust. In the haste to restore services and give
the people a sense that order was emerging, many mistakes were bound to
be made. In too many cases, persons were given serious responsibility and
would later have to be replaced because they had engaged in questionable
or illegal activity.

It took very little time after arriving in Baghdad to appreciate
how difficult achieving normalcy would be. The Western press just never
did really capture the devastating scale of looting that occurred immediately after the war. How does a country find normalcy when most of the
government buildings are either bombed or entirely gutted and burned
by looters? Those realities on the ground conjured the images of vultures

picking clean a carcass, or a swarm of locusts devouring a tomato field right down to the roots. Buildings were stripped clean and whatever wasn't stolen was burned.

I was told that one of our first jobs would be to find the government buildings for which we would be responsible. We would need to enter buildings sufficiently armed in case there was remaining hostility.[7] Then, after the facility was secured, we would presumably meet the Iraqi employees and introduce ourselves as their new managers.

As the senior advisor to the Iraqi Ministry of Youth and Sport, I had imagined walking the halls of that ministry like a newly appointed school superintendent, introducing myself, giving the folks some new marching orders, and hoping to boost morale. Of course, this kind of imagination was one of the many exercises before actually arriving in Baghdad. What we all imagined, as we planned in Kuwait City for the takeover of ministries, was arriving at government office buildings finding people standing by waiting for directions before resuming their work.

Hard Realities

But, of course, what we found was a collapsed state with no functioning government. For several weeks after we arrived, Iraqis were not working or able to work, at least not in the government sector. The small shops and tea salons lining the streets tried to operate. But most people just appeared like they were on an extended sabbatical, roaming the streets and trying to take care of basic necessities.

For public sector workers, there was nothing to do but wait at home and hope. Their country's chief employer, the government, was gone. Their former office buildings were bombed, burned, or looted. And there was little clarity on who exactly would take charge of daily affairs. So, rather than walking into a functioning government, we had to think through a complete rebuilding process.

First, we would need to locate the workers needed to restore government operations, whoever they were. What we needed, more than anything else at that time, was their knowledge and ability. For now at least, their past affiliation was not really the concern.

The best way to do that was to simply take a convoy to the site of the ministry building and hope to make contact with one or two who knew something about it and who could, in turn, reach out to more former workers and invite them back.

We would also need to try to secure payroll lists from the ministry from anyone who had the foresight to take copies with them from the building before the bombing and postwar looting ruined them. In my case, there were no records at all. Nothing could be salvaged from the Ministry of Youth and Sport. Everything had been looted or burned. We would have to organize payroll lists from local community centers and other outposts of the ministry.

We were strongly advised to start meeting with Iraqis. Perhaps we would somehow be able to identify good, capable managers and workers. "Be safe and careful," we were told, but by all means meet with them. Like everything else, that proved to be very difficult. We had almost no technical means of communicating with Iraqis: no phones, no TV services (for broadcasting messages to the people). Like the most primitive societies, we would have to rely mostly on word of mouth communication. Many of the senior ministry advisors simply went to the ministry building site and posted information about times when we would come back.

Because of the small number of available convoys—approximately five for all twenty-four ministries—transportation was very uncertain. We had to sign up for convoys and then wait in line until one was available. We were frequently bumped and had to reschedule for the next day. As a result, often senior advisors could not make it to meetings that had been promised. This did little to help our credibility with the Iraqis.

In these new realities, the recent planning process in Kuwait City seemed so very remote. All the templates, however devised by the best and brightest, pretty much had to be discarded at that point. Doing the job required improvising day by day. We were caught in a continuing exercise of assembling the vehicle while driving it.

As the weeks wore on, we stumbled along trying to build new ministry teams; in some cases we appointed temporary supervisors for divisions. Obviously, we weren't moving quickly enough to fill the growing vacuum. We continued to receive reports of clerics and their militia moving in to take over government buildings. We never had enough security to take and permanently hold a property.

The Ministry of Youth and Sport Facilities

By early May we were expected to have completed an investigation of the condition of our respective ministry buildings and ministry assets. By now most of the key properties of the Iraqi government were clearly identified on the military maps. I could now turn to a map posted on the crowded palace wall and find the grid number for the Ministry of Youth and Sport: MB475893.

Fortunately on that first day, I secured a convoy. We rolled across Baghdad, weaving around wrecked equipment and vehicles still remaining from the war. Finally, we reached the Ministry of Youth and Sport. I had been told that the building had been severely damaged in the bombing. The fact that a ministry—ostensibly set up to serve the needs of Iraq's children and youth—was actually targeted in the bombing campaign spoke volumes about what the ministry was actually used for under Saddam.[8]

Hard as it is for the Western mind to imagine, most ministries had some vital function in maintaining the regime and carrying out police state functions under Saddam. In fact, a majority of the Iraqi ministries carried out a sensitive state security function (in addition to those officially charged with security). Senior officials in all the ministries belonged to Saddam and served at his pleasure.

WHEN I WALKED INTO THE MINISTRY BUILDING, I was once again reminded of the safety training from Fort Meade. We were told again and again to be careful to avoid booby traps and soft surfaces or any surface that could not be clearly seen. Sure enough, as we made our way up the dark staircase with flashlights, we found an unexploded grenade. We called back to headquarters for assistance in sweeping the building for unexploded ordnance.

The building was completely looted and smoke was pouring from the seventh floor. Documents had been set on fire. Obviously, people from the regime had been coming back into the building for unfinished business. We heard many reports of documents being burned; clearly, plenty of Ba'athists remained in the neighborhood around us. Undoubtedly, they harbored deadly designs on reconstruction and on us.

The bombing left the building interior covered with dust and dirt. The grounds were severely littered with piles of papers, broken glass, and window frames that had been blown out of the building. We managed to round up a few documents, but time never allowed for the extent of document recovery that the situation really needed.

Nothing prepared me for the sight of the looting. Throughout the areas of the building that had not been damaged by the bombing, *everything* had been peeled off and carried out. Only concrete floors and walls remained. In a first-floor electrical main room, all of the switches and wires were torn from the walls and ceilings. Except for empty fuse boxes, the entire row of electric panels and switches had been hollowed out and stripped of any metal that could be carried off. It looked like an animal carcass that had been picked clean. A status report on my ministry was fairly uncomplicated: the building was bombed, looted, and burned beyond repair. Later an engineering report confirmed that, due to the structural damage, the building would probably have to be torn down.

With little hope of repairing existing offices and returning to normal function, I spent the balance of my time in Baghdad doing two things: searching for alternative space and finding Iraqis to put in charge of the ministry and the Iraqi Olympic Committee. Finding alternative space for government offices proved nearly impossible because of the large number of ministries that had been displaced. After two months of trying to locate and get approval for a suitable substitute, we secured permission to use a building on the grounds of the Baghdad Zoo near the Green Zone. It had been used previously for youth ministry–related activity.

After visiting the ministry's old building, I walked the streets in the vicinity making contact with Iraqis and trying to determine what was on their minds. The kids were friendly, swarming around our military vehicles, smiling and asking for photos and sweets. Most of the adults were friendly too, but a few gave me my first earful of complaints. They wondered why there was no security on the streets. One said that the soldiers traveling with me were the first he had seen in a week. He made sure I understood that the streets were ruled by looters and common criminals.

Rad Hamoudi and Ahmed Rhaadi

Day by day, we got to know more Iraqis who could help us sort out the old elements from the new. The hardest part of our jobs was trying to determine the character and reputations of Iraqis. I soon learned that the most reliable and trustworthy judges of character in my work with youth and sports were celebrated athlete heroes from the past who had suffered at the hands of Uday. They had enormous credibility with the Iraqi people themselves; in fact, they were among the most popular figures in all of Iraq. I concluded that sports figures who were abused by Uday, and cheered by the Iraqi people, had to be fairly reliable sources of information.

The two most interesting Iraqis who became close advisors were Rad Hamoudi and Ahmed Rhaadi, who were both soccer legends from Iraq's past. Ahmed Rhaadi had been imprisoned three times. His

Ahmed Rhaadi is a former Iraqi soccer star who suffered torture at the hands of Uday, who had been envious of his popularity with the people. He was a genuine hero throughout the country and helped us establish rapport with Iraqis.

treatment was fairly mild; on two occasions his head was shaved, a minor form of abuse used mostly for humiliation.

He also told me about traveling in a motorcade with Uday following a national soccer team victory. The streets were lined with cheering fans, and Uday's initial impression was that they were cheering for him. According to Rhaadi, Uday exclaimed, "I am popular; I am popular." Before long, however, Uday realized that the crowds were not cheering him at all, but rather Rhaadi. For that offense, Rhaadi was promptly punished with imprisonment and cruel treatment.

The popularity of these legendary sports figures became apparent when we invited them into the palace to meet with Jay Garner. Immediately after the two were seated, a long line of young Iraqi custodians formed to greet them. The Iraqi kids filed by and bowed to express honor and admiration.

This kind of credibility could not be manufactured. It was spontaneous and sincere. I came to rely heavily on Rad Hamoudi. He told me much

The prison wing of the Olympic Committee building where athletes were reported to have suffered in a basement torture chamber.

about life in Baghdad under Uday. According to him, "half of Baghdad" was owned by Uday. He provided a very helpful description of the relationship of Saddam and Uday to the corrupt world of money and the central bank. He also advised that we be careful because many of Uday's corrupt busy friends were still around Baghdad.

By the second week in May, the push was really on to get things functioning. Not surprisingly, the more our own government was increasing capacity at the presidential palace, the more an effort was made to establish a broad "matrix" for presenting objectives and tracking daily or weekly progress. We wanted to know where we were accomplishing progress and where we were not.

Measuring Progress

In the effort to make and measure reportable advancements, the outcome that mattered deeply—because so much else depended upon it—was the basic need for getting people back to work. A primary indicator was how many employees were showing up for work. Of course, it was also important to get basic government functions back on line and providing emergency payments to Iraqi workers.

We were urged to make every attempt to get senior technocrats in place to run things so that wherever possible we could begin to put an Iraqi face on the occupation. How many "key positions" had been filled, we were asked. It varied widely. Things had normalized fairly quickly in the few ministries, like agriculture, that played minor security functions during the previous regime and were thus largely intact.

At the opposite end of the spectrum were ministries like mine, in which absolutely no one had returned to work. Thousands of local workers from community centers and the youth ministry wanted to get paid and resume work. But I never met a single senior official who had previously drawn a paycheck from the Ministry of Youth and Sport. I assumed that they were completely spooked.

Next we were asked how soon our respective ministries could be transitioned to Iraqis. For me, the question seemed absurd; there effectively was no youth and sports ministry beyond what my small team was carrying out. No buildings, no personnel, nothing.

At this point, we still had no policy on who among the former ministry officials were eligible to serve. Of course, in my case this was a moot issue. But for many it caused confusion. The early objective was restoring services, which presumably meant that de-Ba'athification would have to wait. For now, we would create a policy on the fly. The only principle enunciated at that point suggested that all except those who abused their offices could serve.

Many ministries, including mine, would basically be starting over. I was beginning to realize that I would have to rely on my own team and the few Iraqis I had come to trust. I put in place two deputies, Ammar Shawkat and Abdul Razak Al-tai.

Personal Responsibility

The various concepts of the individual and personal responsibility represented another feature of the culture clash. Clearly, the local Islamic culture carried an inherent fatalism. The term widely used for the complete mastery over human affairs by the divine was *"Enshallah,"* which is roughly translated as "God willing." In other words, no one is responsible, and what happens or doesn't happen is due to God willing it. The Iraqis felt that most things were beyond their control; if something went wrong, almighty God was directly behind it, and nothing could have prevented it. For example, imagine an Iraqi driving to an important meeting on a bald tire with a slow leak, which he ignored. If he had a flat tire along the way, he naturally concluded that God must have willed that the meeting was not supposed to happen.

Many of us in the West believe in a personal God or, at least, a higher intelligent power that shapes the direction of history. But Western religions and culture also embrace autonomy and responsibility. Those concepts drive our economy and, in fact, our whole civilization. We feel that most things fall

Poor children from Sadr City scavenge metals from the bombed Olympic Committee building. Many buildings, including those that had not been bombed during the war, were stripped bare of all but the concrete and steel structures.

within our control, and if something doesn't get done, someone should be held personally responsible. So, while we see individual responsibility and initiative as a factor in everything, the Iraqi culture devalues personal responsibility.

Often when I confronted Iraqis about something that happened, they looked at me strangely as if I actually believed there was something they could have done about it. Adding to the pattern, of course, was the dictatorship under which they lived and suffered. Shifting blame to someone else is a survival technique in totalitarian societies.

The customs of Iraqi society proved to be major factors in carrying out the official business of government. For one, we were told to expect business to be conducted at a snail's pace. There were rituals that had to be followed. Those rituals included long, chatty greetings involving a lot of superficial politeness. Negotiations were accompanied by endless formalities.

Honor and pride were perhaps the most important factors. Great efforts would be made to confront situations in ways that protected the public face of an Iraqi who had made a mistake. What that meant in the many cases of dishonesty and corruption that would occur is that preserving an honorable public face was of greater concern than the deed itself.

Culture of Deceit

Colonel Kim Olsen, who was top assistant to Gen. Jay Garner, told a story of one of General Garner's first encounters with a large Iraqi crowd. A father cradling his severely injured son elbowed his way to the front of the crowd. Claiming that the boy had been run over by an American army truck and left for dead, he angrily shouted, "I want one hundred American dollars for this atrocity." According to Colonel Olsen, the mood of the crowd shifted quickly from "docile to dangerous."

Then, some from the crowd stepped forward to tell the real story: the boy had been hit by an Iraqi car, and the driver who was responsible had no money. The father refused to take the boy to the hospital because he believed he could extort more money if his son grew worse. The translator accompanying the Garner team told them that they must fortify their hearts against the human suffering around them. Many stories were simply false or partly true or somewhere in between.

The various features of the culture clash found unique expression in the problem of the Iraqi exiles.

Iraqi Exiles

The big solution that was presented to just about every major challenge was to "let the Iraqis sort it out." Unless we Americans wanted to run Iraq for a while, which wasn't the plan, we would need to turn to Iraqis to do so, or at least be the face of our rule. In short, we would need to partner with Iraqis.

A prevailing assumption was that we would help Iraq get on its feet after Saddam by finding competent and trustworthy leaders from a pool of returning Iraqi exiles and indigenous Iraqis who would surface after we arrived. The need to maintain at least a façade of Iraqi participation in the liberation and postwar reconstruction is probably what drove the Pentagon to recruit Iraqi exiles so heavily.

One of the least appreciated aspects of the postwar occupation of Iraq was the Iraqi exile factor. Many Americans know about Ahmed Chalabi, but he was only the most notorious and visible Iraqi exile, who served as chairman of the Iraqi National Congress, the umbrella group. Through Chalabi and a variety of lesser known figures, the Iraqi exile community managed to become a considerable political force in the 1990s, carefully organizing evidence on Saddam's many atrocities and searching out friends in Congress and the Washington think-tank community. To some considerable extent, the decision to liberate Iraq was as much a tribute to this decades-long exercise in Washington relationship building by strategic Iraqi organizations as it was Osama Bin Laden's attack.

The exile community held in common a love for Iraq and a desire to liberate the Iraqi people and carry out vengeance against Saddam. Most of them carried profoundly moving stories of fleeing Iraq for their lives because of some innocent activity that had turned Saddam's functionaries against them. Most of us came to care deeply for them as a community.

On numerous occasions during every stage of my two-year involvement, I tried to help Iraqis who had suffered and needed personal care or connections of some kind. It was impossible to be unmoved by their tragic stories. Our hearts really went out to them, and their suffering was one valid reason we were invading Iraq in the first place, at least in the eyes of us civilians.

Beyond their love of Iraq and hatred of Saddam, little else bound them together. As I often saw in stormy and emotionally raw meetings, they were a fragmented group, torn apart by competing agendas, delicate egos, and ambition. Undoubtedly, some imagined themselves in historic roles following an American liberation. The people who made up the nation state of Iraq were anything but a cohesive group. Neither were the exiles. In so many ways, they exemplified the fractured loyalties and distrust that have been so indelibly imprinted on Iraq's history.

Senior Pentagon planners apparently assumed that at some point in the liberation or immediately thereafter, we would make a move to elevate the visibility of these Iraqi exiles. There was some logic to that, and most hoped that it would prove practical. What group could be counted on to care more about building a free democratic Iraqi state?

But what seemed to matter most was the "optic," the perception, of Iraqi control. Many of the returning exiles had nothing more to offer than the fact that they were Iraqi. To be fair, there were some highly experienced and credentialed doctors, engineers, and planners among them. Several became valued senior advisors and did participate in the interim government. But at least half of them signed up because they were persuaded they would soon be running Iraq. They were brought into the country at enormous expense to the American taxpayer.

Few had any prior experience running government programs. Some, including several who were assigned me, had no education, almost no relevant skills, and next to zero leadership ability. At least three who were assigned to me ranged from mildly disruptive to outright subversive in their daily dealings. They consistently violated policies and refused to change, even when rebuked and threatened with termination.

Two of the Iraqis on my team were committed Islamists—precisely the kind of folks with theocratic tendencies—who (we assured the public) could not and would not take over Iraq. As soon as they arrived, they disappeared to the southern Shiite city of Negev, violating our safety rules and policy on firearms. With no phone connections, I had no way of knowing whether they were dead or alive, but I was pretty certain that if they had been killed while traveling without military protection, I would take the full blame for it. Eventually, after this pattern repeated itself, we just considered them AWOL.

Exiled Iraqi common laborers from the United States, who made an hourly wage working in a warehouse and delivering auto parts, suddenly found themselves making $150,000 a year back in Iraq. Obviously, the contract system was badly out of whack. But this group had enormous political clout back home, before and during the war. By the time details of their performance began to emerge, Jay Garner's deputies fought successfully to delay their arrival. We simply didn't need them, and many in the existing group weren't working out. But when word got back to Paul Wolfowitz that the Americans were obstructing the flow of exiles into Iraq, he starting requesting the names of people responsible. Everybody pretty much stepped back in line. We insisted that we were not against Iraqi exiles; we were just interested in receiving more qualified and trustworthy candidates.

Several of the exiles said that Wolfowitz told them they would "be running Iraq." One openly talked about his desire to be on the governing council, even though these positions were reserved for indigenous Iraqis, not people who were serving on the American government's payroll. Several of the least qualified actually discussed their interest in becoming a government minister. One spent most of his time during midsummer of 2003 drifting around the little power groups that were forming in Baghdad, taking in the latest gossip and advocating himself for public office to anyone who would listen.

I had at least hoped that they would be useful as liaisons to the Iraqi people, if nothing else being able to serve as translators and intermediaries, able to arrange and coordinate meetings. But whenever I assigned them a mission, I would get reports that their agenda, not the U.S. government's, was being advanced. One Iraqi exile assigned to my team showed up three weeks into the operation insisting that he was personally being sent "to run the Ministry of Youth and Sport." This man, a wrestling coach in the United States with no post-secondary education, immediately called a press conference. He announced that he, Iraq's new minister of Youth and Sports, was taking over and would soon be announcing his program.

The next week he helped to orchestrate one of the biggest demonstrations outside the palace gates, timed to coincide with a high-level meeting of Iraqis that we had organized for official business inside. I repeatedly informed them of the rules against unauthorized activity and statements, reminding them that they were Americans and that they worked for the U.S. government. But it did little good. The only solution that ever worked with this man was to encourage him to spend long breaks with his family. I also persuaded him to engage in "assessing the condition" of sports and youth facilities and to get involved in distributing donated soccer balls, both of which kept him on the road and made him very popular.

The working assumption with this group was that Iraq was their country, and they had been transported there by the Pentagon to take it over. So, who exactly were we to get in their way? Again and again, we had to confront this group. At one point, General Garner called a meeting led by his staff lawyer in which he threatened to cancel their contract on the spot and send the entire group home on the next plane. We had a near insurrection on our hands right inside the palace. The meeting was immediately reported back to senior people in the Pentagon. That episode, more than any, sealed in my mind how bizarre it was that people in Washington would conclude that either Garner or Bremer was exercising too much discretion, as though they were on their own power trips. Any person in Washington would have done the same thing under the circumstances. Both Garner and Bremer did their best to make the most out of a severely dysfunctional environment.

I reached the breaking point when I learned that one Iraqi exile on my staff had participated in a meeting in which the murder of a local Iraqi member of my team was discussed (the local man stood in the way of his ambitions). I was furious. This had to be a violation of U.S. law, among other things. Two separate Iraqi newspaper stories reported this same man issuing a call to replace me and make himself minister of Youth and Sports. How could a country possibly get on its feet with this kind of activity going on?

I didn't need my job, and at this point questioned whether I wanted it, but I knew that as long as I (or any other senior advisor) reported up the chain through Jay Garner, ultimately to the president of the United States, this degree of treachery and insubordination would not be tolerated. Our mission was too important. Many in leadership positions turned in desperation to leaking information to the *New York Times*. My case was so delicate that I chose against that path out of a concern for my own safety. I simply waited for my chance to do justice. That chance came when I was able to organize incriminating evidence against the most treacherous member of my team, and it took nothing more than collecting media clippings from the Iraqi press. Remarkably, this was all happening in the open.

I was the only senior advisor during that entire time who actually got an Iraqi Reconstruction and Development Council (IRDC) individual fired for documented subversion. It took a full day of my time working through the issues with lawyers and having to face hostility bordering on hatred from their leader, but it was worth it. I could not stomach the idea that the American taxpayer would be paying barely literate Iraqis to subvert our purposes, and actually increase the likelihood that we would fail.

In the back of my mind I was curious what the American people would think if they knew what was actually going on. Was this episode isolated, or did it symbolize a wider chaos and confusion. It was one of many occasions in which I had to doubt whether those sent by the president to build a new Iraq were even from the same team. If the idea was that this group of Iraqis could help supply a legitimate system of authority available to immediately fill the postwar political vacuum, this was one of the greatest miscalculations and embarrassments of all. Except for the outstanding technocrats, this group had nearly no credibility with the Iraqi people.

Not surprisingly, the technically trained local Iraqis whom we came to work with pretty much dismissed the entire group. It was almost an insult to their pride that we would allow completely unqualified individuals who had been out of the country for ten to fifteen years to step into positions of authority. I tried to assure the local Iraqis that the Iraqi-Americans were mostly there to lend a helping hand and translate.

As it turned out, few of the Iraqi exiles would ever come to gain legitimacy in the eyes of ordinary Iraqis who had suffered under Saddam. That perception by local Iraqis of the exiles was deeply unfair because so many who fled the country under Saddam did so because they had no choice. In many cases their families who remained behind paid the ultimate price by being promptly persecuted or killed by Saddam's forces. They too paid a horrible price and many had heart-wrenching personal stories.

But that was the broadly held perception nevertheless. And it was probably inevitable. After all, the locals had spent those same ten to fifteen years in the cruel squalor of Saddam's police state rather than escape to the comforts of London, Bonn, or Detroit.

The role of Iraqi exiles would prove to be a most difficult, complicated, and contentious issue. The exiles represented a considerable political constituency. In fact, were it not for the years of advocacy in Washington and London, it is doubtful that the case for liberation would have been made. Leading this network was the Iraqi National Congress (INC). The name came up often, and when it came up in mixed audiences it always generated the same awkward reaction.

Whether you were for or against the INC, it was clear that the entire subject of Iraqi exiles was controversial. To the Pentagon, these Iraqis were brothers and patriots, and Chalabi was the Iraqi George Washington; any accusation against him was born of ill motive based upon old battles. But those in the CIA or the State Department were deeply skeptical and carried open animosity toward Chalabi; they regarded him as a criminal. Not even a Westernized Iraqi with a PhD in economics from the Massachusetts Institute of Technology could transcend the tough, treacherous politics of the Middle East. In all my years in the policy arena, I never encountered a single person who generated a deeper polarization than Ahmed Chalabi. The fight over Chalabi symbolized much of the Iraq debate that would follow; there was almost no middle ground.

Chapter 5

Washington's Scramble for a Scapegoat

Garner Takes the Fall

A S THE WEEKS WORE ON, more and more senior advisors reported difficulty with the Iraqi exile staff from the IRDC. Many of these Iraqis had returned because they loved their country and wanted to make a difference. But many had very poor qualifications to serve in substantive roles. Because most had been led to believe that they would essentially be running the new government, it became very difficult for them when they realized that they were our subordinates.

I found it interesting that this group of Iraqis, who had spent considerable time in the West, represented a wide range of ideological and religious thought. Some of the more educated secular technocrats fit in well. Others had very little education or prior experience. Although their opinions were deeply and personally felt, we often found their ideas of little practical value.

Many of them spent their time pursing agendas other than ORHA's. We just tried to ignore that as much as possible. Socially, they kept entirely to themselves. Many became involved in local politics, working to position themselves in the scramble for power in the new Iraq. Some managed to conceal the fact that they were committed Islamists. Yet all were paid handsomely by the U.S. taxpayer to be there; theoretically, they were working for, and accountable to, us.

Garner: Man in the Middle

It all came to a head in mid-May, when General Garner and his top legal counsel, Michael Murphy, called a special meeting with the IRDC to discuss

General Garner mingles with contract security protection.

the growing number of reports of problems and insubordination. Although I did not attend the meeting, another participant told me that it was very charged. Murphy threatened to cancel their contracts and place them on the next plane home if their conduct didn't change immediately. That position, although very courageous, immediately landed Garner and Murphy in trouble with Paul Wolfowitz.

We assumed at the time that some in Washington might perceive Garner's actions in the IRDC case to be insubordinate, though we later learned that he had gotten the call announcing his replacement on April 16. I'm sure that incident played a significant role in causing some in Washington

Paul Wolfowitz on a visit to Mahawil in southern Iraq.

to conclude that he was not sufficiently subordinate. The buzz in the rumor mill suggested that Garner was going to call it quits and just go home or be recalled by Washington. He never did plan to spend more than six months in Baghdad anyway. Six months was how the entire ORHA mission had been presented to him in the first place.

Increasingly we learned about huge conflicts back home, food fights as we called them, especially between DoD and the State Department. None of this bode well for Jay. Usually, this degree of fighting sets up another party to take the fall. As the African proverb says, "When the elephants fight, the grass loses."

I knew that, if they couldn't work things out back home, they would probably conclude that Jay Garner was the problem. He was not politically connected or well known in senior policy circles across Washington. Neither was he very inclined to play politics or the media leak game. And he was also probably too reluctant to respond to every demand that came to him from congressional committees. He had come out of semiretirement and a lucrative position in business, and he planned to be back to his normal life by midsummer.

I assumed this internecine squabbling would endure for only a brief passing phase. I confidently told people that I knew a little about this president and how he worked and that the operative word was "discipline."

The president and his senior staff hated leaks, dissension, and unproductive debate. George W. Bush was the MBA president, and he took the business management model seriously. He was rarely ever more than a minute or two late for a meeting. He reacted viscerally to anyone on his team promoting themselves or their own agenda.

Any lack of discipline in an operation of this risk and this national significance just seemed inconceivable to me. In addition to having been a deputy assistant to the president in the White House, I had talked to scores of people who had worked with him back in Texas. So, based on my own working familiarity with the president, I predicted to a variety of people that corrections would soon arrive. Someone would be put in charge and would soon bring order to the interagency process. Everyone else would fall into line. Because Vice President Cheney and Secretary of State Condoleezza Rice had other major duties, I assumed that it might even be a wartime czar, much like was created for Homeland Security under Tom Ridge. But, regardless of how it would happen, this was a totally disciplined administration; the chaos we were witnessing would not last, I assured myself and others.

I was never more wrong about anything. At the end of my service two years later, very little cohesion existed in the day-to-day management of Iraq at the highest level. The interagency system of coordinating policy was never controlled; at times the State Department and the Pentagon were practically at war. I still do not know why this has been allowed. Many report that the president simply didn't want the facts, and thus was rarely given reliable information on how bad things were until long after corrections would have made a difference. The more likely explanation was that the people responsible for getting him the unvarnished facts were the same people who designed the plan in the first place and thus had serious "skin in the game" and weren't particularly interested in looking bad.

The signs of this enduring chaos came very early, and it would cost some people dearly. As far back as March 30, Garner took me aside for a fifteen-minute conversation on the beach by the Kuwait City Hilton to discuss a variety of problems with personnel and agencies back in Washington. Obviously, even then, he was not getting the personnel he needed. He may not have had the power to demand more. Agencies were given direct orders by the president to free up staff for Iraq, and many simply refused. Typical of agencies fighting for their own turf and prerogatives, they wanted a voice and wanted credit, but they weren't interested in freeing up funds or people. Garner was simply not able to assemble his own team. By this time, the process of appointing people to senior positions was becoming political and ideological, with some names generating major fights.

I knew that Garner was seriously considering not continuing with the next phase into Baghdad. If he had been given to political calculation and reputation rather than patriotism, he would have done so. He knew that he "would be the fall guy." He saw his mission as doomed to fail. But his resignation would have created a huge stir and undoubtedly made things even worse. He was too much of a man and a patriot to do that.

That Garner was not given elevated authority in the first place reflected how casually the postwar transitional phase would be. Several of the senior people forced onto his staff were either not temperamental fits or didn't have the skill sets for what would be required on the ground. For example, Doug Feith sent a senior OSD policy staffer, Mike Mobbs, into Garner's organization to be the "pillar lead" for civil administration. Mobbs was a smart and gentlemanly lawyer but never really had any chemistry with Garner. Besides, he brought no functional complement to the work. We later learned that Mobbs himself had been, at one point, a candidate for Garner's job. No corporate board would ever allow this to happen at the senior levels of a company.

Many blamed Garner for the confusion, but it was obvious to all who served under him that he was given little to work with. Some simply didn't like his style. As for me, I enjoyed a deeply gratifying relationship with General Garner. He bore an uncanny resemblance to my deceased grandfather, who was a larger than life figure. In a letter to friends and family, I wrote: "allow me a word about our consummate leader, General Garner. I love the guy; and he has proclaimed his admiration for me. There's just an unusual chemistry with the two of us. He's one of the greatest motivators I have ever been around; you don't survive around this guy unless you believe as he does there's a solution to every problem. He can juggle fifty urgent problems at once, and believe me these are problems—they are numerous and they are urgent. He charges into rooms and barks out orders, always with a warm twinkle in his eye, never stepping over the line. There's really never any doubt who is in charge. You should have seen him reacting to cell phones going off in the middle of meetings in Kuwait. Ouch."

In my notes home to family and friends in April of 2003, I wrote: "One of my favorite moments was first thing in the morning before the break of dawn when General Garner came charging down the hall to stand with everyone else in the coffee line; you'd hear him coming from a distance, barking out affectionate morning greetings to his troops, always by name. I never saw him fail to remember a name after meeting a person. Not once. When have you last been around a person with such a commanding presence and who could also shed tears at the report of people in need? What a guy."

My assessment of Jay Garner was probably never very objective. I liked the man the moment we met, and as time went on I developed a deeper fondness for him, as he did for me. I have had a long habit of referring to people I admire as "brother" so and so. It was part of the culture I was raised in. I could never bring myself to address Jay (the name he preferred) in any term other than "General Garner." But he often referred to me as "Brother Eberly."

The Dirty Work

During the planning process in Kuwait City, I had been involved in high-minded policy matters relating to concepts of democracy, governance, and strengthening civil society. Well, that was Kuwait City. I realized quickly enough that Baghdad was different. Here, it was "all hands on deck." Here we were, several dozen civilians sent to stabilize and reorganize a country of 24 million people and that country was now in chaos. And we would do what we were told. Here, we would get our hands dirty in the very real work of rebuilding a country.

One story stands out as an example of emergency reassignment. The first morning in the palace, General Garner was greeting people one at a time as he moved slowly through the coffee line. When he saw me, he grabbed me by the arm and pulled me aside. He said "Brother Eberly, I have an urgent job and it's got your name on it." This came to him, he claimed, late the previous night. I assumed he had some kind of midnight revelation.

"Sure," I said slowly, with a mix of excitement and worry. Was something wrong? Was I being reassigned?

Garner escorted me rather firmly into his office, an office that had belonged to Saddam just weeks before. It appeared cavernous and imposing in its empty state. There was nothing on the large desk except a phone. From my White House days, I recognized it as one used for direct calls from the president.

"I've got a job, and it's got your name on it," he repeated, sort of hanging on the end of the sentence for suspension. "The job," he blurted out, is "organizing trash removal in downtown Baghdad." I paused, smiled, and tried to process what was being asked of me.

By nature, Garner moved very, very fast. "Eberly, you're dancing," he growled. Standing there, I felt like a little boy needing to pee. What was flooding through my mind was that this wasn't what I was sent in to do. But I also realized that I had Garner's full confidence as a guy who could fix things. Obviously, that was a real compliment.

"Eberly, you're dancing," he said louder, staring me straight in the eye. Of course, I was taking too long to respond to a man who had been a general for most of his working life. I didn't appreciate that, although he was polite enough to ask, he was giving me a command. All it needed was "yes, sir."

Of course, I agreed and proceeded to organize the trash project without delay or hesitation. While the operation was about garbage, it was a high honor to carry out a presidential instruction and get so directly involved in bringing order to the city. In my letter home, I wrote, "Truthfully, Garner has his priorities right, if you can appreciate what is really urgent here. You can't have an ordered civil society without services and safety."

It was almost impossible to know where to begin such a task in this very alien environment. We all assumed that we would be running mostly intact government agencies. We obviously had not brought appropriate tools for trash removal. Neither did we have the workforce. So, here was a job, ordered by the president of the United States, which could be done only by mobilizing Iraqis. The situation revealed much about our new relationship with this country.

With over 5 million people, Baghdad is about the population and geographic size of Chicago. Garbage collection on a daily basis kept thousands employed and busy. I would need to go downtown, identify and organize an Iraqi team, and begin scoping out the task.

Australian general Keith Schollum, who served as an aide to the Baghdad regional director Barbara Bodine, and I boarded a convoy and headed over to the city hall. We would be the first civilians to visit city hall after the war. We arrived to find the complex heavily guarded by Abrams tanks and perhaps a dozen troops, a number that struck me as far too few. Unlike most national government buildings, city hall had not been bombed and had been fairly well preserved from looting. Long lines of curious and wary-looking Iraqis lined the sidewalks. Many of them shouted out questions about where they could go to find missing loved ones or get some form of assistance.

Larry Eck, an army engineer covering the central region, met us and gave us a tour of the seven-story building. The place was completely lifeless, with the exception of one man, standing on the steps, looking as though he was expecting us for an appointment. Larry explained that the man had been showing up there daily, wanting to know what he could do to help get his city running again.

He was exactly the kind of person we needed. We told him that our mission was to get services restored—trash collection in particular—and we needed his assistance in rounding up a technical team. We asked him to make contact with colleagues in the municipal government throughout the surrounding neighborhoods and bring them back later that afternoon for a meeting.

This would be my first introduction to the tough realities of occupation. Trash removal seemed like a straightforward task. But the size and scope of the problem were staggering. Here we were, facing the need to organize a city-wide operation to remove 60,000 tons of trash that had piled up across the city, and another 2,500 tons accumulating each day, in a city the size of Chicago.

But many of the 234 trash collection stations had been burned or looted. And of the 600 garbage trucks, we were told that 90 percent of them had either been destroyed in the war or stolen. Eighteen hundred workers, three per truck, had all disappeared. Furthermore, the city had no loaders and no trash compacters. Even brooms had disappeared. So here we were, charged with "reconstruction," needing equipment and labor, and we had no money.

Another issue was how this mission could be accomplished without relying on people who knew the city and its systems well. In short, it simply couldn't be done without utilizing the people who had run things before we arrived—those who had served under Saddam. We would have to sort through de-Ba'athfication later; priority number one was service restoration. The objective at this point was continuity, not change. In witnessing the various phases of working with the Iraqis—of first relying on Ba'athists, then later removing them—I was witnessing the unfolding of one of the most difficult and controversial realities of the war. It will be debated by historians for a long time.

We first had to find the city mangers who had formerly directed this work. With no telephone communication, we relied on the original three locals who showed up that first day to deliver messages on foot to their colleagues. Sure enough, the next day at the appointed time, six more key directorate generals from the city government showed up.

Here we were meeting a team of senior Iraqi officials who had just been reporting through the mayor and deputy mayor directly to Saddam Hussein. I could not even imagine what was going through their minds. Recognizing that we needed to get to know them, I handed out pencils and pads and asked them to write their names in Arabic, which I would later have translated. We all engaged in introductions, with the help of my friend and translator, Ammar. I pronounced each name as well as I could, always with a smile, hoping to lighten the moment. We bantered back and forth over pronunciations, feeling increasingly more comfortable with each other.

First there was Dr. Raad M. Hussein, who was directorate general for Baghdad water projects. I refrained from commenting on his interesting last name ("Oh, have you stayed in touch with Saddam, and how's he doing?"). Amir Abulalla Alanzi was reportedly a good engineer; we would probably need his services. Tali M. Jacob was a technical affairs manager. Rounding out the group was a technical deputy, Saed Hussan Hamaid, and the deputy mayor, Duraid Akram Mahwood.

After engaging them as best we could and sketching data and charts on pads, Keith Schollum and I returned to the palace that evening. We had the complete organizational chart of the entire Baghdad municipal system. Now we knew the entire city structure; we could go to work. That kind of information was never made available to us back in Kuwait City because, I suspect, it didn't exist. We just had to show up, do our own research, and hope we weren't shot. That is how most senior advisors went about figuring out who ran things previously. And that's how most got services restored.

WHEN THE ENTIRE GROUP of Baghdad city managers finally gathered together at city hall, I caught a glimpse into how the robotically obedient world of Saddam worked. All had filed in to stand behind their seats along the conference table. Missing was the deputy mayor, the senior-most figure in the group. With great staged fanfare, he entered the room and took his place at the head of the table. He stood facing his colleagues, then raised his straight arm high, with hand cupped downward, and greeted them with the "Saddam salute." What were these people thinking? Did they not know that their time had passed, that effectively we were in charge?

Keith and I got right down to business. We told them we needed their help in designing and carrying out an emergency trash removal operation

I stored about $400,000 in cash in my locked desk
for funding youth ministry activities. It was an "all
cash" system at the time. There were no functioning
banks, and the ministry payroll systems had been
destroyed. To preserve continuity we simply delivered
"emergency payments" of $20 to Iraqi workers at set
times and places.

for Baghdad. Our intention, we explained, was to use the existing system
to organize the project and compensate the workers through an emergency
cash payments system.

Next, we tried to get them to explain how the old system worked.
The details began to emerge. Some of the trucks belonged to the drivers
personally. A contract system covered 30 percent of all work. Much of the
municipal system had disintegrated. Most of the trucks and equipment
previously operated by Baghdad authorities had either been stolen or were
being held in private locations for safekeeping. No one really knew where,
but it was clear that wherever they might have gone, they certainly weren't
available for an emergency mobilization.

Whatever. We knew we could make headway with a job of that enormity only by starting small and starting now. Something had to be done to visibly convey progress to the Iraqis and to the world beyond that was plugged into CNN. If we just stood around talking with our Iraqi friends every day about the problem, that too would be observed.

To get trash removal going, each district needed four trucks and a loader. Given that the personnel and resources just did not exist, we decided to request four dump trucks and three loaders from the army. It seemed like a reasonable request.

But this trash removal initiative became a prime example of the difficulty of dealing with the bureaucracy of our army. We had a huge fight to get even those few trucks out of army command. We would need to have a fragmentary order (FRAGO) drawn up and circulated through the army bureaucracy in order to even get a decision on the trucks and loaders. We resorted to pleading with the army that they were the only source of assets to do the job, and the situation was desperate.

After haggling day and night for two full days, we finally got the order approved. But the approval was on the condition that the equipment would be available for two, maybe three days at the most. Understandably, from the army's viewpoint, there were higher priorities. The demands on them far exceeded the supplies and equipment.

The experience was typical of challenges during the early days of ORHA. What you thought was solved one day, broke open entirely the next, and would probably remain unresolved, all because of too few resources to do the job. Getting approval for the use of equipment was a breakthrough, but no task was as simple as it initially appeared. When one problem was solved, dozens more popped up to impede progress. For example, gasoline was in short supply. That always seemed amazing given that we were standing on a nation that practically floated on an ocean of oil.

We also had to deal with other complications related to the actual content of the trash. We learned that the trash piles contained unexploded ordnance and possibly even some radioactive waste, including uranium. A USAID specialist in hazardous waste management showed up and offered to help address the disposal of dangerous materials. There were also bodies and body parts in the burned-out hulks that had to be removed by the mortuary unit and in accordance with international law.

Finally, on the third day after first arriving at city hall, we all gathered around a Baghdad city map and, working off of military coordinates, charted a plan for the first day of operations. Plotting even a partial operation to remove trash required laying out a strategy for neighborhood-by-neighborhood logistics. We would need to develop a grid to connect assets to location. Because the truck drivers and loader operators could easily become the targets of snipers, we would also need an Army Civil Affairs team working with us for security and force protection.

April 30 was set as "trash day." We had our military equipment, our maps and logistics plans, and an American "can-do" attitude. And we had our press event ready to go. We couldn't help ourselves; we imagined a big civic affair, much like how we celebrated volunteerism and civic pride at home. We hoped that many Iraqis would vote with their feet and come out with shovels in hand to help sweep streets and load trash on trucks. This is what we assumed the Iraqis wanted and were ready for.

I felt a strong push to turn this into a photo opportunity and good news event for the media, generating badly needed confidence. This made sense to me because we desperately needed to get some good news out. The Iraqis as well as the watching world had to see the symbols of progress. Whatever else we accomplished, we needed to show some evidence that Baghdad's trash problem was being addressed.

But we were already staging events and beginning to gloss over hard realities. The press operation came to resemble an American political campaign. I always felt uncomfortable with it, this in spite of the fact that there was a lot of good news that the media refused to cover. There seemed to be a pattern at work: the media would refuse to cover good news while our side would refuse to acknowledge problems; we would engage in more stonewalling and PR, and the media would lose even more trust.

As we approached the big event, we wanted badly to put our American-style template into effective operation, displaying our organizing acumen and inspired civic partnering to the Iraqis and the rest of the world. But the circumstances always had the upper hand. By the time the event actually arrived, other more pressing priorities gained the media's attention. And the event itself proved nearly impossible to coordinate. Just getting a media pool organized and delivered safely across town proved difficult. After several delays in getting out to the media event, I decided I was not needed. Plus, this was also the first of several occasions when premonitions of mine would surface. It was one of three major events that proved dangerous in which my gut told me to steer clear. Sure enough the trucks and loaders came under fire while the CPA team was present. In fact, Dan Senor attended the event and had a very close call. He and his press associate were forced to hit the ground to evade gunfire.

AFTER INVESTING NEARLY A WEEK of intense organizing, I could nevertheless report back to General Garner that we were "standing up" a real trash removal operation. I explained that we were testing the system with small local operations, and that several days later, when a larger supply of trucks and loaders would arrive, we were planning to conduct a large city-wide "trash day," hopefully city wide, to which Garner barked out, "Eberly, I love you." And off he marched. Garner seemed genuinely pleased, and I enjoyed the moment.

Naturally, my colleagues began ribbing me with lines like: "Eberly came in to do the white collar stuff and ended up organizing the shovel and shit brigade in downtown Baghdad." They still talk about that.

Reports from Washington

On April 30, I had a long conversation with Dan Senor (who later became Ambassador Bremer's press spokesman) and his associate, who at the time worked for White House Strategic Communications. They had talked to senior White House communications staff Dan Bartlett about our "rolling political disaster."

Apparently, those whose jobs were largely political were beginning to notice what was all too plain to those of us who had served during the planning phase. At last, they too were concerned about the lack of preparation and information. The telling comment from back home was that "there was no policy shop," meaning that no substantive team was reacting and adjusting to reality on the ground.

What may or may not have been known was that there were plenty of planning documents and strategies. The one that was developed by the State Department was excluded. And the planning strategy adopted by the Pentagon was not really a plan—as that term is normally understood—but rather an assumption that a "brief stay, light touch" strategy was all that was needed. I heard, but never confirmed, reports that Rumsfeld severely chastised anyone who thought a serious Phase IV (postwar) plan was needed.

Dan Senor also reported comments from the White House that "things haven't been thought through" and "there are no resources." That was simple shorthand for what everyone knew by now, which was that there was simply

Ambassador Bremer interacts with Arab world press at a soccer ball donation event at the Olympic village. A spontaneous soccer match was organized with star Iraqi players and Ambassador Bremer. The occasion was the announcement of a large soccer ball donation campaign for Iraqi children, with many Iraqi sports dignitaries in attendance.

too little security. It was conventional wisdom from the first day that senior advisors arrived and had to wait in line for convoys to go out to their destinations and get the process of nation building under way. For some reason, however, it never seemed politically correct to say it. We all knew it was true; we just didn't talk about it. It was a forbidden subject. Most people didn't tell reporters how bad things were because they honestly hoped and believed that conditions would soon improve.

Bremer Arrives

On May 6, President Bush formally announced his appointment of Ambassador Paul Bremer as the presidential envoy to Iraq. By the time the news officially broke, Bremer was on his way to the palace.

We learned long after Garner returned home that he was told on his first day in Baghdad that he was being replaced by Bremer. He told no one. And, throughout his remaining weeks in Baghdad, he worked with an intensity and positive outlook that was inspiring.

I thought the world of Jay Garner. I had come into ORHA through him and we had faced very tough circumstances in Baghdad together. Naturally, my empathy toward him as a man was very high. In my view, he was never given the tools to do the job and was basically betrayed by Washington.

When Ambassador Bremer arrived in Baghdad, we all gathered in one of the palace ballrooms to meet him. Because of the way the transition was handled, the meeting felt awkward. But I instantly developed the highest regard for Bremer. Anybody who could pull off what Paul Bremer did in that meeting deserved immediate respect, and he got it. Bremer was undoubtedly fed lots of disparaging information on the ORHA team from Washington. But he gave no sign of that. Instead, he honored Jay Garner and his team publicly, and gave Jay a lot of credit for his real accomplishments, remarks he would often repeat in Jay's absence, including the following June at his Pentagon homecoming ceremony.

The assembled group that day was, for the most part, not Bremer's hand-picked team. But as the one in command, he would have to galvanize them behind his leadership. By projecting modesty and

Ambassador Bremer acts as ceremonial goalie during the event.

sincere gratitude for the ORHA team, it appeared to me that he had won them over.

Bremer projected tremendous strength. He, after all, had arrived to take over and transform what was still a temporary organization (whose very name implied a soft and limited mission) into one of occupation. I believe that his impressions of his new job description were formed in his May 12 convoy trip from Baghdad International Airport to the palace. The first line of his memoir, *My Year in Iraq: The Struggle to Build a Future of Hope*, was "Baghdad was burning." From that, he graphically recalled the lingering sights of chaos and a country in ruin. I believe that his short experience between being hired and arriving that day provided ample evidence that, contrary to perceptions at the White House and the Pentagon, Garner was not the problem.

Garner and Bremer were both, in my estimation, America's best. I don't want to sugarcoat the controversy that naturally flowed from the tough decisions each had to make. I felt a sincere pride to serve under them. I'm not a military guy, but when either of these men approached, I had a great urge to salute. They both earned our loyalty and respect. Each was able to return home at the end of his tour of duty deserving America's respect for having agreed to take on what was one of the toughest jobs in half a century.

They were very different men, but strong, if not great, leaders. As one who was there, working with both men, I've never been able to join in the public criticism that inevitably followed as their performance and decisions came under growing scrutiny. I've always felt that what each man faced was much like a quarterback who had to abandon the game plan and call "audibles." In my view, they called most of the plays just about right.

The Office of Reconstruction and Humanitarian Assistance (ORHA) immediately became the Coalition Provisional Authority (CPA); it changed in its basic structure almost the day Bremer arrived. Bremer had a well-deserved reputation as a tough, hard-working, and decisive administrator. Almost immediately upon his arrival, memos started arriving on our desks with a boldface URGENT emblazoned across the top. That one word symbolized his approach. It was an approach that was needed and, for the most part, welcomed.

He asked us to make the impossible possible. That was his phrase, and it captured well the mission before us. Anything that could help jump-start a functioning economy deserved priority attention. For example, the "Oil for Food" program had been the only mechanism for the delivery of vital food supplies to the Iraqi people. We had inherited 6,900 contracts totaling $10 billion from Saddam's regime. All of them had to be reviewed and acted upon. That meant getting contracts while also building a list of companies that should not get contracts. The pressure to get services restored presented a classic conflict between the equally pressing priorities of service continuity on the one hand and regime change on the other.

On the contracts, Bremer told us, "step up the pace. This could take years; I want it done in two weeks. That is 3,000 reviews a week." This was, of course, "impossible." But *impossible* was the very nature of Bremer's job (and Garner's before him).

In that environment, there were no weekend or holiday breaks. For example, Bremer called an early morning meeting on July 4. He opened by saying "Happy Fourth of July," and then immediately introduced a long line of urgent work demands. We were failing to communicate our successes, he said. Bremer was always more sensitive about "the optics" of the operation than Garner had been, and I had no doubt that this was pressure coming from Washington. The CPA was in the process of developing a new communications plan to address the problem, and we were to "review and have comments back by COB today." He clarified: "COB means midnight tonight." Bremer typically worked past midnight and slept only about three and a half hours a night.

He demanded that we begin to "push real hard on reconstruction." Bremer declared: "make life better, fast; even if that means having to work twenty-seven hours a day." That was an enormous challenge, especially since nothing was working and we had no money, no security, and no reliable Iraqis to help us.

Bremer was a tireless workaholic. He slept on a small cot on the second floor and then, like the rest of us, in a trailer. He would typically rise at 4:30 a.m., jog several miles, shower, grab breakfast, and head into the office. He might have introduced the world to the fact that America's presence was now an occupation and we would thus stay for a while, but the shelves in Saddam's spacious office were bare. Running across his mammoth desk was a plaque that read "success has a thousand fathers." He ran the CPA like a chief executive officer runs a company. He was very commanding.

Paul Bremer earned my respect. But more than any other person, he will probably bear many of the bruises for what happened during that first summer in Baghdad. He will always be identified with the controversy over de-Ba'athification and dissolving the army.

Running the Government in an All-Cash Society

In a February 2007 House Committee on Oversight and Government Reform hearing, Chairman Henry Waxman asked, "Who in their right mind would send 363 tons of cash into a war zone? But that's exactly what our government did!" Of course, the congressman's imagery carried the day. But it also misconstrued the enormity of the challenge that we faced on the ground in those early days in Baghdad.

You can't build a nation without money, without restoring financial institutions, and without properly dispensing money for those who need it. Therefore, money issues were increasingly dominating our meetings. The greatest struggle by far was getting emergency payments to government workers. By the second or third week in Baghdad, reports were coming back to us that workers were getting restless. We had promised them an emergency payment in the amount of twenty dollars per month just to tide them over. We assumed that that amount would be more than most were making under Saddam, although this proved not to be true. We stressed that this was only an emergency payment to help them out temporarily until a payroll system was restored. There was really no other way to quell the growing disquiet of the Iraqi masses.

But what were we to do in a country that had been ruled by a tyrant and where the banks, like every other institution, were effectively owned by the state? Security was poor, buildings were decrepit, and the nation had no checking writing or electronic transfer capacity. The country's currency, the Saddam dinar, was soon to be rendered null and void. Obviously we were not going to use what was left of Saddam Hussein's banks to begin financing government operations. Whatever banking laws had existed would need to be replaced by new laws.

For those and other reasons, the seemingly straightforward task of "paying the people" would take months of effort to get right. In addition to simply not having Iraqi civilians to work with, there were major communication and transportation obstacles. Too often, the payroll records were either missing or in such bad shape that we would not know who was or was not eligible for emergency payments. Even if payroll records had been available and ready, where would we store our cash? How would we make payments to hundreds of thousands of Iraqi workers?

For the entire time I was there, the new Iraq we were building was an all-cash society. Whenever cash moved, and whenever it stood still, it was under armed custody, either a vault at the palace or, in my case, the upper drawer of the desk in my trailer. I kept $400,000 in cash for the purpose of making emergency payments to teams and athletes.

In the case of payroll, it would take us weeks and in many cases months just to get the emergency payments going, for the simple reason that most public sector payroll records had either been destroyed by the bombing or burned in postwar looting. We would need to reassemble the records with the help of Iraqi workers, which required placing a lot of trust in people we really didn't know. It also required communicating with workers in a country with no radio or telephone and almost no print media communications. In most cases, making payments required making elaborate arrangements with Iraqis. It required organizing separate paydays for each district, agreeing to a specific time to make payments, and then hoping the word got out to the appropriate parties. In most cases, it actually worked.

During the period when many of us were focusing on payroll, senior advisors frequently returned from trips with reports of raucous scenes that nearly turned violent in a number of cases. But there were also frequent and encouraging reports of honest Iraqis stepping forward to help identify corrupt Iraqis who tried anything from double dipping to getting relatives onto the payroll.

The Iraqis who had earned our trust for honesty also had a term for the corrupt former Ba'ath party officials who showed up; the term was "Ali Babba," which meant thief. During Saddam's reign, many of these Ali Babbas made a habit of using the special favor they had as Ba'athists to steal portions of their underlings' checks, keeping them dirt poor. So, naturally, these previously exploited workers helped us to identify the bad guys. When an Ali Babba approached, the honest Iraqis quietly crossed their hands in protest, a gesture that symbolized their desire to see the culprit carried away in handcuffs.

If the cash method of payment was basic, the method of transporting it from one place to another was even more so. One or two people loaded the necessary sum of cash into cardboard boxes or garbage bags and were then escorted to the payment site by tough guys with machine guns. Typically we paired up a member of the ministry team staff with one or two armed Civil Affairs soldiers in order to ensure both safety and honesty in the handling of the money.

By May 25, army captain Lynn Brown, who served on my team, managed to get cash payments to nine hundred local workers. In an amazing scene, and one that became familiar across the entire government during those early days, Brown carried $18,000 in garbage bags accompanied by soldiers with M16s.

The payments were in U.S. dollars, which presented scattered problems in a country still filled with people fearful of Saddam. Some oil refinery workers wanted to be paid in dinars because they feared being caught with U.S. dollars. The existing penal code, which presumably existed until replaced by something else, made cooperation with foreign enemies punishable by death.

The Iraqis we worked with were reliable and cooperative in carrying out this exercise. As it turned out, without our even knowing about it, a number of reliable local ministry workers had been addressing the problem and trying unsuccessfully to reach us. Some of them had spent considerable time reconstructing hand-written payroll records by the time we arrived.

Payroll issues would remain among the most complicated and emotional issues we had to deal with for months to come. As I listened to these Iraqis and watched them work, I was reminded of just how uniform human nature was—there are good people and there are bad people everywhere. When de-Ba'athification was in full swing, stories abounded of both heroism and treachery. In the prosecutorial environment that de-Ba'athification created, all kinds of things happened. Some tried ingenious ways to maintain favor and preserve their place on the payroll. They would lie about their backgrounds or lie about others. Often, we simply didn't have enough information to make uniformly fair decisions. We were given what felt like life and death decisions over people's lives. We would sit around tables going through lists of names, having to announce that "he is in" or "he is out."

Naturally, we had to move very carefully in accepting someone's word lest we encourage score settling and retribution. There was only one way to determine whether a person was good or bad. Although it could not be 100 percent reliable, the best way to test character is simply to watch people perform over a period of time and listen to what others say about them. Bad actors usually have multiple critics.

De-Ba'athification: The Confused Language of Occupation

One of the things I learned from years of attending official meetings is that each one has its own dynamics, usually having something to do with evading tough and controversial issues. I have long taken an interest in the language that is employed to navigate difficult policy territory.

As the ancient Chinese proverb states it, progress begins "by calling a thing by its right name." I've learned that, in government, problems are rarely called by their right name. When discussion suddenly becomes shrouded in jargon and when language becomes evasive, that is a clear sign that controversy or potential division lurks just beneath the surface.

Perhaps the least understood and most poorly resolved issue on Iraq— although it was the subject of many meetings—was "de-Ba'athification," the exercise of removing people with close ties to Saddam Hussein or loyalty to the Ba'ath party from public employment. It would emerge as one of the most consequential and controversial issues because it exposed divisions over core assumptions. Like so many policy decisions, the choices regarding how to proceed were highly complicated. Most critics have concluded that too many workers from the previous regime and its military were thrown overboard with no means to start new lives.

Like the debate over what to call senior ORHA officials, conflicts over de-Ba'athification policy revealed ambivalence in the direction about the nature of the mission. In fact, like perhaps no other issue, this one forced our collective minds to focus with laser beam intensity on real conditions in Iraq.

We didn't know what precisely would replace the old regime, but we assumed that legions of former Ba'ath officials would either disappear on their own or have to be dismissed. But dismissed on what basis and by whom? I sensed that the issue was one of the last to be addressed in the planning process because it symbolized like none other the true responsibilities that came with taking out a totalitarian regime. In phone calls back to Washington, we asked if a de-Ba'athification plan had been worked through or if someone would bring the plan to Iraq at some latter point. We never received an answer.

Regimes such as Saddam's consist of one all-powerful tyrant at the top, a small number of less publicly known but still powerful henchmen just beneath him, and hundreds of thousands of totally anonymous workers at the bottom who have varying degrees of ideological loyalty. Sorting all of that out would be a monumental task.

We replaced a regime that had spent the previous thirty years consolidating its power by eliminating persons who displayed the slightest disloyalty, even those whose only sin was that they were gifted leaders with an unconcealed capacity for independent thought or action. Replacing a one-man, one-party regime with one that would operate along diametrically different lines in the same country presented three equally daunting tasks.

1. By some system of evaluation we would need to identify and root out those who were personally loyal to Saddam or ideologically committed to the Ba'ath party, an exercise affecting potentially hundreds of thousands of people if it included civilian and military personnel.

2. New roles would have to be found for this group of ex-Saddamites (even though they would be reviled by the Iraqi people), lest they move immediately to oppose the new government and become a destabilizing force.

3. We would need sufficient numbers of new qualified Iraqi technocrats for senior positions in the new civil government. And, obviously, they must themselves be free of taint from too close an affiliation with Saddam or extreme ideologies.

So, in effect, we would need to build a new Westernized system of nonpartisan professional civil service. Once again, who exactly would do this? If we trusted the Iraqis with the job, it could quickly evolve into sweeping purges, score settling, and even vengeance killings. The United Nations, which had so strongly resisted the war, had no intention of helping the Americans out by taking over these functions after the war. If we Americans alone bore such as delicate responsibility, it might appear arbitrary and ruthless.

From the early days of Pentagon meetings to the planning process of Kuwait City, no other issue so focused the minds of planners regarding what we were about to undertake. The sheer scale of this operation was shocking for anyone who focused on it for long. To be done right, it would take lots of time, staff, and money, the very things that the senior planners wanted to avoid in the postwar period. It surfaced the real issues that went directly against the grain of the early assumptions ("light touch, brief stay"), suggesting that the "enter-exit" nature of the mission would be a breeze.

The very exercise of de-Ba'athification sounded harshly draconian, the kind of thing an occupying power would do. For that reason alone, the term would be avoided. When the true nature of this de-Ba'athification procedure became apparent, various voices started calling for a softening of the concept. Uncertainty and controversy can produce a great debate over words. We were caught between what circumstances on the ground required and what maintaining political perceptions demanded. We wanted regime change, but we didn't want to be seen as taking over and fundamentally refitting an entire country. But neither were the Iraqis ready to do that on their own. To not do this job would have been to seek "regime change on the cheap," as it would later be called.

The net result of this conundrum was that a variety of euphemistic terms emerged as alternatives. I wasn't sure whether it was local creativity at work, or high-level direction coming from Washington. Either way, the new terms only further exposed the ambivalence of our core mission and whether what we were about to do could be accomplished with a "light touch."

The most evasive term to surface during the Kuwait City planning process was "suitability screening." For its brief life, this term reassuringly took the focus off the more radical surgery that had to be done. Suitability screening made it sound like we would come in like an outside firm under contract and conduct benign interviews over coffee to determine competence and aptitude, maybe administering Myers-Briggs exams along the way for extra confidence in our professional vetting.

This was the kindler and gentler phase of the planning. Once again, the phrase "light touch" made its appearance. At that point, we were informed by senior officials that "party membership was not a disqualifier." Instead of rejecting hardcore Ba'ath party officials and senior government bureaucrats because of their loyalty to the previous regime, we were now attempting to determine their suitability to serve.

Occasionally, it was mentioned that "good capable people will just rise to the top;" it was not our job "to anoint people." We would merely help to ensure a rapid transfer of government. We in the interim civil administration would simply guide this along as "helpers."

The theory behind this approach seemed to be that perhaps with a little persuasion and a seminar or two they would become skilled and impartial Western-styled bureaucrats. The general principle was to "depoliticize the bureaucracy," getting rid of party hacks and ideologues, while keeping the technocrats, which made the job sound a little like American urban government before the great civil service reforms of the past century.

That seemed like a reasonable plan, but just how would we determine skill levels or personal loyalty? Presumably at some point the interview would have gotten into the question of past loyalty to Saddam or association with the Ba'ath party, but that alone would not be a disqualifier. And how would we or anyone else apply this to hundreds of thousands of bureaucrats?

What public service system did we want? In the course of this, I volunteered to assist in producing the early draft of a guidance paper on producing a new professionalized public service. I was in touch with nongovernmental organizations (NGOs) and government agencies such as the Office of Personnel Management (OPM) and USAID back home. Periodically we all allowed our imaginations to race. In reality, Iraqis did what they knew and what came naturally; they immediately turned to hiring relatives and engaging in personal profiteering.

Complicating the project even further was the need to clean house across an entire nation. If we were going to get rid of senior bureaucrats and political leaders at the national level, we also needed to reach down to the eighteen provincial governates and probably even to the municipal level. It was assumed that we would quickly reach out to "community leaders" and achieve through them a speedy restoration of security and stability needs. We would also partner with them in meeting humanitarian needs. This would be solid public service, generating goodwill and morale.

Both of these objectives—setting up a suitability screening system to determine the worthiness of hundreds of thousands of Iraqis and a systematic outreach effort to hundreds of cities and towns—required personnel and resources we simply did not have. Not remotely. Only once or twice during the planning process did I hear anyone mention the need to possibly contract with a qualified firm to come in and conduct interviews with Iraqis. Whenever this level of requirement surfaced and someone mentioned the estimated $100 million price tag, the conversation almost always changed.

There was an ingrained tendency to simply hope that the necessary processes and systems to do these tasks would somehow emerge from the locals in Iraq and we'd figure it all out when we got there. Plus, what was the point in ramping up such elaborate systems if we intended to leave after three months? Again, the answer was that presumably the Iraqis could sort it all out.

The contradictions were painfully obvious. To leave those who ran Saddam's dictatorship in power was tantamount to inviting infiltrators to the table. As we would learn soon enough, Iraq had a deeply treacherous political culture. Failure to remove known dangers would have doomed the new government. Conversely, to throw overboard a group that previously had all the power and privileges and leave them with no hope of meaningful employment and no expectation of political status would almost certainly drive many of them into armed opposition. To indiscriminately get rid of them or to keep them would invite trouble. Either way, they were a potential danger and deserved priority attention.

If priority attention could not be given to this paramount challenge, it was because, like everything else we faced, we simply didn't have the resources or staff and were thus between a rock and a hard place. We faced these dilemmas in April and May, and staff didn't start arriving in sufficient quantities until July. Not until midsummer in 2003 was the conclusion drawn that the entire operation was impossible without a big infusion of cash from Congress.

An emergency congressional appropriation of $18 billion would not be passed until September, six months after liberation. All we could do about any of these challenges in the meantime was to issue policies and pronouncements without the means of implementing them. That is why ORHA and the Coalition Provisional Authority in Baghdad became so isolated from much of Iraq.

Those of us who were on the front lines of dealing with reorganizing the Iraqi ministries that had existed under Saddam were painfully aware of this and spent a lot of time anticipating what might happen. Unlike the decision makers back at the palace or those huddled together in Washington, we were on the streets and could see what was happening with our own eyes.

In my own case, I had one of the more vivid firsthand experiences with the difficulty when I reassembled some of Saddam's top lieutenants in the Baghdad government in order to meet the first and most urgent priority of resuming services—getting 60,000 tons of garbage removed. I did so knowing full well that all these same officials would likely be removed when the next urgent priority, de-Ba'athification, kicked in. There was no conceivable way we could confront the widespread disruption of services without first assembling the directorate generals from the previous regime. The government had been shut down and there was no way we had the means to operate it.

We certainly didn't have the means to remove 60,000 tons of trash that had accumulated on the streets of Baghdad during the war. And only the Iraqis knew how to make the water and sanitation services run. In other words, we needed the very people who had served under Saddam.

These were the remarkable tradeoffs that we had to deal with on the ground. In defense of Ambassador Bremer, it took the wisdom of Solomon to know where exactly to find the center of balance. And no one really knew what to do with Saddam's senior bureaucrats, given our other priorities and limited resources. Rounding them all up and putting them in a detention center was hardly an option. Neither was it an option to drive them out of the country where they could help organize funds and logistics for the incipient insurgency out of sight from our intelligence services.

Where do you want your enemies to go and what do you want them to do with their lives? Do you want to hold them close or cast them away? Enemies who have been cast away or driven out of the country can often do more damage from a distance. And the people from Saddam's regime truly were enemies of the Iraqi people.

What critics fail to appreciate is just how hated Saddam's people were. Even with the eventual de-Ba'athification policy, most of us had to deal with Iraqis who were outraged that the government we were putting in place contained some figures from the previous regime.

A huge, powerful, and lavishly indulged elite class existed under Saddam. Prudence suggested they had no place in the country's future. Those who felt we went too far should consider what we were getting rid of: senior Ba'ath party leadership; the upper crust of the entire multi-layered police state apparatus, including intelligence services and Saddam's own special forces; most of the military brass; cabinet ministers and their deputies; and senior directors across the ministries.

To provide good jobs for Ba'ath party officials or to offer what in effect was a severance package to send them on their way would itself have led to an insurgency against the coalition by ordinary Iraqis. Many of Saddam's civilian and military subordinates had already amassed considerable resources, especially those at the very top. Much of the looting that occurred was fueled by the anger that Iraqis felt toward the wealth and power that had been hoarded by Saddam's government.

There simply was no easy solution. And with thin resources, Bremer had to announce an edict and hope it worked out reasonably well. He knew at the time that corrections and adjustments might have to be made later. And they were.

A scene from a going-away party for General Garner at the presidential palace pool.

Whatever one's view of Bremer's approach to de-Ba'athification, there is little doubt that the insurgency that would emerge by midsummer in 2003 received significant help from Sunnis and Ba'ath party leaders who had been stripped of power and left with nothing. But even with the benefit of hindsight, it is hard to imagine how that could have been avoided.

A similar set of circumstances surrounded the Iraqi army and its status. As Bremer has explained, the army was already disbanded and dispersed, in addition to being largely incompetent. Few deny that the elite intelligence and security forces had to be removed. But as with the civilian officials, no one was sure what exactly to do with them.

Jay Garner proposed a civilian conservation corps to employ some or most of them, and parts of his plan were eventually adopted. It was one of those issues for which there simply were no easy answers. It may take generations for the millions of people who drew power and privilege from Saddam to buy into a different kind of future. Alternatively, they may decide to drive the country toward civil war and permanent division in order to avoid minority status in a Shiite majority Iraq.

I was in the senior staff meeting the morning that Ambassador Bremer made the announcement. When it became apparent that what we were talking about was an extensive housecleaning of the existing senior officials of Iraq, a palpable sense of shock hit the room. Many of the senior advisors were already working with senior Ba'ath officials in order to address the more urgent task of restoring government operations, just as I had been. We knew this decision would mean dismantling and disrupting the structures we were putting in place.

I had the feeling that Bremer knew at the time that this would be one of his most audacious and controversial moves, and he would need to be decisive and unflinching in presenting it, come what may. Decision was more important than precision. The complainers in the "interagency" back home would have spent three weeks picking the plan to death. I admired Bremer for his decisiveness and action.

Many who have focused their postwar criticism on the sweeping de-Ba'athification fail to appreciate how deeply entrenched the Ba'athist culture was in Iraq. Saddam helped create that culture and he exploited it for regime preservation, but he was only its head. A balanced view of the Ba'athist problem would appreciate that whether most senior Ba'athists were preserved in the government or driven out, either way they would remain a problem that could take decades to solve.

Chapter 6

The Sketchy Postwar Plan
How to Assemble a Vehicle While Driving

T HE PROBLEMS ASSOCIATED WITH DE-BA'ATHIFICATION could not be isolated from the larger issues of Iraqi and Islamic culture. Those issues were enormous and would deeply affect our prospects for reconstruction, transforming governance, humanitarian assistance, and all other issues in the U.S. relationship with Iraq.

The debate over "clash of civilizations" is perhaps overblown; human beings do have a lot in common when it comes to core aspirations. But the Americans who served in Iraq could not have been injected into a region, culture, or religion that was more alien to their own. The overwhelming weight of commentary offered by soldiers and civilians, returning home after service in Iraq, centered on two seemingly contradictory observations: "the Iraqis really do want a better life for themselves" and "the Iraqis are not ready for our kind of democracy." Both statements are more or less true.

Human beings universally want to be treated with dignity, and they hope for better, easier, more prosperous lives. While that is as true of Iraqis as Americans, it is also true that, for reasons of their history as well as their religion, many Iraqis are not ready for, or interested in, the rough and tumble democracy that the United States hoped to establish in Iraq. The question that surprisingly few people from our team ever asked was: Are the Iraqi people ready to take the giant leap from being Saddam's subjects to democratic citizens? It is almost impossible for enlightened Western minds to imagine that anyone might not be ready for our way of life, or might be uninterested in adopting core elements of it. It takes time on the ground in a place like Iraq to fully appreciate how difficult it is for people who for decades were prisoners shuffling along with steel ankle bracelets and chains to be transformed immediately into graceful long-distance runners.

Much was made of Iraqi elections and the ink-stained finger, ostensibly the symbol of democracy. But in retrospect, the real symbol of an incipient democratic culture taking root would have been a million Sunnis and Shia shaking hands. Casting ballots is certainly an important part of democracy, but it ensures only that the popular will is expressed. It does not mean that sound democratic practices will take root in the soil. Democracy can, and often does, produce "illiberal" outcomes.

If electoral democracy requires democratic citizens to work, so does running the daily affairs of government. As we planned to reorganize the Iraqi government, conversation often focused on the hope and expectation that an army of technocrats would rise quickly to the top after years of stagnation and forced conformity and bring about a quick turnaround in public administration. That was our hope.

One senior person speculated openly that while the Iraqis were awaiting their liberation, some might have already met and formed committees to deliberate over these matters before we even got there. Perhaps liberation had been anticipated and prepared for inside Iraq. Would some reorganization occur spontaneously? The truth on the ground was quite another matter.

Building democratic nations out of the ashes of tyranny is difficult work. We tend to think that all it takes is aspiration and drive, since those are the central parts of our Western liberal individualism. But Iraqi society combined two challenging features: traditionalism and tyranny—rigid cultural and religious traditions and a police state. One of the most difficult challenges and least discussed aspects of creating democratic citizens are psychological and social factors. How do you transform a people who have been victims of a culture of terror, informants, secret police, and lies into citizens capable of trust, compromise, and collaboration?

As is common in police states, the modus operandi under Saddam was psychological control through intimidation and fear. Imprisonment and torture were used systematically to spread a fear like a thick fog over the populace. Because totalitarianism is based in lies, it generates a culture in which truth, as we understand that term, is largely nonexistent.

The culture of lies and deceit that Saddam created was so pervasive that it might have been the very thing, ironically, that finally doomed him. Those who survived his rule described how government and military

Meeting with my military aides to plan cash dispersements across Iraq.
Providing payments to Iraqi workers required carefully scrutinizing lists of former
government workers.

officials often just told Saddam what he wanted to hear in order to avoid
death. Books by former officials, such as Mahdi Obeidi and Georges Sada,
detail how many of the fateful miscalculations made by Saddam—for
example, in the Iran-Iraq war, the invasion of Kuwait, and his program to
develop WMDs—were based on completely false reports. Most reports were
presented with the intent of appeasing Saddam's rage and flattering his ego.
They weren't even close to the truth.

Saddam's view of his military capacities was so grandiose that both he
and his information minister apparently believed their own propaganda
in the lead-up to the American military invasion. All of this was a result
of advisors and generals telling him what he wanted to hear out of fear of
displeasing him and possibly being imprisoned or shot. It was far safer and
more convenient to avoid the truth. So, most did. For years before the war,
Iraq was one monstrous system of dictatorial ego at the top and pervasive
terror at the bottom.

Torture is the worst and most extreme form of brutality precisely
because it destroys people's humanity. Regimes that rule through terror
create deep and lasting psychological pain and abnormalities. Torture and
terror do strange things to people's minds, including those who haven't
experienced it firsthand. The abuse under Saddam was so pervasive that
just about everyone had a family member or relative who had experienced
it. And the symptoms of the ever-present threat of political abuse are much

like the effects of domestic abuse on its victims. In the presence of constant fear and intimidation, people go to great lengths to avoid a recurrence of the pain. It becomes a part of the mindset.

This, of course, is foreign to Americans steeped in an individual-istic culture of personal entitlements, broad civil liberties, and expansive freedoms of expression. The American character, so open and trusting, is in part the cause and in part the effect of our legal and political system. It is so ingrained that we take it for granted. We never give the slightest thought to the possibility that government agents are secretly monitoring our words or that a close associate, even a family member, would rat on us if we criticized the leader.

Such actions are forms of group psychological bondage. For reasons that only psychiatrists can explain, many in Iraq and other police states willingly informed on a friend or relative in the apparent belief that such action was morally justified. Of course, as a practical matter, such is often seen as necessary to keep food and services flowing.

The youth programs I inherited carried many examples of children spying on their own parents and teachers. We completely removed six hundred people who were associated with the Youth Fedayeen—the orga-nization responsible for programs designed to brainwash kids into blindly following Saddam and his son Uday.

In cultures shaped by vicious rulers, the government reigns through fear and intimidation, and the people survive by lies and treachery. People will do almost anything just to survive, including, as one Iraqi put it, develop "multiple faces." He told me that Iraqis may have ten different faces, and you have no idea which is the true one. I thought about that often as I encoun-tered Iraqis who seemed unusually friendly to me. Which of the ten faces was I seeing? Sadly, in too many cases I learned later that some of the most openly friendly were also the most corrupt and treacherous behind my back. Several who appeared genuinely worthy of trust were undermining me.

WE REALIZED THAT IF THE EARLY POSTWAR PERIOD did not go well in the eyes of the Iraqis, they would have a hard time putting their confidence in the new government, whatever form it took. The conditions for building trust and confidence could be put in place only if there was sufficient law and order. Naturally, many people remained fearful and distrusting long after we arrived. The chaos and criminality that followed the war created a dangerous power vacuum; Saddam, his sons, and many of his most vicious loyalists were still at large. Many Iraqis harbored doubts from the 1991 experience that we would have the courage to finish the job or stay if the going got rough.

These are the very transitional issues that preoccupied some of us back in Kuwait City. A small number of us had a deep interest in the philosophical and moral foundations of democracy. Democracy was made for democrats. It is impossible to have a functioning democratic system, even with advanced constitutions and rules and procedures, that lacks democratic citizens. Democracy is about people. That means the daily habits, attitudes, and practices of its citizens are central to its success.

Democracy depends upon such attitudes and habits as trust, collaboration, and compromise. But, in Iraq, those "habits of the heart" were neither taught nor practiced. Trust, perhaps the most vital ingredient, was impossible for most Iraqis beyond a small radius of family and tribe; no one could ever know the possible consequence of telling the truth. When people cannot share their views or criticisms openly for fear of being heard by informants, there ceases to be any point in even having independent opinions or judgments about anything.

Fear and intimidation also create twisted incentives in the realm of employment. The path to steady employment under Saddam consisted of lavish displays of obedience, never taking risks, never speaking one's mind, and doing only what one was told and no more. Workers neither wanted nor were allowed to engage in activity beyond a narrow radius of prescribed work. Of course, that kind of system destroys productivity. Even the most qualified administrators were conditioned to work within narrowly defined boundaries and never initiate or be creative.

Prior to the war, it was often stated that Iraqis were unusually well educated for the region, especially in technical fields, and therefore Iraq was uniquely ready for the future we would deliver. But "the educated Iraqi" was something of a myth. Iraq had an astonishing number of university-trained engineers, but that was because engineering was one of the few subjects allowed.

The Iraqi university system did not offer anything resembling what we in the West call liberal studies, which is about developing critical thinking skills and the knowledge and practice of freedom in a competitive democratic society. Dozens of subjects that might have helped Iraqis take charge of their own personal and national destinies, such as political theory, social psychology, or public administration, simply did not exist in

Iraq. Not surprisingly, Iraqis had almost no understanding of how public agencies might be organized to reflect standards of nonpartisan professionalism, free of cronyism or corruption. There was no such thing as a Western liberal education anywhere in Iraq. There were no courses or textbooks on liberal values in the universities. Neither were there phone or Internet connections with the outside world that might have encouraged this broader view.

It is true that Iraqis did not lack ingenuity. But such creativity was generally technical in nature. For example, when it came to fixing switches or pumps at power stations, jerry-rigging irrigation or sanitation systems, or hobbling together functioning cars from the parts of a dozen others, many of them were master mechanics. The country's aging infrastructure would have been far more dysfunctional had it not been for the technical proficiency of the Iraqis.

This ingenuity was often cited as the reason Iraqis would likely be proficient at building a democratic nation. It was actually the reverse. They had all been conditioned to be little engineers, people who could fix things, but not to reason or to be reasonable. So many were trained in engineering and other technical fields under Saddam because they were being conditioned to use their engineering skills to function like mindless cogs in a totalitarian system, not to be imaginative or resourceful. Anyone who showed leadership talent was viewed with suspicion. So, naturally, people behaved like sheep.

In fact, in a perverse sort of way the ingenuities in practical tasks that did exist—and theoretically could have been used to build a great nation—were stymied by the very oppressive system that favored their talents in the first place. They were neither a threat to dictatorship nor useful by themselves in advancing democratic practices. They just existed like property of the state.

It took me a while to figure out why Iraqis with advanced degrees showed so little imagination and were so lacking in initiative. Sometimes, I wanted to say, "Hey, you have your freedom; do something with it." Even now, years into the occupation, I still receive emails from colleagues who are mystified by the refusal of Iraqi government officials to take charge and implement programs. Even the best-educated Iraqis showed little resourcefulness and waited to be told what to do long after they were put in charge. From my own experience, the few who did rush forward to seek authority and responsibilities often had their own agendas.

Iraqis took justified pride in their accomplishments in technical fields, but few skills possessed by an engineer are significant for shaping a free society or a democratic system of government. Nothing is more convincing about the positive moral and practical power of freedom than seeing it negated.

The notion of objective and impartial management of government—based on the science of administration, transparency, and democratic values—was foreign to the Iraqis. Where would they have learned these things? Certainly not under Saddam or by attending conferences in the West. Positions and favors, based strictly on standards of professional merit, administrative competence, or nondiscriminatory hiring, were never given. Many of the jobs under Saddam went automatically to the favored Sunnis. In the climate of score settling that quickly emerged in the new Iraq, hiring by religion or ethnicity would continue, with only new categories receiving the preferential treatment.

The concepts of shame and honor are, perhaps, the least understood characteristics of traditional Islamic cultures throughout much of the Arab world. In shame and honor cultures, it is instinctive to look out for family or tribe. In fact, it is dishonorable to *not* do it. Great attention is given to preserving one's public reputation. And the man of real standing is the one who valiantly fights for his kin and community and helps them to prosper.

Our commitment to individual merit and nondiscrimination is based upon American-style individualism, which simply doesn't exist in much of the Middle East. In fact, a leading cause of anti-Americanism there is their rejection of the fragmenting and alienating effects of individualism and its first cousin, crass materialism. What does exist is a tribalism combined with strict religion that has been shaped over millennia of struggle against invaders and hostile autocratic regimes such as the one we were replacing. Traditional societies feature a hunger for group affiliation and identity that is simply foreign to Western liberal societies.

Today, Iraq moves in a continued and palpable shift toward loyalty to family, tribe, and mosque; for safety, for dignity, and for identity. The trust that we Americans are trying to build is projected at the level of mass society and nation state. But Iraqis are content to experience trust in smaller circles.

Of course, culture matters generally. But it matters deeply (in cases like Iraq) where success requires a rather abrupt change in culture. The tendency to embrace custom, tribe, and strict religion, as we quickly learned, affects everything. For example, many Iraqis had come to experience regular handouts under Saddam's quasi-socialist state. Of course, that social welfare assumption forged an expectation that they will be taken care of. America, as an occupation force, was expected to be the new provider of those handouts.

Religious culture also undermines personal innovation when it views individual initiative as undermining the patriarchal tribal system of distributing benefits and protections. When the pursuit of change is seen as a heretical undermining of authority, then it affects the basic openness to freedom. And fatalistic views of success and failure and wealth and poverty will always reduce the enthusiasm for private enterprise.

All of these deep cultural patterns, which are not particularly obvious to the naked eye, took quick effect after liberation. Almost immediately after handing government agencies over to the Iraqis, one could detect a flurry of hiring and contracting based on family or tribal connections. Hiring a blood relative in America would be seen as nepotism; in Iraq it was treated as a moral duty.

As soon as the Iraqis got to form their own government, cabinet and subcabinet slots were handed out like spoils. At one point, after the transfer of power, we discovered that most if not all of the key staff in the Ministry of Youth and Sport were from the same city in Iraq.

Any nation's cultural nuances radiate through all its institutions, laws, and attitudes. That is a large factor in why the postwar planning for Iraq was insufficient. Had Iraq shared even some of our Western assumptions, the job might have been more feasible. But because it didn't, our task was extremely large and lacked a historical model. Those of us in the ORHA team spent thousands of hours—first in Washington, then in Kuwait City, and finally on the ground in Iraq—wresting with the details and ramifications of these issues.

The six weeks spent in Kuwait while working on postwar plans produced a huge amount of detailed operational plans covering the widest range of functions. We were always discouraged by senior Pentagon liaisons who came and went from the compound from getting too serious about transforming the governing structure of Iraq. After all, we wouldn't be there for long. We'd restore services, correct a few humanitarian problems, and leave.

But the lack of a Pentagon plan for Phase IV and this repeated discouragement did not prevent the senior team under Garner from developing

A team meeting with Ambassador Bremer in his presidential palace office.

highly advanced guidance for the postwar reconstruction of Iraq. Here are but a few of the core tasks:

Finances

Managing the finances of a replaced regime was certainly one of the biggest challenges of reconstruction. The domain of money and the economy was the sector that presented as great a challenge as physical security. We would be taking over the entire financial infrastructure of a country that had been run by a dictator. Obviously, that economy would have to put it on a radically new footing if it was going to emerge in new form. We would need to first take firm control over the existing fiscal affairs of the Iraq government, and return it to some semblance of normal functioning in order to avoid a catastrophic collapse. If this mission failed, it was hard to imagine the country holding together.

We would also need a framework for quickly organizing the resources for postwar reconstruction. Obviously if we inherited a bankrupt country with a massive foreign debt, an antiquated and poorly functioning infrastructure, and only a trickle of oil production, Iraq would be a collapsed state and completely dependent on the United States. The worst conceivable scenario would be to end up with a failed state with a flat or rapidly disintegrating economy.

Payments for public workers, pensioners, private relief, and the functioning of government would be one of the most urgent priorities. At least initially, that funding would have to come out of whatever Iraqi assets we could capture and hold, with the rest presumably coming from the American taxpayers.

Perhaps multilateral institutions like the World Bank and the International Monetary Fund (IMF) would come in and help; maybe European powers would swallow their pride and participate as well. Within a short time of his arrival, Bremer realized that the cause would be completely lost without a huge supplemental from Congress. That was the $78 billion (for combined civilian and military expenses) that Congress quickly allotted. The finance team would also have to come up with a plan for a new currency and a monetary policy that would prevent explosive inflation. That is a common problem in postwar environments and one that could quickly complicate economic stabilization goals.

The longer-term goal would be to establish a new regulatory regime that would build a modern banking system that was sufficiently private and independent. In addition to new laws to license and regulate banks, new foreign exchange polices would be needed to replace Saddam's practice of manipulating foreign exchange earnings for personal enrichment. New systems would be needed to encourage trade and financing for private enterprise in a market economy.

But the most urgent need was to simply re-open banks, which would likely be raided by Saddam's people on their way out of town and in need of new reserves. Above all, now that the Iraqi government would effectively be ours, we would need cash in sufficient supply to pay the daily costs both of running the Iraqi government and to cover the expenses associated with the plans we were developing in Kuwait City.

Covering the central bank and treasury functions during the early days of ORHA and CPA was a team of veteran financial experts from the U.S. Department of Treasury, including Van Jorstad, George Mollinax, and David Nummy, each of whom had extensive prior experience in situations like this (such as in Bosnia and Kosovo). The finance team would have to sort through the byzantine system that Saddam had in place for financing his operations and paying workers. We knew the system would be in a state of collapse and would probably be lacking cash reserves. Since the existing corrupt system of dispersements would probably not be recoverable, a new temporary system of payments, along with pay scales and job schedules, would have to be established. Hopefully, we would do it well enough to reassure the Iraqis and maintain peace.

Some cash is dispersed for us to make emergency payments to Iraqis. All transactions to operate business and government were done in cash during the early months.

We assumed that at least some cash, perhaps in the neighborhood of $1.3 billion in Iraqi assets, would be recovered from Iraqi vaults and frozen accounts and applied to funding postwar rebuilding. This money would be organized in a central location, and, with the help of Army Civil Affairs units, emergency payments in cash would be moved through the ministries' teams to Iraqi workers. These assets would probably be sufficient to fund government operations for a month or two.

What was needed, however, was an infrastructure to finance the emergency operations of the entire Iraqi government that would now be in our hands. That meant that each of us would take over the budgeting and management of our ministries. Under the direction of Nummy, we would all be expected to come up with an emergency budget for our ministries covering the first six months.

Of course, sitting in Kuwait City, it was very difficult to know which assumptions would prevail. We were told that our budget calculations should anticipate the need to repair damage and resupply equipment. In Kuwait City, we had no idea if we would be entering government buildings with fully functioning systems in place, much like a bus full of passengers waiting for a new driver, or if structures would be destroyed and most personnel dispersed. In the majority of cases, the latter was true. Most of us arrived at our ministry buildings to find nothing there. The buildings were either totally destroyed or severely damaged by the bombing. Those that survived the bombing were hollowed out by looters. They were like haunted tombs.

Even if buildings had not been bombed, burned, or looted, and the workforce had not fled, we would still have had a monumental financial management challenge. Nummy described pretty accurately what we would find in Iraq. He predicted that most major assets, especially cash, would have disappeared, leaving little cash on hand to pay civil servants. We would have to do our best to find and sort through local ministry financial documents, which hopefully would survive in some form. We would need to calculate wages based upon historic data, assuming it was available. If not, we would need to establish the facts through interaction with Iraqi officials. We assumed we would be able to hire locals for basic temporary staffing purposes to cover such functions as transportation and interpretation.

We could only speculate on personnel issues: how many employees there were and how they were organized. We knew almost nothing about how national, regional, and local governments interacted. We would need to figure out how to integrate these units of government.

After getting an emergency budget in place for short-term operations, each of us would prepare a "steady state" budget—reflecting current levels of activity—by which funds would be allocated for the balance of 2003. A second phase would involve laying down the broad outlines of a full-year budget for calendar year 2004.

Every ministry would need money—lot's of it. Few postwar rebuilding issues concentrated our minds more than financing and managing government functions. If we didn't do the job, and we didn't secure the necessary funds, who would? If we were to leave town shortly after arriving, as was implied by the guidance, who would be responsible for these operations? What would happen if we just abandoned these responsibilities "to the Iraqis," the term often thrown out as the catch-all solution to everything? Of course, there was no such thing as a typical Iraqi. They were as diverse and divided as any society anywhere, yet without the ingrained democratic habits to deal with their differences.

The biggest disconnect between the realities faced in Baghdad and the messages filtering in from the high command was on issues of reorganizing Saddam's ministries. Our job with the ministries, we were told and reminded, was to simply "get them started." We would presumably get them in operating condition, supplied and functional. The question of future control would be left entirely open. We were often told "we don't want to dramatically change what is there." And yet the "what was there" was the entire machinery of a tyrannical state—corrupt, dysfunctional, and totally collapsed.

If the idea was to liberate Iraq and put in place the foundations for a democratic society with a competent, professionally run state, how could we just leave without putting in place new systems and far-reaching reforms?

Trade and Commerce

Iraq did not have a dynamic private enterprise that could have maintained itself while the government went through a process of reorganization. That would be a huge problem. A large portion of the population was effectively subsidized by the state, even if they were in the "private sector." A majority of Iraqis worked for the government, the military, or state-owned enterprises. And they would have to be paid.

The primary source of wealth in Iraq was oil; much of the state ran on the basis of oil revenues. Because there was very little need to encourage an independent entrepreneurial business climate, Saddam was content to build the economy largely on the basis of state-owned enterprises. Naturally, it would be more beholden politically to him. So, how does a country transition out of the old and into a new private economy when much of the old economy is state owned or controlled? In fact, the economy was part of the corrupt regime itself.

An able team from the U.S. Departments of Commerce and State, led by Ambassador Robin Raphel, organized a transition plan to take Iraq from the statist industrial system toward private ownership, markets, and trade. The two greatest obstacles to that plan were (1) the food distribution system that existed under Saddam, the Oil for Food program, and (2) state-owned enterprises. The Oil for Food program, put in place by the UN during the period of sanctions for the purpose of ensuring an adequate food supply for the Iraqi people, had become hugely corrupt and inefficient. Working with Frank Ostrander and Sue Hamrock, plans were developed to steadily introduce private enterprise and replace sanctions with trade.

Civil Justice

The need to transform Iraq's legal system and the abusive legal culture it spawned was just as important and urgent as the economic conversion. What passed for a legal system in Iraq was effectively an extension of Saddam's tyrannical system of intimidation and control. Like everything else, the law was pretty much what Saddam wanted it to be. The entire system was arbitrary and widely feared.

If we were going to remove Saddam, we would also need to remove the legal structure that treated Iraqis like captives and subjects and establish a system of civil justice grounded in individual rights and impartial law. In fact, little else was possible without it. If we truly wanted to position Iraq for a democratic future, every vestige of totalitarian law should be uprooted and replaced. If we did not do that, Saddam's police state could easily have continued without him.

Local police, courts, and corrections were all assumed to be inept and corrupt. Their powers to operate independently and impartially under Saddam were severely limited; the real decisions were made arbitrarily and by authorities often operating under direct orders from Saddam or the Ba'ath party. Therefore, at a minimum, we would have to create a new and dramatically upgraded professional police force, new courts with independent judges and prosecutors trained in Western judicial standards, and a modern corrections program that would clean up the wretched prison conditions.

Bill Lantz, a legal specialist from U.S. Department of Justice with a broad background in what is called transitional justice, led the planning for justice reforms. He presented a plan for the professional administration of courts, developing new standards for judges and prosecutors, and new procedures for judicial appointments. We would need to convert Iraq's "Supreme Law College" into a training system for modern professional legal practitioners.

Joining Lantz was Dick Meyer, who would review a variety of functions that fell under the Iraqi Ministry of Interior. One of the most abusive and feared Iraqi ministries, Interior Ministry oversaw a range of police state functions such as internal security and surveillance, prisons, immigration, and border issues. It also managed presidential properties such as farms and palaces. By administering the eighteen provinces of Iraq, the Interior Ministry effectively extended Saddam's political and security control over the entire country. Not surprisingly, the ministry was crawling with Ba'ath party agents.

The core challenge of the legal team was to satisfy the expectations of the people that they would now have a system based on rule of law, not brutal force. Even with Saddam gone, Iraqis would have little confidence that they were safe in a legal system built by him unless we acted boldly to establish a system of rule of law. They must have confidence in a new system, "a shield not a sword," grounded in the rule of law. No more arbitrary arrests or imprisonment, no more torture and slaughter. No more mass graves.

The heart of reforming the police state was transforming public administration to civilian oversight with new standards for public service. I worked with the Civil Justice team to prepare a new nonpolitical system of public administration. We also needed to form a legal framework, under international law, in order to take command of Iraqi resources and assets, work through thousands of existing contracts, and resume control of a variety of state functions.

Ruling by Decrees

Iraq under Saddam was a personality cult. His image permeated to the smallest corners of daily life in Iraq. The changes that would abruptly come for the Iraqi people—just by virtue of removing Saddam—would likely be welcome, but also be highly disruptive and disorienting. A new occupying power would, obviously, need to inform Iraqis about the status and plans of their new government. That was particularly true in the areas of security and law.

Initially at least, in the emergency environment in which we operated, we would need to set policy by decree. Bret Barkley, an army lawyer, became the "proclamation czar." Our all-around "legal beagle," Bret would coordinate the numerous public announcements, hoping to reassure the Iraqi people that life would get back to normal soon under new humane rules.

We were asked to help think through the policy of public declarations that would have to be made upon arriving in Baghdad. Public statements would be made in several categories. The highest-level legal order was the "proclamation," which could be issued only by Gen. Tommy Franks. General Franks' proclamation would explain the broad powers of the occupying forces and their civilian components, and spell out the specific authority that would be conferred downward from him to the senior civilian administrators. Perhaps the most important proclamation in this category established that the coalition had clear military authority under international occupation law. The hope was that occupation, as that term is understood militarily, would be brief.

When we got to Baghdad, we found that the coalition military presence was the only security that existed. If we didn't do it right, there would be none. We had to be the cop on the beat. Much of the debate during the early years of the administration made it clear that providing civilian security was

Coalition Provisional Authority staff gear gets loaded up at the Baghdad airport for a flight to northern Iraq to witness an Olympic Committee of Iraq election.

not the mission that the Pentagon had in mind for the U.S. military. Their conviction was that the military doesn't do that well and that's not what the military is for.

We in ORHA would issue "directives," nonbinding public messages designed to give Iraqis important information on developments and directions to go about their daily lives. The technical means of delivering messages to the Iraqis remained uncertain; communication systems had been destroyed. New media outlets would have to be created. Perhaps temporary broadcast systems would need to be erected by the military. We considered creating an "official" gazette that could be circulated among the Iraqis.

Many of these public announcements had to do with basic services, workforce issues, the maintenance of order, or dealing with legal matters. Great emphasis was placed on the need to create a sense that life was returning to normal. But what exactly that meant for a people who had never lived under what we consider "normal" was unclear.

For example, early on, we felt it would be desirable to issue a "back to work" message from General Franks urging all government workers to return to their former place of employment. But where would they report?

Once we arrived in Baghdad, General Garner would also sign and publicly release written statements delegating authority to each of the ministry heads. We, in turn, would issue decrees and statements as necessary to run day-to-day affairs operating within the authority that had been delegated to us.

Many functions of the Iraqi government had to be declared null and void by decree. For example, in my sphere, great confusion remained about whether the Olympic Committee that had functioned under Uday was still valid (he had used the National Olympic Committee of Iraq as a corporate entity for his personal business dealings). Many of his cronies were still operating in and around the sports scene. We knew we couldn't move forward with a reorganization plan unless or until we eliminated the existing organization.

National Defense

National defense was one of those major functions of great concern but was basically above our pay grade. Therefore, it rarely came up in group meetings. There were people in ORHA, however, assigned to address postwar military requirements. They would work on their own plans as complements to the more comprehensive plans that were expected to arrive from Washington.

Washington was apparently searching for a very senior defense official for the job of senior advisor for national security; a variety of names were floated, including that of a former CIA director. At some point, we learned that Walter Slocomb would be coming in, although he would not arrive in Baghdad until midsummer.

In the meantime, ORHA planning in the area of defense would be led by Paul Hughes and Carl Strock. They faced the huge task of thinking through what could be done with the existing military. How could soldiers be converted to a civilian reconstruction force, and how would a new military be transitioned to civilian control?

The defense working group would have to develop plans for dealing with the multi-layered complex of security organizations that Saddam had built. In addition to the standing army, level upon level of secret police, spying operations, and elite military commanders had reported directly to the presidential palace.

The elite security apparatus around Saddam and his family performed much like a mafia. Most were from the minority Sunni community, and many from Saddam's tribe. What would be left of them, everyone wondered. Where would they go? Would they yield to the new reality and be eager to work with us?

I caught only an occasional glimpse into the restructuring of Iraqi national defense. Each day, as we would go around the circle and place issues on the table for consideration, interesting questions about Iraq's postwar security would arise. For example, a defense analyst asked, "How fast can we turn the Iraqi army around?" His question came back to mind in the months and years that followed because it reflected thinking at the time, that there would be an Iraqi army left standing to turn around.

The working assumption, at least at this stage, was that we could not get rid of all security ministries, just clean them out. We would need to find reliable people to work with. But how? The focus of a defense reorganization would be on ensuring that the new state was thoroughly demilitarized; all military functions must be put on an independent and professional footing and led by civilians.

The initial matrix for the team was dubbed DDR, for "demobilization, disarmament and reintegration." The plan clearly was to first separate the Iraqi army from the fighting roles, at least for a while, and to reintegrate them into productive roles in Iraqi society. On another occasion, it was mentioned that "no one be put in place who had a past role in defense," implying that perhaps the changes would need to go deeper.

Military administration would be supplied early on by Army Civil Affairs. They would be moved into position as quickly as possible and then begin to assess what indigenous capacities for leadership could be tapped. The country would need security, but the intent was never to have the coalition forces be the complete answer to Iraq's postwar law and order needs.

To have a secure future in a dangerous and unstable region, Iraq would eventually need to be supplied with armaments to replace those that had been destroyed in the war. Therefore, some combination of domestic military production and foreign procurement would have to be resumed at some point. Iraq would need a program to develop arms and a skilled armed services.

Borders and International Affairs

The American occupation would also be immediately responsible for Iraq's international business and relations. Foreign affairs would be especially tricky. The entire foreign policy establishment was corrupt and was involved in sensitive regime business such as espionage.

Requiring immediate attention was the need to recall Saddam's ambassadors, deal with international donors and debt, and develop new temporary legal authority for conducting foreign policy. We would have to work through the status of Iraq's treaty agreements and bilateral relations.

Presumably, one of the most vital functions after the liberation would be securing Iraq's borders. With the collapse of Saddam's government, it was not at all unreasonable to expect that elements from neighboring countries would have designs on Iraq. Everyone knew that Iran and Syria had regional ambitions. Both were staging areas for the wandering extremist elements in the Middle East that could quickly migrate into Iraq and make trouble.

Strangely, there was almost no discussion about the need to establish a strong border after the war. Like everything else, border policy would be ORHA's responsibility and yet there was only one person available to work on it, and he arrived very late in the process. A Justice Department specialist in border and customs issues arrived only two days before our departure to Baghdad. For weeks, he would be the only one focusing on the complex issues of border security and customs. After only a short time in Baghdad, he went home. It would take years to effectively address the border problems; the persistent problem of porous borders would become a major factor in the migration of foreign fighters into Iraq.

Culture and Religion

Of great political sensitivity was the function of culture and religion. Most Arab and Muslim countries have ministries of culture. We realized that, in taking over an overwhelmingly Muslim country, this would be a particularly delicate function for us.

Paradoxically, many Muslims view America as both a Christian country and one that has drifted from its religious heritage and roots. Many Muslims see America as a Christian enemy and at the same time a land of lapsed religious belief and too secular. Those combinations severely complicated our attempts to gain their respect. Much of the talk in Kuwait City, not surprisingly, focused on our need to present our government as secular. Hopefully, we could put in place a Western-style secular, or at least nonsectarian, government.

It was just assumed at that time that America would not accommodate an Islamic state. Under Saddam, the government had become quite secular. Iraq was unique as a Muslim nation; religion was confined largely to the private sphere. Might we ultimately do away with the Ministry of Religion altogether? Perhaps it would at least be possible to use the ministry to encourage interfaith dialogue and cooperation.

There was wide recognition that whatever we did, we must show respect for the Iraqi people. Two broad principles were established to project that respect: (1) we would honor Iraqi values and religion, and (2) we would not meddle in private and religious matters. To communicate that respect, we discussed a variety of "high-impact" projects that were sure to be noncontroversial and would likely generate goodwill. For example, we discussed reopening and refurbishing the Iraqi Museum, which was filled with valued antiquities that made Iraqis proud of the ancient civilization of their homeland. We also discussed restoring and transferring the palaces and gardens, used by Saddam for his own self-indulgence and glorification, to the Iraqi people.

The cultural sensitivities were a particular focus for the team members who had extensive experience in the region. Ambassador Barbara Bodine was brought in as the Baghdad area regional director, but also to advise on issues of local customs and culture. Bodine had much to say about Arab traditions. Discussions in her presence often turned to winning Iraqi trust

Meeting with leaders of the Interim Committee to Administer Sports. This committee was set up to oversee rebuilding institutions that had been run by Uday and his cronies. Every attempt was made to include all segments of Iraq society.

and the need to reach out to interest groups and civil society organizations if they existed. We should miss no opportunity to extend basic courtesies to them as Arabs and Muslims. To be effective, she advised, we would need to be accessible, visible, respectful, responsive, and patient. Ambassador Bodine shared with anyone who would listen her strong view that only patient and respectful interaction with the Iraqis would earn their trust. She called it the "tea strategy," in which we should talk about their lives— about family, kids, uncles, and aunts.

I thought her guidance on how to respect the Iraqi people was urgently needed. That included reaching out and promoting people-to-people ties and developing community programs. We needed to immediately focus on education, youth, and community. Her ideas ranged from art therapy, to "seeds of peace" initiatives, to providing small grants for summer schools.

This was an entirely sensible approach. I sympathized with it because of my deep concern for winning the hearts and minds of youth. At the same time, I had to wonder how practical it was in the face of urgent conditions for a nation lying in ruins. As it turned out, I never heard much again about those ideas after arriving in Baghdad.

Health and Social Services

From what was being reported to us in Kuwait City during the war, it appeared that there was no immediate threat of a public health crisis.

For all Saddam's faults, like many dictators, he did make investments in the country's infrastructure, including hospitals and clinics. Though the hospitals were in a shambles by the time we got there, there had been no epidemic in a long time.

Given the relative stability of public health conditions, every effort could be made through USAID and NGOs to turn available resources and energies to building a modern health care system with upgraded hospitals. The Ministry of Health was one of the most corrupt of all. Its extensive procurement system for medical supplies was rife with self-dealing and bribes. Existing officials would need to be removed down to the lower levels, and the ministry would need a new procurement system, one that no longer merely filled the pockets of bureaucrats.

Many social service functions simply didn't fall neatly into boxes. We called these "cross-cutting" functions because they involved responsibilities from various ministries. Coordinating these clusters of responsibilities (for example, across all of the finance and economic ministries and the wide array of social programs, including Youth and Sport, Education, and Labor) would be "pillar leads." Iraq had a very porous social safety net under Saddam, but there were programs for pensioners and a department of labor. That would be managed by USAID veteran Karen Walsh. From that post, she would attempt to strengthen Iraq's social security system and advance the needs and interests of women.

The assumption was that at least some of the Iraqi population might be displaced by the war and need temporary housing, and some of the housing complexes in the urban areas close to bombing targets would be severely damaged.

Higher Education

The chief function of the Ministry of Higher Education (MoHE) was to administer Iraq's university system. The MoHE and the university system it served employed 50,000 people. It carried out some sensitive functions under Saddam, including training engineers and scientists who would preside over Iraq's weapons programs, including WMDs.

The MoHE had little independence, but it did manage to develop some strong programs from which its administrators took justified pride. Drew Erdman, a sharp, young Harvard PhD, presided over higher education. Drew's job was to restore the legitimacy of the university system, separating it entirely from its prior political role and service to the state. University administration would have to be set on an independent foundation. Professors would be encouraged to incorporate the principles of Western liberal education in revising curricula and teaching methods.

Perhaps the greatest priority was more practical—dealing with the trauma of the war. Getting the universities open in time for the fall semester would be a big accomplishment. Like so many other key Iraqi institutions, universities were heavily hit by looting.

Electricity

Few functions would be more important to postwar rebuilding than quickly restoring Iraq's electrical power generating system. By midsummer, temperatures would rise to 125 degrees by midafternoon. The lack of power for air conditioners and refrigerators would be a crisis. The electricity team, led by Andy Backus, declared its purpose as offering the people "safe and reliable" services as quickly as possible. That service would establish a new rate structure so that the financial viability of the system could be improved.

Most other vital services in Iraq were dependent upon electrical power. The failure to fully restore electricity was one of the greatest sources of grief among the Iraqis in the year following the liberation. It symbolized the downside of liberation; the Iraqis may have gained their freedom, but in many other respects life would be more difficult for a while.

For the most part, the electrical grid was spared from bombing. But a combination of factors, including looting, extensive sabotage, and worn-out equipment, meant that electricity service did not reach the expected and needed levels.

Rajiv Chandrasekaran described the value of electricity to our venture (and the significance of its absence) in his *Washington Post* column: "In Baghdad, a vast city of high-rise buildings, bustling markets and scorching summer temperatures, most residents received more than 20 hours of electricity a day before the war—enough to run elevators, air conditioners and other staples of modern life. Today, the capital got about eight hours of power. On Tuesday, it was even less. . . The persistent blackouts—U.S. and Iraqi specialists blame sabotage, looting, war damage and the failure of old equipment—have transformed a city that once was regarded as the most advanced in the Arab world to a place of pre-industrial privation . . ." [1]

Information

One function of a free and open society that we Americans take for granted is an independent media. It is almost impossible for us to imagine what might be required for a country to move immediately from a state-controlled media, dominated by a totalitarian ruler, to one in which news and information would flow from free sources.

Bob Reilly, who was the senior advisor for communications, described the official news organizations run by the Ba'ath party as "all Saddam all the time." We never found any independent media, not even an underground press. Electronic communications technology, including such simple devices as cell phones and Internet access, was strictly controlled under Saddam. Saddam and Uday controlled the media by infiltrating the entire media apparatus with Ba'ath party ideologues and loyalists. Of course, they reported anyone perceived to be a danger.

Liberated Iraq would need new message delivery systems and new radio and television transmission capacity. A new generation of journalists would have to be recruited and trained in professional and independent journalism. In all likelihood, new media outlets would have to be established and managed with American assistance.

A variety of other state functions also depended on a modernized communications system. It would be impossible to create an open society within Iraq or to open the country to global communications, travel, and trade without upgraded telephone service and efficient modern air traffic control services, seaports, and telecommunications operations.

Irrigation

Because of the sheer number of ministries, some senior advisors had to do double duty. Steve Browning, who already covered health, also agreed to cover irrigation (Bob Mcloud handled water and sanitation issues). Iraq's largest economic promise was probably in the area of agriculture. Thanks to its good fortune in having the Tigris and Euphrates rivers flowing through the land, the potential existed for the rapid development of agriculture through an irrigation system that had been built under Saddam. But it had fallen into disrepair. The rivers were heavily polluted, and waterfront facilities were poorly maintained.

The extensive dams and reservoirs were used by Saddam to oppress his own people, the most famous case being his drainage of the swamps in the south in order to displace the Shia population that had fled there for livelihood and protection.

Oil

Implicit in the planning for regime change in Iraq was the idea that, since Iraq had the second-largest proven oil reserves in the world, we should be able to use these abundant natural resources to fund the country's path to freedom. In fact, very optimistic predictions were projected on how the postwar reconstruction would be funded by the rapid return of oil revenues. Paul Wolfowitz confidentially expected that "Iraq will finance its own reconstruction."

That would require making sure the existing Iraqi oil production system remained operational. If the experience of 1991 was any guide, we could confidently predict that Saddam would set much of the country's oil fields on fire as his regime was collapsing. Gary Voegler organized an expert team of planners for the oil sector. They would be responsible for putting out oil fires and getting refinery capacity restored. Once stabilization was achieved, priority number one was to aggressively boost production and begin to market Iraqi oil.

The expectation of Iraqi oil paying for the reconstruction just never worked out. Postwar reconstruction costs ballooned beyond the capacity of Iraq's oil production. Additionally, the production itself was constrained by antiquated equipment and sabotage.

Human Rights

Clearly, a major priority would be to help post-Saddam Iraq come to terms with the systematic abuse of human rights they suffered under his reign. The people would be looking for evidence that justice would be done for the violence that was carried out against them.

Leading the effort for ORHA was Sandy Hodgkinson, a young lawyer from the State Department. Sandy's concern was that every effort be made to prevent reprisals and a new cycle of abuse. Working with the Justice team, Sandy planned for transitional justice and the documentation of human rights abuses. Any law or practice that perpetuated the police-state powers of Saddam's regime would need to be immediately suspended, including the old penal codes, political courts, political prisons, and arbitrary prosecution system.

It was vitally important to help the Iraqis come to terms with the psychological and social realities of the oppression they suffered. At one point, it was suggested that a truth and reconciliation commission be established. Countries with deep and painful histories must find a way to put the past behind them. Obviously, glossing over abuses hoping to forget them does not work.

Transitional justice would certainly entail erecting systems for holding key people accountable, and perhaps setting the stage for eventual war-crime trials. Stretching across every ministry and critical government function would be a systematic attempt to recover and preserve documents confirming war crimes and other criminal offenses.

Decentralization

One of the cross-cutting goals that emerged and was widely discussed in Kuwait City was the need to decentralize control of the country. ORHA had a superbly qualified expert on decentralization in Chris Milligan, my USAID colleague who was instrumental in me getting on the team. He devised a comprehensive strategy for devolving authority away from Baghdad out to the provinces.

Iraq's eighteen provinces were little more than administrative outposts ruled dictatorially by Saddam and the Ba'ath party. If a new system of participatory democracy was to take root, we could encourage it by building capacity at the local level through citizen councils and strong local government.

Decisions under Saddam were all made in Baghdad, with even much of the work of local employees controlled by central bureaucracies. The dominant national product, oil, also strongly reinforced the top-down nature of the government. Creating new habits of independent thinking and acting would require a major overhaul. The centralized power structure, which worked in parallel with the Ba'ath structure, needed to be dismantled.

Milligan's plan called for bottom-up governance. "Democracy," he said, presciently, "is not an election; it's what happens between elections. . . Democracy will have to be built on a small scale, from village to village, from the bottom up." Iraqis, who had never experienced democracy, would need to learn it on a small scale if they were to practice it successfully as a nation.

How could a new democratic localism flourish without placing new strains on a nation comprising three large ethnic or sectarian divisions? The alternative was not to continue the domination of Iraq out of Baghdad. But, on the other hand, too great an emphasis on building regional or local political capacity could lead to balkanization because of the deep divisions.

Certainly balance would need to be preserved between strong national government and all subnational governments.

Very little was known about Iraq's provinces, municipalities, and villages. The Kurds had already gained a certain autonomy and freedom of operation. They would likely press for more, putting strains on the new national government. Perhaps whatever lessons we learned from the Kurdish experience in building strong regional government would have wider applications.

One approach was for national ministries to set standards, while leaving much operating responsibility decentralized in the hands of provinces and municipalities. This approach would also entail fiscal decentralization.

This was Milligan's work, and it made a lot of sense. He cited the experience of Indonesia in which provinces were strengthened in ways that preserved the nation. One thought was to have some of the national ministry workers transferred back to localities.

Whatever we did, we would have to be serious, bring sufficient resources to bear, and prove that there were benefits to a particular approach. That would mean promoting the widest participation in local decision making and reconstruction. If the Iraqis themselves were not able to help build local capacity, it would be far harder to find national solutions.

The military did not have sufficient troops to fully secure the liberated towns and villages of Iraq as they moved north. And ORHA had its own severe staffing limits. So, with few exceptions, ORHA operated in Baghdad at the presidential palace. Coordination with the northern region (Bruce Moore) and the southern region (Buck Walters) proved difficult during the early months. The two regional directors had very few staff, and communications were difficult. The challenge was tantamount to governing California with fifty people in Sacramento, three in Los Angeles, and three in San Francisco.

Logistics

We would not be able to do our jobs without adequate resources and logistical support. Central Command (CENTCOM) did not appear to be stepping forward to develop the level of support that ORHA needed, so we mobilized on our own as best we could. Between Garner's deputies—Jerry Bates and Ron Adams—and a Civil Affairs team assembled under army colonel Tom Baltazar, an entire system of logistics, communications, and support came together.

With a limited amount of emergency money, Jerry Bates engaged in some quick contracting to get vital services and assistance (like securing interpreters). As it became clearer that the Baghdad reconstruction operation would require major mobilization, a massive army of contractors would steadily arrive for work in Baghdad and back home at the Pentagon.

Equipment, supplies, transportation, and mechanical issues were covered by "gasoline Bob," a feisty army colonel who had a reputation for walking right over nay-sayers or grumblers. Anything in the area of basic supply needs—sanitation, food, water, and just getting around—fell to Bob.

For our official transportation needs, the army operations unit working with us secured 140 brand-new Chevy Suburbans. All Arab streets and roads were clogged with old Toyotas, dented like tin cans. Not surprisingly, when we realized that the Suburbans stood out like sitting ducks in Baghdad, many of us turned to beat-up old cars with tinted windows to evade detection in the hostile neighborhoods of Iraq.

The Suburbans might have been perfect for rural Kenya or Honduras, but not the violent urban terrain of Iraq's budding insurgency. They were "soft-skinned," a term that entered the public debate, describing the vulnerabilities of the vehicles to RPG attack. Even the heavier army Humvees were eventually refitted for improved protection against the daily onslaught of rockets and improvised explosive devices (IEDs).

OUR PURPOSE WAS TO RUN A GOVERNMENT and rebuild a nation, but this would not be like moving into a furnished office suite in downtown DC. This mission required attending to the most mundane issues in order to get by day by day. While still in Kuwait City, we were told to expect nothing in Baghdad to work electronically and, therefore, our connectivity would be very limited for a while. We would need computers and phones, and electricity to operate them. Assuming we would have access to the Iraq electricity supply, we would need adapters in order for our electrical cords to work.

Mugged by Reality

Everyone shared in the responsibilities of getting the most basic tasks accomplished. Moving into Iraq was like being parachuted into a remote and exotic place, where we would restore and operate the government in a country the size and population of California. We all wanted desperately to do it right. Every area outlined in this chapter represented an opportunity of historic possibility as well as historic adversity. The planning for each ministry should have matched the historic dimensions of the challenges we faced. It didn't.

In a June 21, 2004, article in the *Washington Post*, Rajiv Chandrasekaran interviewed John Agresto. John had been brought in to oversee Iraq's university system, taking over in midsummer for Drew Erdman. Like other challenges, this was an enormously important area; we had to get it right. Chandrasekaran captures something that still haunts most of us ORHA senior advisors:

" 'Like everyone else in America, I saw the images of people cheering as Saddam Hussein's statue was pulled down. I saw people hitting pictures of him with their shoes,' said Agresto, the former president of St. John's College in New Mexico. 'Once you see that, you can't help but say, 'Okay. This is going to work.'

"But, the Iraq he encountered was different from what he had expected. Visits to universities he was trying to rebuild and the faculty he wanted to invigorate were more and more dangerous, and infrequent. His Iraqi staff was threatened by insurgents. His evenings were disrupted by mortar attacks . . .

"His plans to repair hundreds of campus buildings were scuttled by the Bush administration's decision to shift reconstruction efforts and by the failure to raise money from other sources. His hope that Iraqis would put aside differences and personal interests for the common cause was, as he put it, 'way too idealistic.'

" 'I'm a neoconservative who's been mugged by reality,' Agresto said as he puffed his pipe . . . 'there were mistakes, things that didn't work out the way we wanted,' he added. 'We have to be honest with ourselves.' " [2]

Chapter 7

Surreal Life in the Presidential Palace

A False Sense of Security

For the first week after arriving at the presidential palace, it was so empty you could walk an entire corridor without passing anyone. You could also hear the sounds of distant footsteps and voices echoing through the marble halls. By late May, the place was congested with people. The CPA was rapidly changing, and the Republican Palace was being transformed. Cubicles were installed in every room to maximize space; even the hallways disappeared as temporary offices were constructed out of plywood.

To accommodate the influx, large ballrooms were converted to sleeping quarters and filled wall-to-wall with cots. We even used the rooms that had previously been avoided because of the spine-chilling activity that occurred in them under Saddam. What happened in those rooms was so hideous that many considered them haunted. The so-called encounter room, used by

A full replica of the presidential palace that was on display in the rotunda.

Crater from a bomb attack close to the Republican Presidential Palace. What became known as the Green Zone where we set up operations had been the scene of heavy fighting during the final stages of the war, and there was much damage to buildings.

Saddam to interrogate and sentence people to their fates, had been converted to a multi-faith chapel. In this room, with its elevated platform and gold-plated chair once occupied by Saddam, Iraqis reported hearing him proclaim, "There is one God and I am he."

The stories of what happened in that room were chilling. The lucky ones were brought to the palace, tortured mildly, and then driven back to their homes in government cars. They were dropped off and given wealth for all to see that they were now owned by Saddam. In other cases, he cut off their ears or tortured them with hot swords. Those accused of serious crimes against Saddam were imprisoned or simply taken out and shot.

Now the room was used for more transcendent purposes as soldiers and civilians alike gathered there for quiet prayer and meditation.

Throughout the long, hot days of summer, we enjoyed great dinnertime conversation and stories, often late into the night. Those times and stories revealed the best and the worst, the highest and the lowest, that human beings experience.

By late May I was truly grateful to have come in as a senior advisor. We had been delegated real authority under ORHA (and then CPA) to reorganize and rebuild the government ministries to which we were assigned. Our jobs also required lots of contact with the Iraqi people.

The Bureaucratic Impulse

We were also beginning to see the arrival of a large administrative staff. And they promptly turned to doing what administrative staffs always do: build a bureaucracy. In my Washington years, I've noticed a certain pattern: government administration tends to centralize, to gather, to stockpile, and build protective barriers against the people it serves. Its impulse is never to release or decentralize. The bureaucracy that began building in Baghdad that summer would, in time, become increasingly confined to the Green Zone and more and more isolated from the Iraqi people.

Many who arrived during this time period ended up spending most of their days in the living and working quarters inside the Republican Palace. It seemed that increasingly and inevitably, the centrifuge of bureaucracy pulled them away from actual program work and contact with the Iraqi people. In the classic organizational drift from "mission to maintenance," the bureaucracy demanded more and more time for itself. Entire systems were moved in to equip and support a sitting bureaucratic army.

The early days of ORHA were austere and severely under-resourced. With limited staffing and little support, each person was pretty much on his or her own. If you wanted paper, pens, or paper clips, you had to go searching for them on your own. We had one copier for the entire civil administration wing, then two after a couple of weeks, and then another one when the second one broke down and parts were not available. After waiting for days for replacement parts, we were told by a technician that "KBR [Kelly, Brown and Root] ordered them." Then he added, "No one ever planned for this size of operation." Of course, my reflex thought was, "No one planned . . . *period.*"

For those of us who had to build ministries from scratch, we had no choice but to be out and about engaging Iraqis. We often traveled without convoy protection because none was available. For our time outside of the presidential palace, we all got to see some significant change. As a result, we all carry unforgettable memories and a sense of at least some accomplishment.

In May and June real progress was made. Of course, when breakthroughs happened—and they did happen—my colleagues were eager to tell the story. In particular, a number of the ministries (mostly, those that were not military targets and had not been bombed) were getting on their feet. In fact, there was talk of a rapid transfer of perhaps a half-dozen ministries to complete Iraqi control.

Most, however, were struggling badly. It was easy to form overarching opinions about the enormity and complexity of the mission as it unfolded, and the likelihood of success. Quite apart from our own assignments to particular ministries, our collective task as a group offered a bird's-eye view of how reconstruction was going generally. Many of my notes home to family and friends captured that.

Freedom and Certainty

On June 21, I wrote to my family:

> The biggest challenge in a country like this is managing the tremendous economic trough and social turmoil that follows the conflict. One great need that all human beings have is freedom; but another is some measure of certainty. Unfortunately, a sudden burst of freedom in a place like Iraq is accompanied by a major rupture of what was known and considered commonplace by the people. Even though most Iraqis celebrate Saddam's departure, it is hard to capture how suddenly the pattern of their daily lives was transformed—in a hundred consequential and unsettling ways.

> In the past, before Saddam was removed, they woke up every day knowing pretty much what to expect. Now they don't know. The uncertainty has a painful impact on the psyches of many. And in the case of at least some, their lives are actually worse because of the disruption of basic supplies and services, and will be for a while to come. It is difficult for people to celebrate their new freedoms, if freedom means having a harder time, at least under our current circumstances, feeding your family and protecting from common thieves who kidnap, steal, murder or rape.

> The country was a basket case before the war, and obviously it is bound to get worse for a while after the war, but with Saddam Hussein gone who else is to be blamed but us from this point on? The unemployment rate was 50% before the war, yet the anger of the unemployed is now directed toward us. The economy prior to the war spent at least one third of its domestic production on the military. Today, the Iraqi military is gone, but what do we do to employ the millions who worked for the massive military, intelligence, spying and prison operations? What do you do with these folks? The issues are always harder than they appear on the surface.

Then, there is the issue of basic services, like water, electricity and sanitation. Because Saddam Hussein spent most of his shrinking national treasure on the military and carrying out wars against his neighbors (reconstruction from the 8-year war with Iran alone cost Iraq $250 billion), he was always postponing repairs of basic infra-structure. Most water, electricity and sanitation systems are not working better, not because of anything we have done, but because the parts and equipment needed to run these systems are completely out of repair and outdated. Iraq's industries require 4 kilowatts of electricity to operate, yet the existing system is incapable of producing it, which means we decide who gets it and who doesn't.

Most of the stories among the senior advisors in mid-June revealed the great difficulty in jump-starting ministries. We didn't have cash. Many of us still lacked even temporary offices, leaving many Iraqis working at home. With security worsening and too few conveys to cover the entire group, we were forced to do more and more of our business with the Iraqis in the palace rather than downtown Baghdad. Inevitably, that created a reality gap between the Iraqis and the Americans.

Our growing difficulty in being transported safely around Baghdad pointed to a fact that was privately discussed but publicly withheld—the CPA had still not really entered Phase IV of the operations. That "postwar" phase had not yet commenced because the violence had not yet been suppressed. So, we were technically still in Phase III.

Naturally, that restricted our visibility and presence in the neighbor-hoods of Baghdad. As a result, a growing number of municipal buildings and even schools in the provinces were being taken over by armed Shia declaring Jihad. Other public facilities such as prisons and courts were being overtaken by squatters. The little site security we did have early on was now declining because coalition troops were being diverted back from serving police functions. They were needed in the regular army functions of "killing bad people," as one of them put it.

In other words, the war wasn't really over.

Erosion of Security

It didn't appear to most of us that much of the daily functioning of Baghdad was actually under our control. In the massive vacuum that was created by our inability to establish order and stability following the war, other dynamics just took over. It didn't appear that the Iraqis took us very seriously. We couldn't even control the squatters moving into the many high-rise apartment and office buildings right there in the Green Zone, which had been abandoned by the senior Ba'athists. More and more we could see Iraqis standing on balconies and drying laundry within view of the palace.

Who precisely were these people and what would we do with them? Kim Olsen, Jay Garner's chief of staff, told a funny yet disconcerting story about visiting one of the Green Zone buildings the first week after arriving. It was General Garner's first day at the palace and his first trip out. He wanted to make contact with the people, so he and his companions stopped to talk to some Iraqis. After a brief conversation, Garner asked if he and his party could meet their families. They were invited into the apartment complex. After sitting down, General Garner asked one of the gentlemen what he did. The man answered, "I am a Republican Guard colonel." Then they discovered that the entire apartment was filled with people who had served in Saddam's personal Republican Guard.

Kim's immediate thought was, "Oh my God, we're all going to die."

Garner asked the colonel what he planned to do next, to which the colonel replied, "It depends on what you do next." From April 20 until June 1, Garner engaged in seventy-eight such meetings with Iraqis, gauging their attitudes and letting them vent, as he explained to me.

On more than one occasion during the first three months in Baghdad, we speculated about the frightening mismatch that would confront us if a popular uprising were to develop. The coalition forces would be far too thin to repel it. In such an event, we would have had to be airlifted out of the palace. That never happened for the simple reason that Iraqi opinion was too divided and the politics were too splintered. At that point, most Iraqis feared the possible return of Saddam, who was still at large, more than they feared any other thing.

BY MIDSUMMER, THE DAILY RATES of oil production and electrical generation were getting worse, not better. And nothing we tried seemed to improve that decline in services. In early July, stories multiplied about organized crime activity and sabotage, especially in the oil sector.

According to one CPA staff member who was tracking this activity, the bandits who were attacking the ministries and vital infrastructure "made Jesse James look like an amateur." Gary Voegler, from the oil ministry, said that it took a particularly sophisticated type of sabotage to bring oil refineries

A tall mural featuring scud missiles decorates Saddam's "encounter room," where many forced confessions of his enemies took place over the years. Saddam used this room to determine who would be put to death, who would be tortured, who would be imprisoned, and who would be set free. Most of the architecture and art conveyed images of Saddam as a great Arab warrior.

to a halt, but somehow the Iraqi saboteurs succeeded. Few people working on reconstruction carried more pressure than Gary. Getting oil production on track was central to every other objective. At one point, I asked Gary privately how he was doing. "Some days," he said, "are bad; some days are awful."

So, obviously, the bandits were very sophisticated and quite determined to stop progress. They frequently succeeded. They shot up railroad cars, dismantled and looted buses, and removed railroad tracks in order to derail trains. With simple AK-47s, they shot up and disabled electric lines, transmitters, and pumping station generators. Suspicions grew that criminals and insurgent sympathizers were infiltrating into ministries. In too many cases there was simply no way of knowing the workers' loyalties.

The net result was that the infrastructure—for which we were now responsible—was working sluggishly at best. We had almost no resources available to replace obsolescent parts and equipment. On any given day, a large portion of the electricity and oil ministry staffs worked to repair the damage from sabotage. One morning, as we were listening to an electricity ministry representative's description of just how bad the electricity service was across Baghdad, our lights promptly went out.

The general threat levels continued to worsen. On July 10, the popular and enjoyable weekly trip to the ancient city of Babylon had to be permanently canceled. It was simply too difficult to provide protection for the thin-skinned vans carrying staff to and from the site.

That was a small inconvenience compared to the increased threats to our Iraqi friends and staff. One of my Iraqi ministry deputies, Abdul Razak, found a picture of Saddam Hussein on his doorstep. It was delivered by Ba'athists as a threat. Furthermore, as he and Ahmed al-Samarrai, my advisor for Olympic Committee affairs, traveled extensively to reorganize sports clubs, they increasingly came face-to-face with armed hostility.

My Iraqi team pled for more security protection. When we couldn't offer it, they requested permission to carry guns and to assemble their own team of bodyguards. Even though we were supposed to enforce CPA gun rules, I had a hard time discouraging them from acquiring their own protection. Whenever I traveled with Iraqis in their vehicles, I was always astonished at the pistols and machine guns lying on the floor or under the seats. Because the government couldn't provide security, the Iraqis quite naturally turned to protecting themselves.

The heightened security created another problem. It was harder and harder for our soldiers to tell friend from foe. If only one in a thousand was a foe but looked like everyone else, they all belonged to the same suspect category. Soldiers securing the palace had no choice but to be on high alert for the possibility of intruders slipping through the checkpoint.

I understood their dilemma, but it posed a variety of problems. Fewer allowances could be made, even for people with passes. Growing security problems have a way of eroding trust and mutual respect. More and more of my Iraqi friends and staff—even senior officials—reported feeling humiliated by their treatment from American soldiers on their way into the palace. By late June, every person was strip-searched and every vehicle was examined. As a result, we had a harder time reaching the Iraqis outside of the palace, and they had a harder time getting through to see us in the palace. Unavoidably, this created high walls between us and the citizenry.

On May 22, Ammar, my trusted Iraqi advisor and friend, was dragged from his car while waiting in the concrete "cattle chute" at the entrance to the Green Zone. He was beaten severely by an army captain. When he got to

One of Saddam's presidential thrones, which we placed in storage along with possessions from the palaces of Uday.

me, his face was bloodied and swollen. Ammar, understandably distraught, insisted that he had compliantly showed his CPA identification tag as well as his German passport when ID was requested. He had also spoken in clear English, hoping to show that he was an official. Ammar believed he was being attacked because of his ethnicity; he said the captain accused him of "being uppity."

I was furious and confronted the captain. After an angry exchange, I demanded that he return with me and offer a direct apology to Ammar. But as he and I turned to leave his guard post, I caught a glimpse of the crowd of Iraqis pressing in on the American soldiers; in that moment, I felt a surge of sympathy for him. As we walked together silently, I felt a mix of anger and pity, blame and respect. His was an exceedingly difficult and dangerous job, and there was no easy formula for making it through a day without such incidents. In his mind, he was surely doing what he thought was necessary to protect the rest of us from a suicide bomber. I told him that and, after the apology was given to Ammar, considered the case closed.

It almost didn't matter who was right or wrong. What was clear was that the insurgency was changing our relationship to the Iraqi people. More and more stories like this circulated among the Iraqis, giving them reason to doubt our motives and character.

The troops had my sympathy, and I was very reluctant to make their job harder. They too were doing the best they could with the limited resources they were given. The soldiers we mingled with at the palace had their own stories of being endangered because of military overextension. One young reservist described being assigned, along with only one other soldier, to an isolated spot—at night—in order to provide security for a hospital's fuel supply. In the pitch black of the night, the two soldiers could see the outline of a nearby house. They could also see shadowy images of Iraqis hanging out of slightly illuminated windows, pointing AK-47s their way. Then two armed Iraqis in black clothing approached them. The Americans were outgunned and really had no choice but to abandon their post and run fast into the night. The reservist added that he and many of his associates were rushed to Baghdad with little training for the kinds of security challenges they were now facing.

By the summer, many of us—civilian and soldier alike—had to regularly deal with unruly crowds that organized to make demands on the Americans. In some cases, they were struggling for control over a ministry. These encounters produced remarkable stories of courage and ingenuity. One advisor witnessed an especially skillful soldier step into the middle of an angry Shiite gathering. The soldier demonstrated a new and very effective experiment in crowd control by telling the armed Shia that he was instructing them to do two things. First, he said, they must point their guns in the opposite direction of the crowd. Second, they must all join in smiling, which they promptly did. Hostility was replaced with smiles and even laughter at least for a brief moment.

By late June, we had to contend with a growing number of death threats against ministry officials. More and more Iraqis who were working with us were being killed. Obviously, that sent a chill through the ranks of our support staff. In a single week, an interpreter and the new Iraqi head of taxation were gunned down. A growing number of Iraqi contract workers were shot for no reason other than that they were helping to supply services and supplies for reconstruction.

The erosion of security soon even affected our food supply. Our meals were mostly American-style buffet food, brought in from Kuwait and elsewhere by KBR. Lunch usually consisted of sandwiches, salads, fruit, and dessert. Dinner was the basic meat and potatoes. We had steak on special days. We all stood in long lines at the chow hall, civilians intermingling with soldiers in their desert camo uniforms and machine guns strapped over their shoulders. Chow line familiarity drew us together as many talked about family and kids at home and what they were missing.

In addition to the Americans, growing numbers of staff members came from dozens of other countries: African Berkas, Mozambican minesweepers (same continent, but very different people), and a variety of other ethnicities. The place was starting to feel like the UN.

In the second week in July, we began noticing that some food items, such as vegetables, were in short supply in the mess hall. The reason? KBR contract drivers were being killed; three had been gunned down by snipers that particular week.

Although we felt relatively safe behind the thick sandstone walls of the palace, the rows of aluminum-skinned trailers on the palace grounds that served as our sleeping quarters were another matter. Gunfire was increasingly directed our way from just beyond the compound. One ORHA staffer two doors down from me discovered a discharged bullet lying on the floor; it had penetrated her ceiling while she was away. Later, another CPA staffer found a bullet that had penetrated his pillow while he was at work.

After a month or so of very intense work, we all increasingly took the time and found the means to turn off the stress and worries. When the Al Rasheed Hotel reopened on the oppose side of the Green Zone, we often took trips over there. It was a great place to enjoy some time fraternizing with CPA colleagues. On the first floor was a dimly lit bar with leather sofa chairs. On the top floor was a disco with a wide, brightly colored hardwood dance floor. The dance floor was surrounded by restaurant-style booths. It was, according to numerous eyewitness accounts, a favorite spot for Uday Hussein. In fact, he reportedly shot up the place in one of his many rages.

Of course, there was a certain poetic strangeness watching CPA colleagues dance to loud, thumping music under the strobe lights in Uday's old playground. It was there that we often celebrated and marked the departure of ORHA group members. We had all come to Baghdad together and had all developed what my roommate Terry Sullivan, a retired and decorated navy SEAL, called "combat closeness." So, it was sad and sentimental to see them leave. One by one they were mostly gone by midsummer. They were slowly replaced by new senior advisors coming in from Washington.

Various views of the
presidential palace,
including its four
two-story busts of
Saddam along the top.

The Great Disconnect

While things were grinding along steadily in Baghdad, by mid-June we were clearly having major complications with the provinces. It was the familiar litany of too few civilians, too little security, unreliable Iraqis, and very poor communications.

With limited electricity and communications technology, it was very difficult to get the message out to coalition staff—let alone the Iraqis—in the eighteen provinces of Iraq. Robin Raphel, who had been working on trade issues, attended a meeting of business figures in the south a month after her ministry had announced a "tariff holiday" (an emergency initiative designed to eliminate barriers to trade and to jump-start commerce). She discovered that, because of poor communications, no one knew about the meeting, not even the coalition staff working there in the region.

The army was basically in charge, but it wasn't always careful enough about who it put in positions of responsibility. Because the military and civilian staff in the provinces of Iraq had no more capacity than we had to properly check the backgrounds of the local Iraqis, the wrong people were filling positions. In many cases, locals managed to take over by electing themselves or getting appointed to positions. They then promptly turned their positions to personal advantage. We heard many stories of them profiting from government funds, hiring relatives, and even selling land that was not theirs.

While the controversial policy of dismissing senior Ba'ath officials from the government would generate all of the public debate, this was an equally consequential problem. Removing senior Ba'athists was only one part of the problem. In too many cases, Iraqis with no affiliation with the previous regime who stepped forward to serve were simply no different.

Attempts were made to organize more cohesive governance teams to sort through these problems. But if we were making a lot of decisions in Baghdad on the fly, the regional staff members were working entirely on the basis of improvisation. There was a great "disconnect" between their decision making out in the provinces and the established CPA policy in Baghdad. Email, if it was operational at all, often took days to turn around. Very often, the only solution was for regional staff to travel to Baghdad just to find out what was going on. The result was that the provinces were a mess.

Not all news was bad. A lot of positive buzz in Baghdad left us hopeful that somehow the chaos in government was not preventing Iraqis from enjoying their new freedoms and building new lives. In fact, we were constantly irritated that the media seemed steadfastly resistant to telling the positive stories.

Plenty of evidence suggested that, in spite of the difficulties, very real progress for many Iraqis was beginning to happen. The number of cars had quadrupled (jamming intersections with long lines of traffic and clogging gas stations). Shops were doing a brisk business. Satellite dishes were going up on more roofs. More and more media and entertainment programs were being broadcast into Iraqi homes, offering connections to the wider world that hadn't existed under Saddam. Real estate values had increased tenfold. I was never interested in sugarcoating reality, but it seemed there were twenty-five negative stories for every positive story in the media.

By July, attacks were routine and security was becoming suffocating. Over dinner at the Al Rasheed, a colleague told of going to a restaurant with Ambassador Bremer. They stopped on the way to do an interview for CNN (ironically about improved security in Iraq). Just before going live, an RPG went off just outside the studio, causing everyone to hit the floor. Bremer just sat unaffected waiting to go live. He concluded the interview and they proceeded to the restaurant, where he enjoyed his evening meal surrounded by his bodyguards.

Although the danger never seemed to faze Bremer, I could see that it was taking its toll on our team. By midsummer, our army friends were wearing down under the heavy pressure. Many of our Army Civil Affairs people were being shot. The Civil Affairs unit covering the Ministry of Higher Education had just suffered its third casualty.

I had grown to deeply appreciate my Army Civil Affairs team. Although they belonged to their own army organizations, they were assigned to my team and felt like family. On July 2, as I sat at my desk at the Republican Palace, I watched Janice Albuquerque take a call from her headquarters. Someone from her unit had just been killed and another seriously injured. She suppressed her emotions while completing the conversation, replying calmly, "yes sir, I understand sir, I will be right there sir." After hanging up the phone, she paused a moment, breathed deeply, and her eyes welled with tears. Then, with tears streaming down her face, she said, "When you hear about death affecting someone you don't know, you just move on. When it hits home, it's another matter."

According to Janice, many of her Army Civil Affairs friends who had served in Afghanistan reported that it was not like this in that country. They could tell that their presence was increasingly being rejected by the Iraqi

Major C. David Long in a makeshift office at the presidential palace.

people. One soldier told me, "In Bosnia, all of the factions welcomed us. They liked us. It was much safer there. This place just defeats you. Everything is five times harder than it should be."

Major C. David Long, my chief of staff from the army, told me that he spent a fair amount of time counseling people about family situations (he was a pastor in civilian life). "Now," he said, "my wife, who has been a rock of Gibraltar, is sick." He worried about the men and women he served with. He said "many had fought to come, and now are fighting to leave."

Major Long also told me about the incredible difficulty in dealing with the army command structure and bureaucracy. It was an eye-opener. I appreciated the army enormously, but I also learned what kind of unwieldy and frustrating bureaucracy it could become. As Major Long said, "The Army is an efficient killing machine, but the moment it stops it becomes an impossible bureaucracy. The Army wants to take its own time making decisions, but when it has decided on something, then it wants everyone else to snap to attention."

I understood perfectly; I had waited two months for final authorization to occupy an office for the Ministry of Youth and Sport. But when the decision was finally made, I was told to move immediately or they would give the space to someone else. It didn't seem to matter that the office could not yet set up our computers or that printers were not available. Again Major Long supplied a fine summary, "When the Army makes a decision, they don't care whose day it ruins."

My worst experience with army bureaucracy came in the case of the soccer ball donation project; as time went on, it became progressively more bogged down. We couldn't distribute them ourselves because of security. So, the army had to do it, but they were lost in a system of impossible regulations. By the fall of 2003 when I had returned to Washington, I had accumulated an inch-thick file of emails about the fiasco. Major Long spent an amazing amount of time trying to get the soccer balls to Iraq. Finally, I was told that "Janice is preparing a PowerPoint presentation for a meeting at which a decision memo will be drafted." All for soccer ball distribution.

I soon realized that people on the higher end of the army food chain were angling for control of the project, in the hope of getting a promotion for themselves. According to my army friends, doing time in Baghdad was an almost sure way to advance a military career. Many were surprisingly open about their search for credit and career advancement. Some would go to extraordinary lengths inside the bureaucracy that formed at the palace; they stayed up into the wee hours of the night writing lengthy reports for their superiors.

According to my army friends, many people were obsessed with credit and career. "Everyone is chasing medals," one of them said. "Colonels will get bronze stars for service. No one cares about Iraq; they care about their little piece of it."

Chapter 8

The Sociopathic Son
Cleaning Up after Uday

EACH ORHA (OR, LATER, CPA) senior ministry advisor assumed the leader-ship of a specific Iraqi ministry. Our intent was to clean up the ministries and restart them as soon as practical, under Iraqi control. My assignment was the Ministry of Youth and Sport along with any other sports functions. These would seem to represent innocent and nonpolitical activities. But the previous minister of Youth and Sports was Uday Hussein, Saddam's eldest son and senior member of the regime.

What I encountered in my new role gave me a periscope into one of history's most gruesome chambers of horror. Ralph Waldo Emerson said that every institution is the lengthened shadow of a man. Uday Hussein's grotesque shadow had lengthened across the nation and even lingered across the very job I was given. I felt like I caught sight of his very shadow slinking

The façade of Uday's main residential palace was destroyed in a bombing campaign.

away out the back door as I walked in the front; I remain haunted by much of what I saw (personally as well as through eyewitness and official reports).

Much of the indescribable dysfunction and demonic cauldron of evil seen in Iraq is traceable to one of the most hideous families to ever live on Earth. To understand the shadows and undercurrents of what we faced, and continue to face, in Iraq, you have to peer into the darkness of the Hussein family.

Uday: Portrait of a Monster

Uday was a volatile and erratic figure with a hunger for cruelty. His life story, from his early years as a boy to his last days, was one of capricious abuse of others. The Saddam family may have ruled by an ideology, by they lived like gangsters.

Eyewitnesses of Uday's decadence and rage were always struck by how much he seemed to revel in and live for it and how self-indulgent and lacking in purpose it was. According to the accounts of Iraqi exiles and a long list of victim's families, Uday murdered at will and tortured with zeal. In all of the testimony that surfaced from people who knew Uday or encountered him—friends, bodyguards, cooks, and female victims—there are recurring adjectives: loud, vicious, paranoid, sadistic, jealous, and violently moody. Professionals who studied him consistently used clinical descriptions: psychopath, sociopath, megalomaniac, and sexual predator.

It is a rare creature of Earth about whom *something* good cannot be said; everyone must possess some redeeming quality or make some contribution, however trivial, to civilization. Not Uday. His was a demented existence; he started low and moved inexorably downhill as he steadily lost his mental grip.

While ordinary Iraqis suffered in poverty, Uday spent his days developing opulent palaces, exploiting women, and acquiring fast cars, expensive liquor, and hard drugs. To come close to Uday's habitat was to encounter the unmistakable signs of debauchery and dysfunction. When I surveyed Uday's primary residence, I saw several rooms fully dedicated to medicating the man. Drugs, including bags of pills and medicines, and needles were strewn across the floor of the bombed palace.

Uday lived a reckless and exquisitely self-indulgent life. His huge personal staff included a purchasing department complete with personal shoppers who were sent to Dubai or Europe on a regular basis to satisfy his vanities. One report suggested that he employed several people just to maintain an accurate count of his inventory of liquor, clothes, and exotic animals held at various palaces. Several staff were maintained to satisfy his lust for fine imports. He spent enormous sums of money importing cigars from Cuba and fashionable items from Europe, including cars, women's and men's clothes, liquor, films, and music. He maintained hundreds of expensive cars in an underground parking garage, ranging from older rare collections to brand new Mercedeses, Bentleys, and Jaguars.

One room in his personal palace contained row upon row of fine women's dresses, which he apparently kept for girls he wished to dress up for major official events and parties. While his taste in women's fashion was strangely and incongruously traditional and tasteful, his taste in male clothes was bizarre. He apparently kept several staff busy just scouring the Internet for the latest fashion trends in Europe. The palace floor was littered with printouts of models dressed in the latest and oddest; Uday had scribbled comments along the pages' borders. Included were printouts from trendy fashion magazines such as the Italian *Vogue L'oumo*.

Uday, according to friends, hated being seen wearing the same clothes or shoes as anyone else. He had to stand out. He had to dominate. He was frequently photographed in public wearing coats and trousers of lurid colors, outrageous by local standards. In the rubble of the bombed building, there were mountains of his own personal collections: piles of gaudy belts with brass and silver buckles and rivets, stacks upon stacks of shoes of every imaginable style. Apparently a fan of Russian pop music, Uday had collected hundreds of CDs from his favorite Russian artists.

His concubine palace, a seedy and tasteless imitation of the Playboy Mansion, was obviously reserved for continuous sexual indulgence. The walls were lined with pornography. A table in the main room featured a statuette of a nude couple in foreplay. Lining the rooms were beds and large sofas with pillows. Outside was a large swimming pool with a concrete and tile bar built into one end. Behind one palace was a personal zoo in which he kept lions, tigers, and cheetahs.

History carries many examples of state-sponsored violence carried out for political purposes, such as Germany's Hitler. But in many ways this was worse. Adnan Jabbar Saddi, of the Human Rights Organization of Iraq, said, "Hitler was mild-mannered compared to Uday." [1] For Uday, violence and brutality were a personal sickness that served no known ideological purpose.

Uday's younger brother, Qusay, was also ruthless. But he was moderate by comparison, always disciplined and discreet, always well dressed and orderly. Qusay was more trustworthy and less inclined to bring embarrassment to the first family. He was said to be squeamish about reckless killing and had an aversion to being close to blood, whereas Uday was explosive and bloodthirsty, often engaging in the killing himself. For this more "responsible" approach to managing things, Qusay steadily gained an elevated role and was assumed to be the second most powerful man in Iraq.

While Uday reveled in drunken partying, Qusay soberly built a power base that made him Saddam's undisputed heir apparent. He was clearly gaining in power, entrusted to manage the most politically sensitive missions—the Elite Republican Guard and the intelligence forces. From a national security standpoint, he was clearly the insider. Qusay was entrusted by Saddam to carry out the brutal crushing of the Shia in the south following their uprising after the U.S. military liberation of Kuwait. Uday did manage to maintain a role in state security as head of the Fedayeen Saddam. But that paramilitary force was not militarily serious.

As it became apparent that Qusay was increasingly being groomed to succeed Saddam, relations between the two sons worsened. Relations within the first family were so dysfunctional and tenuous that, just before the invasion, Uday was reported to be quietly plotting his own coup. And, according to journalist Peter Arnett, Uday was plotting an insurrection against his father. Saddam was reported to be fearful of him.

Clearly, Saddam came to a point where he had enough of Uday. After Uday murdered his father's favorite bodyguard, Saddam banished him to Switzerland. On another occasion Saddam retaliated against Uday for shooting and permanently crippling his beloved half-brother; Saddam ordered bodyguards to torch several dozen expensive cars from Uday's collection. To further humiliate Uday, Saddam confiscated his palace and threw him, as a common criminal, into Radwaniya, a prison known for especially harsh conditions.

Uday was apparently beaten severely in the prison, and at one point was observed swollen and blue over his upper body. The experience reportedly left Uday even more filled with rage, especially as it became apparent that Saddam's affections were shifting to Qusay.

The reason so much is known about Uday's violence is that he often carried it out with audiences looking on. Uday is said to have executed a personal guard with an electric carving knife with horrified palace guests looking on. Often he used his walking canes—designed to conceal swords and 9mm pistols—to injure or kill people in his presence.

Uday fell irreversibly out of contention for power and slid deeper into violent pathology as the effects of the 1996 assassination attempt took their toll. The attack, which nearly killed him, provoked a stroke that left him partially paralyzed and subject to frequent seizures. During the attack, he took life-threatening shots in the chest, abdomen, legs, and pelvis. The doctors said that he would never walk or have sex again.

With months of the best medical care Europe could offer, Uday recovered both functions but only slightly. Walking became difficult, so he acquired hundreds of canes. Numerous hospital beds and wheelchairs were found in the palaces. When sex became impossible, he resorted more and more to sexually perverse violence, and developed a particular obsession with violating young virgins. Doctors were frequently called to the palace to pick up women who were left unconscious from severe beatings. Often they were young brides stolen away from their weddings at Uday's orders.

The family story is too tormented to describe. There was sibling rivalry from the beginning under a father who was distant and tyrannical. Both boys experienced the worst combination of father absence and father abuse. Saddam was in prison during Uday's infancy because of a failed coup attempt against the regime he eventually replaced. During the years of Iraq's war against Iran, Saddam was gone for long periods of time. According to family friends, there were long periods during Uday's tender years when he saw his father only several times a year.

Other reports suggested that Saddam familiarized his sons with cruelty at an early age, which included introducing them to various torture techniques and forcing them to overcome any revulsion they might have toward it. Uday, from an early age, was vulgar and flamboyant while Qusay was quiet, disciplined, and calculating. More than anything, they were both spoiled and encouraged to develop abusive ways. The story is told of Uday's elementary school being forced to single out Uday each week for recognition as the best student even though he was disruptive and mediocre. Uday is said to have already acquired a taste for cars and prostitutes by age fifteen.

Saddam gave him sports, youth, and media activity to rule over; he did so from the beginning with maniacal brutality. He ran the broadcast media; Iraq's largest daily newspaper, *Babil*; and *Al-Zawra*, a weekly published by the journalist union he headed. Journalists had their heads shaved for no reason other than displaying independence or offending Uday in something they wrote. Former aides on radio programs reported having their feet beaten with rods by Uday for such minor offenses as getting the grammatical emphasis on a propaganda broadcast wrong—slights that Uday believed put him in a bad light.

Many suspected that Uday was given dominion over sports rather than sensitive issues of security because he behaved so erratically in the affairs of state. With Uday in security issues, Saddam would have taken on many more internal enemies than he already had.

Uday, first named chairman of the Olympic Committee in 1991, used the committee as his personal playground. He was routinely unopposed and re-elected in mock elections with his armed bodyguards encircling the assembly where the vote was being cast. The Olympic Committee under Uday became an instrument of state coercion, financial corruption, and sadistic personal abuse. He made a fortune trafficking in supplies and equipment (banned under UN sanctions), which he used in turn to subsidize his lavish and abusive lifestyle.

Many stories of Uday's treachery were confirmed by multiple eyewitnesses and became part of the legend. Human rights organizations, journalistic investigations, and local eyewitness accounts have established that the abuses of athletes were extensive and ranged from mild to severe. Thousands of athletes were tortured, many so badly beaten that their careers ended. Others refused to return out of fear. The lucky ones received a beating, or public humiliation by having their hair shaved, or prison time in the basement of the Olympic Committee building. Uday applied an imaginative and chilling range of torture techniques, including common beatings, electric shock, the dismemberment of a hand, or the removal of ears or tongues. On the extreme end, there were reports of Uday having enemies thrown to starving wild animals he had caged behind his palace.

According to INDICT (a British human rights watchdog group that took a particular interest in Uday and his Olympic Committee abuses and spent years trying to get the International Olympic Committee, or IOC, to investigate), Uday ordered prisoners to be dropped into acid baths. INDICT also confirmed reports of Uday forcing track athletes to crawl on newly poured asphalt while they were beaten. Others were thrown off bridges.

Defectors told stories of soccer players being jailed and forced to kick a concrete ball after failing to reach the 1994 World Cup finals. One soccer player claimed he was dragged through a gravel pit and then dunked in a sewage pit so that infection would set in.

Uday's beatings, unpredictable and violent, were not limited to enemies. He beat friends, bodyguards, and maids for offenses so trivial has having body odor or laughing inappropriately at a comment. Bodyguards witnessed everything from mundane clubbing to beheadings. Obviously, what they saw made them dangerous to Uday. So, for them to attempt escape from Uday's control meant certain death. To succeed in an escape meant injury or death to their families.

Uday kept a special prison in the basement of the Olympic Committee building. I visited it on several occasions; I have heard Iraqis describe the screaming that came from the cells. One of his favorite torture techniques was a medieval practice of hanging the victim upside down and beating him on the soles of the feet. In this practice, called *falaqa*, the victim was hoisted by bodyguards onto a beam; his knees were fastened with plastic straps to the beam so that his head and bare feet pointed toward the floor. With the feet at a convenient height, Uday would club the feet until they are badly swollen. After hanging for some time, the victim would be lowered to the ground and forced to dance, producing excruciating pain.

The most commonly reported offenses involved young beautiful women. Uday routinely had guards snatch young women for him, usually at posh pubs and restaurants. His habit was to enter private clubs accompanied by bodyguards and select the women who would be forced to accompany him back to his palace.

His most common practice was helping himself to another man's wife, sharing her with his bodyguards after he was finished, then killing her or returning her to her family badly bruised. In cases of young virgins who were snatched from weddings, the grooms reportedly often took their own lives due to the shame associated with the circumstances.

One man reported that his attractive seventeen-year-old daughter went missing for a week and was reported to be held inside the Olympic Committee prison. The father's attorney confronted Uday with documentation. Uday looked at the papers and threatened to break both of the lawyer's legs if he ever returned. One of Uday's bodyguards shot the man in the foot as he left. When the girl eventually showed up at home, she had been repeatedly raped. Father and daughter fled, but both were tracked down and shot.

Death to the Sons

On July 22, Uday and Qusay Hussein were killed in a shootout with coalition forces in Mosul. This was a big day for everyone. I felt the impact in a very clear and perhaps personal sense because Uday had previously been at the center of the twisted world I was trying to transform. In one sense, he had

The burned interior of Uday's residence, including a wheelchair used by Uday. There were several rooms with burned medical equipment, evidence of the permanent damage Uday sustained from a 1996 assassination attempt.

remained a shadow presence because he and his brother had been at large throughout my entire leadership of the Ministry of Youth and Sport. As for Iraqis, Uday, along with his brother and father, symbolized one of the great obstacles to a new future, filled, we hoped, with possibility.

I was invited to attend a hastily called press conference at the convention center, where more information about their deaths was expected to be released. Given that the conference center was within the Green Zone, I drove myself over there in a Suburban. I had to park in the rear because the front of the building was closed to traffic. Just as I exited my vehicle to make the two-minute walk to the entrance, the night sky lit up with gunfire; it was like the Fourth of July. The gunfire was rapid, loud, and continuous. At first, I thought we might be under attack by angry remnants of the regime. However, the gunfire was actually an outpouring of Iraqi joy. This was my first encounter with the Arab custom of celebratory fire. It didn't take long for my basic self-defense instincts to kick in; after all, when bullets go up, they also come down, and with deadly velocity. By the time I got to the convention center door, army soldiers were yelling at us to take cover inside and away from windows.

This was also clear evidence of just how many guns were still out there. Whether used for friendly or hostile purposes, an abundance of guns in this culture was a deadly fact of life. The next day, our intelligence liaison informed us that 50 Iraqis were killed and 130 injured from the discharged bullets that fell from the sky. Incredibly all of this firepower was in celebration of the deaths of Uday and Qusay.

For those who suffered in Iraq, the deaths of Uday and Qusay may have been a bigger event than the capture of Saddam. Uday and Qusay may have lived lives of conflict and sibling rivalry, but they came together at the close of their father's regime in an attempt at mutual survival.

Relations between the brothers were strained, but in one of their last acts on the way out of Baghdad, they pulled up in front of the Iraq central bank and, like a latter-day Jesse and Frank James, forcibly withdrew a billion dollars in cash. A bounty of $15 million each was placed on the heads of the two sons. Yet they survived for months without being reported, apparently blending into a village fairly comfortably and enjoying the comforts of a friend's hospitality. They were killed after a lengthy and intense gunfight in the small town of Mosul just an hour north of Baghdad. Their last act was dying together.

By the standards of honor in Iraqi culture, by fighting and not surrendering they died more heroic deaths than their own father. Even Qusay's fourteen-year-old son took up a machine gun and battled the American forces until a volley of antitank missiles was fired at the house, destroying them all.

THE DAY AFTER THE ANNOUNCEMENT, I was showing a *New York Times* reporter through the large warehouse of materials we had taken from the palaces of Saddam, his wife, and two sons. There, in one section of the warehouse, was a stack of pictures of the two sons when they were young. The boys looked so harmless, like any other toddlers. In fact, I saw hundreds of family photos at various stages, similar to what you might find rummaging through my own storage closets. The sons were pictured at picnics, shooting geese with their father, playing sports, and graduating.

They had grown to be full partners in their father's crimes. Now, they were dead, riddled with bullets. For their crimes, the two sons met a just fate; no sympathy arose for them. Yet I thought about the mother of these two boys; she was still alive out there. Of course she would be grieving. What a tragedy. I also wondered how different that family story could have turned out if the father and his sons had chosen to truly build a strong nation rather then enriching themselves and becoming brutal dictators in a repressive and paranoid police state. How that one father and his two sons would affect the entire world.

Yes, we could celebrate the death of the tyrant's sons. But what a tragic story it was—for the Saddam family, and for all of Iraq.

After the bodies were recovered, the Coalition Provisional Authority took the unusual step (on the advice of Iraqis) of releasing pictures of the two dead sons with distorted faces. At the risk of offending devout Muslims, the step was taken because many Iraqis would not feel comfortable getting on with their lives unless or until they saw firm evidence that Saddam's offspring and potential successors were dead.

When that confirmation came, everyone suddenly felt free to vent their relief that, after suffering humiliation and bone-chilling fear, Uday and Qusay were finally gone. The people poured into the streets, dancing, shouting, honking horns, and (in accordance with tradition) firing machine guns into the night. Tracer rounds could be seen arcing their way across the Baghdad sky. Iraqis described feeling like they were at a celebration feast. There was no disputing how vile and vicious most Iraqis regarded Uday. The venting was unmistakably cathartic.

As the man who replaced Uday, I understand some of what the Iraqis felt. Although I never saw him, I daily lived with the stain of his time and place on Earth.

The Ministry of Youth and Sport

Incredibly, the Ministry of Youth and Sport could have been used to build international esteem for Iraq and Saddam's family. Instead, it was perverted and turned into another grotesque feature of the regime. What could have been used to build ties to the wider world became another source of Iraq's isolation under Saddam.

Throughout the 1990s, Uday made international news for the abuses he carried out on Iraqi athletes. Hideous crimes against innocents were inflicted for no reason other than that Saddam's or Uday's egos had been offended in some way. History records nothing else like it.

The abuse was often and widely reported. In the early 1990s, ESPN did a special broadcast on the torture of athletes under Uday. Also widely reported was the activity of a special ethics committee established by the International Olympic Committee (IOC) to investigate allegations. Most in the Iraq athletic community were angry at the international community for being so slow to act on the abuse. The IOC defended its inaction by stating its policy of staying out of politics and government affairs, whatever the cost. In this case, that cost was severe. Thousands of Iraqis suffered.

For more than a decade, Iraqi sports programs were mostly cut off from the world. For that and other reasons, we believed that the issue of sports was critical and the stakes were very high. If we succeeded, it would do as much as any other single thing to boost Iraqi pride and give them a sense that they are back as a legitimate nation.

The Olympic Committee Building

The nine-story Olympic Committee office building took two direct hits during the bombing campaign. A large part of the structure had collapsed completely and the sides of the building were blown off. The grounds were covered with strands of mangled aluminum sheets. Crumpled window frames dangled, clanging like wind chimes in the hot summer breezes.

When I visited it for the first time, I saw a dozen poor young males crawling all over the broken glass and metal debris. They were loading donkey carts with scrap metal and stretches of electrical wire. It would all be melted down and sold for a pittance. My Iraqi aide told me they were from Sadr City, the infamous slums of Baghdad. They lived very hard lives but were warm and friendly kids. I didn't have the heart to stop them. What were they making, a dollar a day at the most? They were probably helping their families survive. Plus, they were hauling off only scraps, which now served a useful purpose.

We climbed and picked and threaded our way through the twisted wreckage of the building, picking up documents that might be of use. But I kept thinking of reports of a secret prison and torture room in the basement. It seemed inconceivable that this activity could have gone on in what was a tall modern office building, much like you would find in any city. Later, many Iraqis escorted us to the sites from where loud screams had been heard. They grimaced when recalling the experience.

On our way back to the palace, we got stuck in heavy traffic. Slowly, as the weeks wore on, city life began to pick up. Of course, that translated into frequent traffic jams. There were no cops and few American troops. When traffic stopped, it stopped; there was no quick way to fix the problem.

We were slowly crawling beneath an underpass and into one of the most dreaded sites in all of Baghdad. We had all heard numerous reports of grenades being dropped or shots fired at cars. Several of my associates had experienced very close calls. Every time I passed through that area, I had the very real sense that if I went home injured or worse, it would be due to a moment just like this one. We were relieved to have inched through the underpass section, but the worst part lay ahead.

The most feared experience was riding in a convoy and watching the lead and rear vehicles, which had .50-caliber turrets mounted on top, become separated in heavily clogged traffic circles. After coming to a dead stop, we were surrounded by a dense crowd of Iraqis, some pressing up against the Suburban. Although these times presented opportunities to get out of the vehicle and greet people, they were also very dangerous situations. Should I make eye contact? Should I be friendly? Or should my demeanor repel troublemakers?

The prospect of being hit by an RPG was ever-present and frightening. An RPG hitting the side of a Suburban would have created a hole in the vehicle a foot wide. The exploding RPG would turn the interior and its occupants into a furnace with millions of bits of red-hot shrapnel. Mortars or IEDs were worse. An exploding IED would toss the vehicle like a toy into the air, and then drop it in a smoking mass of incinerated steel and flesh.

If native ingenuity was in short supply when it came to the challenges of building a new nation, it existed in abundance when devising lethal and inexpensive ways to wreak havoc and death on the coalition forces. In fact, the IED became the symbol of resistance. "Improvise" is the word for the creative smarts that Iraqis brought to the business of killing their American liberators. By early 2007, three thousand U.S. servicemen had lost their lives in the Iraq war, and more of them had been killed by IEDs than by rifle fire, car bombs, or mortar attacks.

In testimony before Congress, Gen. John Abizaid described the IED as the perfect "asymmetric" weapon—"cheap, effective and anonymous." It was striking how little effort or intelligence was required to frustrate the most powerful and sophisticated army in the world. The bombs are easy to construct, easy to bury, and difficult to detect. They are made from old explosive materials taken from artillery shells and munitions. Typically they are placed just under the road surface or hidden in garbage or even the carcasses of dead animals.

In early May, we had intercepted messages from Saddam's death squads indicating that they were targeting General Garner for a roadside ambush in heavy traffic. According to the intercepted message, the ambush would smash into the lead vehicle, bringing the convoy to a stop. Then, while the occupants of the lead vehicle were being machine gunned, a truck with an RPG launcher would fire through the second vehicle carrying Garner. No survivors.

Anyone who spent time on the streets of Baghdad during that period was struck by, and would always remember, what they saw in people's eyes. Iraqi faces registered a range of attitudes, from acceptance and even gestures of friendliness all the way to real and scary hostility. You could feel eyes watching from everywhere.

Most of them wouldn't dare confront or taunt us when we were sandwiched inside a heavily armed convoy. But on the street separated from the heavy guns, we were vulnerable. All we had for self-defense were 9mm pistols, which we gripped firmly in our hands while burying it out of sight between our knees.

Olympic Sports: Starting Over

The most urgent task for my team was reorganizing Iraqi Olympic sports. There was no dream for the Iraqis like getting an Iraqi athlete or team qualified for the 2004 Olympic Games in Athens. It may have seemed like wishful thinking, but Ambassador Bremer insisted that we do everything within our powers to make it legally and procedurally possible for the Iraqis; we weren't the athletes, but we could certainly do our part. In fact, Bremer adopted that goal as one of his highest personal priorities. Bremer was himself an accomplished athlete. Even into his sixties he started his day with a run of several miles.

Few entities were more tangled with corruption and abuse than the National Olympic Committee of Iraq. Ahmed Rhaadi, who had been flogged and imprisoned by Uday, supplied much of the background on the business dealings of Uday. According to Rhaadi, "half of Baghdad is owned by the Olympic Committee." He continued, "parking lots, horse racing clubs, media outlets, and even a Pepsi franchise." Some Olympic Committee bank accounts held $2 billion in Iraqi dinar.

Hard as it is to imagine, under Uday's domination the National Olympic Committee of Iraq served as a corporate front for a lot of this activity. Before we could build a new organization, we had to make certain that the old structure had been completely dismantled, legally and financially. Otherwise, much of the organizing for new positions might have been motivated by an effort to gain control over the finances and enterprises that Uday had operated through the committee.

On May 8, Jay Garner signed a decree abolishing the Olympic Committee. It read very simply: "The National Olympic Committee was an instrument of torture, repression, and corruption for the prior government. It is hereby dissolved." The decree then proceeded to address all of the property and enterprise holdings that fell under the Olympic Committee's control: "All assets of any kind of the National Olympic Committee, Uday Hussein, or any entity associated with them, are the property of the Iraqi people. Those in possession of such property may not sell or dispose of it; they must hold and preserve the property until directed to surrender it to an appropriate authority. Those who violate this order will be held accountable and will be subject to such punishment as a coalition or Iraqi authority may direct."

There simply were no shortcuts. The long and arduous path would require a bottom-up reorganization of all Iraq sports, by legitimate means and with the approval of the IOC. In order to be legitimate, Olympic committees had to be elected in a national assembly, which itself had been elected by "the base" of that country. In Iraq, that was hundreds of local sports clubs and twenty-nine sports federations.

To get to a legitimate national Olympic committee, we would have to start at the very bottom by organizing hundreds of local elections in the towns and villages of Iraq; it would take months. Since we were the occupying power, we also had no choice but to remove the corrupt Ba'ath party element through which Uday had worked to dominate the clubs and federations.

Although international sports bodies would argue with us and resist that action (believing that sport must always be independent of government), it was the only humane and just thing to do in light of the history. We came under heavy fire from the Federation of International Football Association (FIFA) for attempting to remove well-established soccer officials who had served under Uday; and we came under heavy pressure from Iraqis for not going far enough. The Free Iraq Olympic Committee, the exile group that saw itself as spearheading the reorganization, constantly pushed for more change. Bremer was emphatic about the need to remove Ba'athists, and correctly so. And, as we discovered again and again, the Iraqi people themselves wanted the old element out.

Experiment in Democracy

All of this left us with a problem: we could use our power to eliminate people, but we could not use that same power to dictate who would replace them.

Those who served under the new order would have to be chosen through a process organized by the Iraqis themselves. We claimed the right to remove past sports officials, even though, under the IOC, sports are supposed to be independent of government. However, we could not simply and arbitrarily put new people in place.

At this point, we knew that although this was tricky business, there was no other way to proceed. We were the only people who could start the process of reorganization. No one else within Iraq or elsewhere was in any position to do it. In late May, I decided that the only way we could accomplish the task of replacing the old element and properly elect new leaders to the federations and Olympic Committee was to choose a new group of credible and untainted Iraqis who could do it for us. So, we formed the "Interim Committee to Administer Sports," made up of outstanding athletes, coaches, and sports authorities who were without taint and had the backing of the Iraqi people.

Under normal circumstances, a committee like this, generated by the government or an occupying power, would be accepted as legitimate. But these were not normal circumstances. The problem was that we really didn't know who these people were. So, Ammar engaged in broad consultations across Iraq. I decided that the only way the process would work and not blow apart was if there was near consensus on everything done during the early stages. Once the committee was up and running, they could make policy on their own by majority vote.

So, over the course of several weeks, we assembled and circulated a list of respected Iraqis. Hoping to secure the cooperation of the exile group, we created a couple of positions for members of the Free Iraq Olympic Committee. It was only fair that members of the exile community, many of whom themselves had been driven out of Iraq by Uday's abuses, be welcomed to participate. We would also need the full understanding and cooperation of the regional and international Olympic community. Ambassador Bremer insisted that I ensure that if we did our part, the IOC and FIFA would not stand in our way.

In early May I convened a meeting in Kuwait City with senior officials from IOC, the U.S. Olympic Committee (USOC), and various leading sports officials in the Arab world. We knew we would probably need the assistance of regional authorities and neighboring states to rebuild the program; we would need to consult them from the beginning. This group would serve in a support role for the months to come, in solidarity with Iraqi athletes. And they seemed genuinely interested in helping the Iraqis.

After spending a day assessing the state of each of the ten leading Iraqi sports areas, we decided to focus on the top seven. Realistically, the rest would take years to redevelop. For those seven areas, we would work tirelessly to get the athletes resupplied and into training, and make sure the teams were properly coached, funded, and reconnected to regional competition. The proof of our effectiveness, we realized, would be if several athletic teams actually completed all of the necessary qualifying rounds in regional competition. Frankly, I don't think there was a person at the table who actually believed an Iraqi team would even get to the games in Athens, let alone come within one small step of winning the bronze medal.

We planned to have our first organizing meeting for the Interim Committee to Administer Sports on May 25 at the presidential palace. I was confident that if we could elect a president, officers, and several committees, I and other CPA personnel could afford to pull back and let them do their work.

The entire episode proved to be a remarkable early experiment in democracy for Iraq. In fact, this effort to reorganize sports by means of the ballot was the only experience of its kind during the first several months of the occupation. We hoped that if we succeeded in introducing democracy at the level of associational life in Iraq, it could be modeled out on a national level.

WE HAD NO IDEA HOW THE ORGANIZING MEETING in Baghdad would work out, given that people had to travel in from the farthest reaches of Iraq. When the time arrived, the new committee members were ushered through the elaborate security process and escorted to their seats in one of the many ornate meeting rooms of the palace. Many of them stared in disbelief at the vast, opulent surroundings of the palace. Never before had Iraqis been given access to their ruler's lavish dwelling.

When the group was fully assembled and the roll was taken, we realized that everyone made it except the Kurdish delegation from the north. But we proceeded with our plans, and spent the first two hours allowing people to be heard and working toward a consensus over approach.

That was my first introduction to how the Iraqis themselves viewed their country. A lot of commentary focused on the evil past under Uday. Equally great attention focused on the future and the need for ethnic and regional balance in the distribution of power. I would realize the significance of their ethnic and sectarian consciousness only as the months and years progressed. There was constant pressure to increase the number of Shia and Kurds, who at least initially were underrepresented in the group.

One of thousands of pictures of Uday placed in storage. One can only speculate whether Uday personally killed the individual over whom he poses with a sinister smile.

While I acknowledged their basic point, I balked at the idea that representation on the committee be proportional rather than merely general in order to ensure that the Shia in the south were in no way undercounted. The fact that the previous regime had ruled dictatorially through the Sunni minority set the stage for the political dynamics that would rule the country for years to come.

While we were focused on diversity and balance, I managed to persuade the group to accept a female, which they did—but only one. She was Imman, a celebrated track star from the early 1990s.[2]

We ended that first day by allowing all participants to place names in nomination for the position of president. I promised that the next day, after tallying all the nominations, the three individuals getting the highest number of recommendations would be presented to the committee for election. Then, the top vote getter would win the presidency. I was pleased at how well this elementary experiment in democracy was going.

Somehow, the delegation of three Kurds from the north made it to town the next day and joined the meeting. When I began to review what had happened the previous day and how we were planning to proceed, one of the Kurdish members asked to be recognized. When I did so, he proceeded to give a long and impassioned speech about the problems the Kurdish people had under Saddam in receiving recognition and fair treatment. He was worried that, because they lived in the far north, the

Kurds on the committee would likely be overlooked by the mostly Baghdad committee. He concluded his long talk with the suggestion that the only fair way to proceed in light of the Kurds' absence the previous day was to re-open the nominating process for additional candidates, presumably to add a Kurd to the mix of nominees.

This felt like the opening of Pandora's box. I was concerned that by reopening the process, everything would unravel. I filibustered for a while, talking about how imperfect and imprecise democracy was. I quoted Churchill, who said that "Democracy is the worst form of government, unless compared to all the rest." I explained what a quorum was and the principle of majority rule as well as minority rights. I further explained that, had the three Kurds been present the previous day, the outcome would have had no effect on the final vote. Without stating the obvious, I hoped they caught the fact that, even if a Kurd had been nominated, he could easily have been voted down by the non-Kurdish majority.

But I clearly sensed that many in the room (and not just the Kurds) felt that my approach was not fair. So, I decided that winning and maintaining the group's trust based upon the consistent practice of fair play was too important. I announced that I would ask for a show of hands on the matter and if a majority voted in the affirmative, we would re-open the election for fresh nominations. I further explained that the top vote getter today would automatically replace the lowest vote getter from the previous day in the group of three finalists. This was democracy on the fly, but everyone received it as fair.

Before taking the vote, we took a break. Ammar came to me, ashen with anger; "They are not ready for this," he said. He argued that I would have to be ruthless; it was the only way they understood. I quietly informed him that if we didn't get started on a sound democratic footing now, as we are starting a new phase of Iraq life, it would never happen. I was prepared to take that risk. I needed to win their trust by being completely straightforward and truthful with them.

When the group was reconvened and the vote cast, a majority chose to add a new name. Expectedly, that addition was the Kurd who had made the speech. But when it came his turn to accept his nomination from the group, he announced that he was withdrawing his name for the sake of the greater good; that his only intention was to make certain that the Kurdish concerns were heard and honored. He was only testing our fairness. He added that the committee would probably need to be led by someone from

Baghdad, and concluded his remarks by making a strong appeal for Ahmed al-Samarrai, a Sunni.[3]

I will never forget the sense of solidarity and trust that existed that day. I felt like anything was possible. It was my best day, by far, in Iraq.

Reorganizing the Ministry of Youth and Sport

Not only did Uday's official functions include the Ministry of Youth and Sport and the Olympic Committee, but some military functions fell to Uday by virtue of his being a part of the first family. Saddam had given both Qusay and Uday sensitive security functions, presumably because the entire first family was at constant risk of assassination or being overthrown. For Uday, the most vital and sensitive security function was controlling the Youth Fedayeen.

He ruled over a tangled web of corrupt official and private operations. Obviously, they would have to be disentangled. I kept inheriting more and more functions for the simple reason that Uday had his hands in so much and no one else had been assigned to addressing them. When issues relating to anything in the world of Uday came up, the response was: "take that to Eberly." Because of all I knew and had seen, to be the "gatekeeper" to Uday's world was more than a little creepy.

By the time Ambassador Bremer arrived, we had assessed the nature and scope of the Youth Fedayeen and concluded that the entire organization had to be abolished and rendered illegal. At one point we leaned toward abolishing the entire Ministry of Youth and Sport. But when I briefed Bremer, I explained that under international law we were probably not authorized to make changes of that magnitude. Besides, much of the ministry was involved in legitimate community activity. In any event we could use the ministry to win the hearts and minds of Iraq's youth, as we had earlier hoped. Bremer agreed with my recommendations and requested that we maintain a small, lean headquarters and work toward decentralizing the programming.

Uday also presided over a huge business empire, which included a considerable portfolio of real estate. Uday had several palaces in the immediate vicinity of the Republican Palace. Uday's principal residence, which was within a very short walk of the main palace, took a heavy hit from several 2,000-pound "bunker buster" bombs in the early stages of the military campaign. In rummaging through the bombed-out remnants of these palaces, I couldn't help but be amazed at the power of our bombs as well as the enormous strength of the structures that Saddam and his cronies built for themselves. America was the only nation on Earth that could deliver this kind of damage; it was obvious that the structures were built by Saddam with that eventuality in mind.

There were large craters where the structure took two direct hits—massive damage where large pillars of concrete and reinforcement bar were blasted into a tangled web as though they were balsa wood. Much of the surrounding structure was slumping inward toward the epicenter. Lying along the front of the building was a massive slab from the palace's façade, easily two feet thick and weighing many tons. It had been blown at least twenty feet.

Yet, not far from the center, most of the structure was relatively intact, suffering damage only to the ceilings, walls, and contents from the concussion and the fire and smoke that followed. Remarkably, however, several entire wings of the palace remained structurally sound, testimony to the extraordinary measures that were taken when the building was constructed. An entire basement bomb shelter remained completely intact without so much as a crack in the wall. The only damage was heavy soot from the fire that swept through the building following the attack.

Three additional palaces, as well as other buildings, were still full of Uday's possessions. Something would need to be done with the contents of the palaces that survived. I recommended to Jay Garner that we organize the remaining contents for storage and possible use in the future by an Iraqi museum. He agreed. With that mandate, I spent countless hours in the weeks ahead prowling through the palaces and the surrounding grounds, organizing a plan to transfer the possessions of Uday and his family to the Iraqis.

The acres of open space around the palaces were tilled by large bomb-proof tanks in order to clear unexploded ordnance. In most of the fields and among the palm trees lining the streets and back alleys around the palaces, deep trenches and narrow holes led to large underground bunkers and weapons caches. Aboveground, numerous troop barracks with sleeping quarters and lockers were still filled with military uniforms, helmets, dog tags, gas masks, and personal toiletries. Many Iraqi soldiers died in the final hours of the coalition assault, but large numbers had apparently abandoned their posts and fled. Several of the underground bunkers were storage facilities for what seemed like every imaginable kind of exotic machine gun. Some were gold plated with ornately carved stocks. I could only assume they were used by elite troops for official functions.

The other objective in searching the palaces was to attempt to recover any evidence of human rights abuses. On several occasions when I returned to the Uday palace, I was accompanied by Sandy Hodgkinson, the human rights

Brad Clark at the "renamed" Tallil Airfield in Iraq.

lawyer with the State Department, and Brad Clark, a lawyer who served on our civilian reconstruction team. They wanted to find bunkers, torture chambers, and confirmation for some of the many stories of abuses that were in circulation. We looked for and found a large underground bunker that, according to some local stories, was used for occasional abuses. This basement complex was built to the size and function of a luxury home. It felt a little like an underground train station, fairly deep underground with heavy concrete slabs on all sides. The dark and haunting home had walls as thick as eighteen inches and two layers of steel "bank vault" doors, which were designed to protect against the most severe bomb concussion. The doors must have worked as designed; the entire basement bunker system was largely unaffected by the direct hit of at least two 2,000-pound "bunker buster" bombs, which struck during the opening stages of the military campaign.

Touring the palaces gave the clearest sense of Uday's decadent way of life. I'm not sure what the palaces were named under Saddam and Uday, but they were given a variety of creative names by the troops who camped on the grounds. In addition to the heavily bombed main palace that served as Uday's personal residence, there was the famous "concubine palace," which, as the name suggested, was the place where Uday apparently kept multiple women at any given time for his pleasure.

Although it had taken a serious pounding, we saw several large rooms with ornate tiles and sculptures that looked like they had been used for entertaining. Several bedrooms appeared like tawdry replications of the Playboy Mansion. Most of the doorjambs had erotic themes engraved into the wood and copper frames, the surest sign that Uday had illicit activity in mind when he had architects design the building. According to military personnel, large supplies of porn videos, statues of nude couples, and paper pornographic posters were found.

Adjacent to the two main palaces, two smaller structures were apparently used mostly for events and storage. The smaller one was packed with guns, ceremonial swords, and tack and saddles. This, the "warrier" house, was apparently used for state ceremonial purposes. The second smaller palace, dubbed the "party palace," was filled with tacky furnishings that were described as "velvet Elvis." Stacked from floor to ceiling in one room were crates of liquor. Other rooms contained anything from children's toys to appliances. One entire room was filled with imported pottery and vases.

An Infamous Inventory

In a May 5 memo to senior ORHA officials, I requested a policy on what to do with the contents of Uday's palaces. I mentioned that Colonel Colins had guided me through six facilities belonging to Uday, "two palaces, three warehouses and a bunker." I stated: "we need a policy to decide on how to sort out and store these materials, and perhaps release some ordinary household belongings to ORHA for immediate use." I added: "two other palaces not visited today—the main residence, which was totally destroyed, and the 'concubine' palace—contain no objects of value."

I listed the contents of the "warrior house" and "party house" palaces as: Royal saddles and ceremonial garbs

- A room full of silverware and silver pottery
- A room full of gifts, mostly toys for children, Olympic memorabilia
- Decorative ceremonial swords
- A tack room full of decorative saddles and other riding gear and uniforms
- A room full of liquor, including a wide variety of expensive scotch and wine

- A fairly large collection of official and royal uniforms, helmets, hats, plumes
- A large collection of ornate knives
- Pictures of Saddam Hussein family

I listed the contents of the warehouses as:
- 138 Lladró porcelain figurines
- Large collection of carved and decorated walking canes
- Ancient Bedouin weapons
- A large collection of fine sofa chairs wrapped in plastic
- A room full of fine pottery, gold plated vases and glasses, china, rugs
- Crystal bowls, gold-lined chalices
- Ornate chests of drawers
- Large gold-plated model of Uday palace in glass viewing container
- Hundreds of common household items including kitchen appliances
- Sony and Panasonic electronic musical equipment, cameras
- Computers and other devices.

I listed the contents of the underground bunker next to the warehouse as:
- Collection of ornate gold and silver plated weapons
- Official and Presidential uniforms

What was peculiar about Uday's palaces and possessions was just how many symbols of his violent and decadent lifestyle emerged. The most astonishing discovery was of a collection of 197 walking canes that apparently entered Uday's inventory after he began his physical decline following the assassination attempt against him in 1996. The handles of the canes were carved into the shape of heads of wild boars, a cobra, a giraffe, dogs, hawks, or horses.

Most of the canes on the list, which were ornately carved in hardwood, ivory, or various precious metals, were actually cleverly concealed weapons. Dozens had narrow razor-sharpened swords on the inside ranging in length from nine to twenty-six inches. An undetermined number of canes were engineered with elbows just below the handles that opened up as 9mm pistols.

A significant debate took place regarding what items should be considered common and released for use by ORHA and what should be preserved for an Iraqi museum. Perhaps the greatest dispute of all involved the disposition of Uday's alcohol supply, an inventory large enough to fully supply a liquor store—4,002 bottles. Included in his collection were old and rare wines and

Portraits of Uday and Saddam outside of Uday's palace.

liquors, including Cotes du Rhone 1994, Nuits-Saint-Georges 1994, Moet & Chandon Champagne Brut 1992, and Louise Roederer Cristal Champagne 1988; very rare thirty-year-old Whyte & Mackay scotch; and a large collection of cognac and Johnnie Walker scotch. If the volume of inventory was any indication of drinking preferences, Uday apparently preferred Johnnie Walker Blue Label and Remy Martin XO Special, of which there were 149 and 142 bottles, respectively.

AN APRIL 15, 2003, ASSOCIATED PRESS STORY carried a partial inventory of Uday's possessions.

"His personal zoo has lions, cheetahs, and a bear. His storehouse has fine wines, liquor, and heroin. His house has Cuban cigars, cases of champagne and downloaded pictures of prostitutes. . .

"Uday Hussein's compound is in a back corner of the Presidential Palace compound, a small city that boasts six-lane avenues, traffic lights, and a hospital. U.S. Soldiers who occupy the grounds said they believed Uday's portion included a house, a warehouse, a gym, a gaudy house for women, and a zoo.

". . . There were bottles of Cuervo 1800 tequila, Danska vodka and Delamain cognac, as well as Chimay, Corona and Miller Genuine Draft beers. There were bags and boxes of pills and medicines everywhere— ginseng fortifiers, heartburn medication and Prozac—and HIV Antibodies Screening Test Kit." [4]

What to Remember, What to Forget?

A short distance down the road was an entire industrial park that appeared to have been created just to supply the presidential family's palaces with furnishings. One shop housed stone and tile workers. Another was used by fabricators of ornate steel structures, another by stone sculptors. One entire building was stacked full of ornately carved chair frames and stacks of fabrics used to manufacture the gold-enameled armchairs throughout the palace.

Colonel Colins, who managed all the real estate in the Green Zone, designated a warehouse close to the palace for temporary storage of goods that appeared to be official items of state—gold trophies, mountains of Persian rugs, china from Japan, a gold-plated chest of drawers, glass vases, hundreds of silver chalices, and crystal bowls. There were enough possessions to fill a dozen 18-wheeler trucks.

I took *New York Times* columnist Robert F. Worth on a tour of the vast supply of treasures. He wrote, "The inventory lists 193 canes, half of which slide open to become swords or guns. There is a strobe light, a fog machine and 4002 bottles of wine and liquor, including a rare mid-1960s Cabernet Sauvignon worth $3,500.

". . . For the moment, the objects, neatly catalogued on an 18-page list, sit locked in warehouses and storage rooms in the main palace that the American-led alliance uses as its headquarters here.

"Because of their historical value, some of the items may be retained for a museum or documentary record of Saddam Hussein's rule, said Don Eberly,

Bombed sections of Uday's palace. It came to be known as his "concubine palace," where he was known to keep women.

an American official who has spent the last few months sorting through Uday's legacy of corruption and cruelty.

" 'Do they want to put this in a hall of remembrance, or do they want to forget it all?' Mr. Eberly asked." [5]

AND THAT, I CONCLUDED, was a very serious question. Iraq had rolled along for millennia. Saddam and his sons had appeared on that land only very recently. Would the nation want or need to remember them and their times at all? It is the same dilemma faced by Jews about Hitler and the Holocaust. Remember. Forget. Remember. Forget. The tick-tock goes on and on.

But one thing I knew. All of us working on the front lines of Iraqi reconstruction and humanitarian assistance were almost obsessed to do our job with the larger witness of Hussein's victims in mind. That infinitely larger plumb line pulled us through our own specific job assignments, personal heartbreaks, and the horrid discoveries buried in the sands of time. We would do what we did for those who died. We would also hope that those directing and equipping our jobs would understand and support us. History demanded it.

Chapter 9

Youth are Iraq's Future
Rebuilding a Ministry from Scratch

THE MINISTRY OF YOUTH AND SPORT was one of the smaller ministries. But in a country in which a majority was under the age of twenty-one, any effort to win hearts and minds and productively engage the young was bound to have serious consequences. The factors contributing to terrorism and insurgencies are complicated, but those filling the ranks of extreme movements are overwhelming young males with few other options.

In environments of political chaos and social instability, young males have always supplied the manpower. Examples of angry and idle youth being mobilized for revolutionary purposes include the Russian Bolsheviks in 1917, the Hitler Youth, the young fighters who brought the Ayatollah Khomeini to power in Iran, and the Taliban.

The planning for postwar Iraq paid far too little attention to employment opportunities for young males. Spending several hundred million dollars—out of tens of billions—in reconstruction money on providing youth a future would have yielded a substantial return on investment. At various times during the first two years following the invasion, proposals surfaced to provide opportunity for the young, including the concept of a youth corps. But funds were always more urgently needed for other things.

The debate that ensued following the release of the "Baker-Hamilton" report in late 2006 focused on many shortcomings, but the problem of unemployed youth did not escape comment. Army lieutenant general Peter Chiarelli, the top field commander in Iraq, was quoted as saying that tackling unemployment could do far more good than adding U.S. combat troops or more aggressively pursuing an elusive enemy. Chiarelli said: "We need to put the angry young men to work." He added that "a relatively small decrease in unemployment would have a very serious effect on the level of sectarian killing going on."[1]

In postwar Japan, General MacArthur realized that he had to move quickly to establish goodwill with the Japanese. So, he introduced them to baseball. The abstractions of democracy were passed over during the early stages for a far more important function: simply establishing activity to engage the otherwise idle and frustrated young.

We did our utmost to use sports to bring the nation together, with at least some success. No activity in the Arab world compares to sports as a means of channeling fanaticism into socially constructive activity. We did manage within weeks of arriving to stage a contest between the two major national teams in Baghdad's al-Zawra stadium after several delays due to security. It was a jubilant event for the 10,000 spectators. For the first time in decades, Uday's powerful presence was not felt.

The event proved that factions were prepared to leave violence at the door when sporting events are being staged. Former Iraqi soccer star Rad Hamoudi watched from the stands as a small squad of U.S. soldiers watched from the edge of the field, and the capacity crowd cheered. One observer at the event was overheard informing an official, "my experience in the Arab world is that soccer is far more important than politics." We worked overtime in concert with FIFA, the international soccer ruling body, to get a new domestic soccer program organized, with a special focus on preparing a national team for international tournaments and, eventually, Olympic competition.

Jump-starting the Youth and Sports Ministry

Few activities in the Arab world are more important than sports. Sports was bigger than any other news, including politics. It often dominated the front pages of Iraq's newspapers.

Various Iraqis captured that priority for us early after arriving. One said, "when sports is going strong, other problems will take care of themselves." Another predicted that if Iraqis could preoccupy themselves with sports, tranquility will result. He said, "Get sports going and it will be quiet again in Iraq."

The most revered figures from Iraq's past were sports celebrities. They received a hero's welcome wherever they went. And unlike anyone associated with politics, they were trusted. Athletes were among the least likely to pursue political power or personal financial gain, which made Uday's abuses of them all the more absurd. Several were so revered that they practically became advisors to CPA.

We realized that the vast majority of kids in Iraq had almost nothing to do with their time. Even the major sports clubs and community centers had very limited supplies. The farther you went from Baghdad, the more you saw kids kicking homespun, taped-together balls.

Back in Kuwait City, I had worked with the American soccer community to organize one of the largest donation campaigns for the Iraqi people. Getting the donations was fairly easy; getting them transported to the region and then across borders was a nightmare. But on June 2, we rolled out the first phase of the soccer ball donation program. Joining Ambassador Bremer and me on a soccer field at the Olympic village were famous Iraqi athletes, luminaries from the sports community and many from our temporary Olympic Committee. It proved to be one of the happiest days and one of the most successful media events that happened during my time in Iraq. Dozens of cameras and reporters from all over the region covered the event; it was televised far and wide. Without doubt, the event showed our sincere desire to do all we could to help normalize life in Iraqi neighborhoods and bring smiles to the faces of kids.

Saddam's Perversion of Sports

When I first arrived at the youth and sports ministry, the literature strewn around the grounds was filled with revolutionary slogans, all bearing the image of Saddam. The cover of one prominently used brochure (see appendix D) detailing the purpose of the ministry featured a quote by Saddam: "All comrades working in the field of youth and those who are concerned in this sector either within the formal or party formations should realize the importance of this sector and the importance of the saying 'who gains youth guarantee the future.'" It was signed: "The militant leader President Saddam Hussein."

FROM THAT, THE BROCHURE PROCEEDED to explain the purpose of otherwise harmless activities such as sports, science, culture, youth centers, and sports stadiums: "The leadership of the party and revolution has paid a great attention to the youth sector which is considered one of the most prominent vital elements in the movement of the new Iraqi society which its pillars have been fixed by militant leader the President Saddam Hussein."

It went on to explain that stadiums and youth centers enable the regime to enlist the youth in "defending the country against invaders, and foiling imperialistic and Zionist conspiracies."

The Ministry of Youth and Sport was basically killed as a legitimate organization in 1990. According to our Iraqi friends, at that point much of the regular programming to serve the children of Iraq changed and became oriented toward the ideological and even military objectives of Saddam's regime. Throughout the 1990s, the ministry was more and more consolidated under complete Ba'ath control. Many reports told the story of how sports became engaged in military training for the young. The most extreme end of the activity, the Youth Fedayeen, was compared to the "Hitler Youth" movement, complete with extreme indoctrination in Ba'ath ideology and the worship of Saddam. Much of the extreme activity for the youth during Saddam's regime was carried out by senior Ba'athist and military officials working directly for Saddam.

Authority

The U.S. authority in Iraq was pretty simple and clear. Both the right and the requirement of exercising occupation power flowed from the military victory over Saddam's government and occupation law. In other words, our authority was a byproduct of gun power. The coalition arrived, defeated Saddam, and declared itself in charge.

Within days of Baghdad falling, Gen. David D. McKiernan, commander of all coalition ground forces, introduced himself to the Iraqi people through a "Proclamation to the People of Iraq." It was direct and to the point: "The Coalition, and the Coalition alone, retains absolute authority with Iraq. The Coalition will remain in control until it transfers its authority to a new firmly established and internationally recognized Iraqi government."

General McKiernan also spelled out the consequences of resistance to the new authority: "As the head authority in Iraq, I call for the immediate cessation of all criminal activity to include acts of reprisal, looting, and attacks on Coalition forces. Those who commit criminal acts will be apprehended and subject to criminal prosecution." (See appendix A for complete text of the proclamation.)

GENERAL TOMMY FRANKS, COMMANDER IN CHIEF of the U.S. Central Command (CENTCOM), was, of course, the most senior military commander in the theater. To establish civilian authority and administration, General Franks issued a one-paragraph memo on April 28 to Jay Garner, the director of ORHA. It read simply: "As the Coalition Provisional Authority responsible for the temporary governance and civil administration of the

State of Iraq, I authorize you, on my behalf, to reestablish, reorganize, provide oversight, and reform the Iraqi central government ministries and infrastructure for the benefit of the people of the State of Iraq." (See appendix B for complete text.) Acting upon that authority, the ORHA administrator, Gen. Jay Garner, delegated authority for Iraq's ministries to the twenty-four senior ministry advisors.

General Garner's May 2, 2003, memo to me stated: "On behalf of the Coalition Provisional Authority, I am authorized to oversee the reestablishment of Iraqi central government ministries and infrastructure. I hereby appoint Don Eberly as the Senior Ministry Advisor from the office of Reconstruction and Humanitarian Assistance to act on my behalf in matters related to that Ministry (Youth and Sport)." (See appendix C for complete text.)

With that memo, I had conferred upon me wide-ranging authority to reorganize the Ministry of Youth and Sport, to put in place a new organizational structure, to appoint people on an interim basis, and to issue policy orders.

THOSE OF US WHO WERE RECRUITED to serve as senior advisors for the ministries reported first to General Garner and then later to Ambassador Bremer. It was our job to take general policy directions and implement them as effectively as we could.

Curious youngsters gather near the Ministry of Youth and Sport Building.

As it turned out, others also felt they had authority for the ministries. In the weeks after we arrived, U.S. Iraqi exiles began appearing at the palace. Many showed up believing that they had been sent to take charge. In fact, they looked at me suspiciously as I sat at the head of the table presenting plans.

It was difficult to feel like we were on the same team. They were, after all, Iraqis. This was their country; we were there temporarily. So what were we doing getting in their way? In a sense, of course, they were right. But it was already clear that if we left Iraq shortly after the military mission and turned the situation over to some sort of self-organizing process, presided over by Iraqi exiles, it would have been disastrous.

MOST OF US SENIOR MINISTRY ADVISORS did not have the teams we needed. We basically hobbled together staff from the army, from the exiles who were returning to help build the country, and from lower-level Iraqi bureaucrats who had survived de-Ba'athification. Many of the Iraqis simply did not have the education or skills for the work. And a significant number saw themselves as independent actors with their own vision and agenda for control.

Adam, in particular, was a problem. The first thing he did upon arriving was make an announcement to the media that he was the Iraqi minister of youth and had just arrived to take on his responsibilities. Naturally, I was curious to know more about these newly arriving Iraqi officials. Viewing their resumes, I found that one was a car parts delivery person. He was assigned to my team because he had been a wrestling coach back home; my ministry was the only place he might fit in. But we didn't need a volunteer wrestling coach; we needed experts who could help rebuild the ministries.

Adam's greatest desire was to go see long-separated relatives in Negev. That was a reasonable request, except we had no extra vehicles, no security to offer, and no phones. He still wanted to go on his own. We told him that under existing policy we were responsible for his safety and, therefore, we strictly forbad his taking the trip until the security improved. Adam disappeared anyway; he simply disobeyed orders and made the trip on his own. It was the first in a series of insubordinate acts.

Engaging the Iraqis

Unlike other ministries, no one at the senior level of the Ministry of Youth and Sport ever stepped forward to help the new phase of the ministry get started. I had hoped that we could at least learn about the structure of the ministry from Minister Kareem Mullah, minister of youth. Even if the programming was bad and would have to be replaced, we still wanted to build upon structural and management approaches that worked with the existing Iraqi officials. That could ease our way through the transition to Iraqi rule. But when Colonel King arrived at Mullah's home to request a meeting with me, Mullah's disposition toward me and the ministry was made abundantly clear. Mullah told King, "I wouldn't meet with him unless you arrived in an Abrams tank and hauled me away. I am a loyal follower of Saddam Hussein."

The Ministry of Youth and Sport, with only six thousand paid staff, was small relative to other ministries. But it controlled lots of real estate and programs, which, if properly directed, could serve very healthy purposes in the new Iraqi society. For one, the ministry controlled and operated over 230 youth centers in the towns and villages of Iraq. Some were partly controlled by the provinces, and many of the local clubs raised some of their own budgets through lotteries.

This was a country in which government did almost everything; technically there was no private sector or voluntary civil society. Some independent organizing activity existed around local clubs before we ever got there. That suggested that opportunities might exist under our ministry to encourage citizen-led voluntary associations. For Iraq democracy to work would require a thriving civil society through which Iraqis are able to learn the skills and habits of citizenship.

We would need everyone's help to build a new Iraq, and this might be one key way to engage the youth. Youth centers could be organized to promote educational programs and activities in science, art, literature, and personal hobbies.

But it took enormous efforts to get Iraqis to show initiative, even those far removed from Baghdad. They were so used to strong dictatorial leadership from the top. One Iraqi from a remote province managed to reach Ammar, my deputy for youth programming. He requested permission to hold a festival. Ammar immediately granted the permission, which prompted a second request: "Mr. Ammar, tell us your plan."

Ammar replied, "My plan is that I want you to show initiative, and develop your own plan." The Iraqis were deeply conditioned to follow rules and central plans. They also had grown accustomed to receiving very little money or supplies. Under Saddam and Uday, little was ever provided for the youth, and what was available to them, sadly, was destroyed or looted in the aftermath of the war. Most community centers and sports clubs had only old or meager equipment. Or it was missing altogether.

Even the one major investment in youth science education, a planetarium, was completely destroyed. Located next to the new Ministry of Youth and Sport office, the planetarium, reportedly costing upwards of $10 million, had just opened in January. The state of the art facility, about a hundred feet across with a dome-shaped roof high above, was reportedly the largest of its kind in the Middle East. But there it sat, gutted by fire. The only thing left were the sticklike steel frames of the comfortable modern theater seats. To walk through the ashes of the hollowed-out building was a sickening experience. What a waste. What a shame. It would take decades to recover from this.

I SIMPLY COULD NOT BEND IRAQI HABITS. They had a different concept of time, of processing decisions, and of solving problems. Frequently they wouldn't show up at all for meetings. When they did show up, they arrived late and would break away from the main group discussion to chatter among themselves. I felt an unbridgeable gap in our cultures, even though many of the Iraqis had returned from spending some time in the United States.

Several of them carried a remarkable preoccupation with gaining access to cars and equipment. Like all ministries, mine had a large fleet of luxury cars. Of course, most of them were missing, along with other equipment and supplies. Under Saddam, loyal public workers had access to benefits that were beyond most Iraqis. Many were on the payroll and did little more than show up. There were forty drivers on the payroll. Dozens of directorate generals in the ministry had their own cars.

One of the Iraqi exiles on my team, who had served in the Free Iraqi Forces (FIF) before joining my team as part of the American Army Civil Affairs unit, took his machine gun and spent an inordinate amount of time scouring the neighborhoods of Baghdad for the missing cars. Predictably, he frequently got in scuffles with local Iraqis. Again and again, he interrupted more pressing business to demand of me a policy on the cars he was recovering.[2] I finally recognized why the cars were so important. As confiscated cars were steadily lined up in the parking lot across from the palace, it became clear to me that the Iraqis on my team wanted to take personal possession of them.

Despite the contradictory images, I developed a genuine fondness for many of the Iraqis and Arabs. I especially admired their traditional customs and values. Fortunately, several who became my senior trusted advisors were solid men. Others would turn out to be deeply disappointing, turning against me and others in the CPA when it proved convenient. Under my successor, several of the trusted mid-level Iraqi appointees were found trying to steal substantial sums of money.

For a long time, I had entertained the possibility that some of the Iraqis that I had brought onto my team were fundamentally dishonest; they were very clever manipulators. Many of them joked about how ruthless and treacherous they and fellow Iraqis could be. Occasionally, they would reveal that many Iraqis were like "little Saddams"; they behaved honestly only when treated ruthlessly.

In one of our long late-night conversations, one of my senior Iraqi confidants warned me about being too trusting of the Iraqis around me. He described his countrymen as "unprincipled." He said, "they have been taught to fight for themselves and their own small piece of the country, not the nation."

That word—"unprincipled"—came back to me again and again in the years following as Iraq drifted toward fragmentation. In a conversation with Ambassador Bremer after my return, I said that my greatest disappointment was with many of the Iraqis: "They aren't what they present themselves to be." We Americans have many faults, but we tend to be so straightforward and for the most part honest.

More and more reports of corruption arrived at my desk. Two of my senior Iraqis were fighting intensely over charges and countercharges of corruption. One accused the other of cutting his son in on contracts. The other was accused of pocketing some of the money that we were distributing to athletes and sports teams for training. This was exactly the kind of behavior that was rampant under Saddam.

We had no choice but to work with some characters who had cooperated with Uday. In some cases, they had too much expertise and too many official ties to the Arab sports world to be ignored. Of course, it was a risk. It was impossible to know if they would help us or undermine us. Some would appear well intentioned while quietly looking for every opportunity to perpetuate control for their corrupt cronies and continuing the abusive and corrupt practices of the Uday era. We felt strongly that we needed to clean house, even if that meant longer delays.

There were people we never could really figure out. We simply did not have enough information. The best example in my case was Hussein Saed. He was clearly close to Uday but just as clearly he loved soccer and had spent his entire life building expertise and connections. At the time, he was Iraq's only real connection to FIFA, the powerful body that regulated the sport. He even had a seat on the regional Arab world affiliate of FIFA.

He first came to me through Col. Alan King. We met three times in the palace. Although I probed for information on his past activities and current intentions, he pled with me to allow him to continue to serve. He appeared sincere, insisting that he worked with Uday only because, like so many decent people, he had no choice; it was the only way he could continue to carry out his love for soccer. Many throughout Iraq agreed, pointing to sacrificial actions he took to develop the game under very difficult circumstances. He lived for the game, they said.

Others stepped forward offering proof that he was a dark and corrupt character who got close to Uday in order to enrich himself. They claimed that he was Uday's trusted friend, that he was with Uday at the time of the regime's collapse, and even cooperated in smuggling cash out of the country. I was warned that if I elevated Saed, a man with allegedly bloodied hands, there would be a broad revolt across Iraq against us.

In Iraq, it was rarely possible to establish the real facts. Rumors and innuendo were so pervasive and the hard data so difficult to find that we were often forced to just make the best judgment calls possible. Naturally, those calls produced doubts in many.

When Saed asked for authorization to make a trip on behalf of Iraqi soccer to a May 12 regional meeting, I insisted that he not go until the issues could be sorted out. Instead, I sent our two star soccer players from the past, Rad Hamoudi and Ahmed Rhaadi. I authorized them to represent the ministry and the sports community on an interim basis only. Shortly thereafter, the rumors started to spread about Hamoudi—he had left the country in 1991. Among other charges, he had supposedly returned just before the war to take properties and farms. How would I ever know?

When I left Iraq, Saed was still under investigation and the results were inconclusive. I often mentioned that if the evidence against Saed were presented in a court of law, the result would be a hung jury. And a very polarized one. That's how difficult it was to sort through the claims and counterclaims.

OF COURSE, THROUGH ALL THE CULTURAL and relational chasms, our highest short-term priority was to get sports clubs and local community centers operating as quickly as possible so that Iraqi youth would have normal activity. We worked hard to stay focused on those objectives.

Ten prominent clubs in the Baghdad area were organized under a central committee. We realized that, even though this was the structure that had been put in place by Uday, we would continue the organization as it was before, but with new leaders as much as possible. There were teams for youth eighteen years and under, and for kids twelve and younger. Every club received $8,000 dinar a month. Many athletes were employees of the clubs and had no other means of income.

We received enormous help from the Army Civil Affairs units in cleaning up and painting many facilities that had been destroyed. Civil Affairs units from the 254th Regiment, the army reserve's 352nd Military Police Company, and the 354th Civil Affairs Brigade were all involved in organizing local athletic activity. At one point, games were being organized for soccer, basketball, wrestling, weightlifting, and boxing.

But it was difficult to tell whether we were making advances or were being outmaneuvered by the same Iraqis who controlled sports before we got there. There were many conflicting agendas, and we soon realized that a number of sports clubs were being taken over by factions and conflicted territory.

In that rolling cycle of conflict, properties restored after the looting were damaged again. The police club facility that had been painted up and cleaned of rubbish was again looted and damaged. This was so strange to me; some people were more concerned about control than they were about a future for Iraqi kids.

Trip to the Kurdish North

I had always hoped to visit the Kurdish north. It was particularly tempting during the hot summer months because the mountains of the north had a climate that would compare to America's or Europe's.

Anyone in Iraq who could afford to travel at all imagined going there to enjoy the relative safety and comfort and moderate summer temperatures. Many Iraqis I knew just disappeared there whenever they could. To imagine sitting by the area's cool spring-fed ponds and lakes made it feel a world apart.

I had planned to travel to the north by ground transportation, which required going through sections of the country that were not considered safe. So, after the trip was postponed three times, my army chief of staff and I decided to travel there by Blackhawk. A larger group of Army Civil Affairs staff from my organization would drive there separately, meet us on our

President Bush was especially popular in the Kurdish north (Suleimania), as this sign demonstrates. The United States continued to enjoy broad public support in the Kurdish north throughout the occupation.

arrival, and escort us for the balance of the trip. After loading up, we lifted gently up off the helicopter pad with the powerful whirl of the Blackhawk blades and flew out over the city. Flying in and out of Baghdad offered a panoramic view of its many sights and living conditions.

Each helicopter had a crew of three, which included two pilots and a gunner who manned a .50-caliber machine gun that hung out a side door, which remained open. We flew at altitudes low enough that we could almost see into the modest sand-colored two-story homes below. Children scurried around on the flat stone roofs, and bedspreads that were draped over wire lines flapped in the breeze. Along the Tigris River in the vicinity of Baghdad were homes that would have been the envy of prosperous Americans.

Flying low and escorted by a second attack helicopter, we followed the path of the Tigris River north, passing at slightly higher altitudes over lush green fields. Iraq had so much going for it. Just beneath us, some of the finest agricultural lands in the world lay cradled between two ample rivers. It was called the cradle of civilization for good reason. For miles we flew over healthy palm groves and smalls plots of land lushly planted with eggplants, tomatoes, and peppers. Again the mind roamed to questions of whether Iraq might become an agricultural giant again, maybe the breadbasket of the Middle

East, thanks to our actions. The serenity contradicted the stormy reality of Iraq's difficult transition.

Not far out of the city the terrain began to change. The ramshackle homes were surrounded by mounds of trash and pools of sludge. Many of the outbuildings were half finished or abandoned. We saw more horse-drawn carts and fewer vehicles. An hour north of Baghdad, dotting the miles and miles of dusty earth below, we saw circles of tank embankments and concrete aircraft bunkers. Burned-out tank carcasses sat in wide circles surrounded by mounds of barren earth. This was one very heavily armed country under Saddam, but no match for the American air power. Those tanks never came close to engagement.

Another hour north, we saw the mountains and foothills of Kurdistan. Here the country was truly green, and, unlike the suffocating dust of Baghdad, the air was clean. Below us we could see flocks of sheep attended by boys, and women in long red dresses, next to wheat fields of freshly stacked straw. It could easily have been a scene out of Switzerland. The sheep scurried confused in all directions as the Blackhawks rumbled and whirled over them. The shepherds didn't seem to mind; we were welcome here.

We arrived in a remote airstrip in Erbil; from there we would drive two hours to Suleimania. To my surprise, at least forty people were waiting to greet me. I had no preparation for this, but I would be accompanied for the next three days by large crowds of people who simply wanted to express gratitude and were desperate for me to tell them what lay ahead. Only one or two other senior officials had made it to the north since the liberation.

The rural towns along the way were fairly barren and isolated. Progress had passed them by. The mountains were majestic, with UN mine-sweeping operations covering many slopes. They were cleaning up land mines from past conflicts between the Kurds and Saddam's army. I was told that upward of 60,000 Iraqis had suffered land-mine injuries. It was a reminder that this seemingly tranquil place was just another war-torn battlefield in Saddam's Iraq.

It was a beautiful land with beautiful people. They had much to offer the Iraqi nation, as General Garner occasionally remarked. Garner loved the Kurds and they loved him. In one of his first trips into the country, he flew north to meet old friends he had made while leading Operation Provide Comfort in the early 1990s. I was eager to meet them too.

The Kurds I saw were a tough, self-reliant people. They had survived Saddam's terror and a food and fuel embargo. Saddam's repeated assaults on

A scene from my official trip to the north, meeting with dignitaries. The Kurds treated those of us representing the United States on an official basis with lavish generosity.

the Kurdish people in 1991, driving many refugees into the mountains, was the action that created a semiautonomous region in the north with Americans supplying air protection.

In March of 1988, Saddam sent air force jets over Halabja, releasing clouds of lethal chemical agents. Five thousand people died in a single day. Tiny amounts of the nerve agent Sarin were absorbed quickly through the skin and eyes into the lungs and nervous system, causing severe neurological damage and deformity. Saddam dropped thousands of tons of chemical weapons over several hundred Kurdish villages.

Because Kurdistan is a mountainous region, to go anywhere means climbing and descending pigtail curves. Around many of those curves you can look down on lower slopes and see what remains of villages that were exterminated. Nothing but the outlines of concrete foundations remained; they resemble the site of an archeological dig.

As I was hosted by locals, people presented pictures to me, photos of the dead as well as the living who had experienced the chemical attacks. The entire region was still haunted and traumatized by the butchery of Saddam. Survivors had terrible brain damage, deformed limbs, and burned skin and were kept mostly out of sight.

The most difficult picture was of a father cradling his curly-haired toddler daughter tightly in his arms. The picture might have suggested the two were taking a nap. But, no; they were both dead from gas extermination, with burn and boil marks all over their skin, and eyes frozen wide open with a look of excruciation on the father's face. It was another one of those occasions when I knew that Saddam had to be removed. Of course, it was the right thing for us to do. I also wondered how these Kurds would deal with their anger and hatred toward the perpetrators. This was life as hard as it gets, all because of a monster.

In Iraq, the lucky ones were those who died a relatively painless death. Just as in the Shiite south, thousands in the Kurdish north were loaded at gunpoint onto army trucks and delivered to hastily dug graves, where they were slaughtered execution style. Corpses were covered over by bulldozers.

Gangland-style shooting was the easy and preferred exit. Detention was far worse. Kurds described torture victims being attached to meat hooks and hung from the ceiling of prisons with electrodes attached to various parts of the body. The Kurds were able to preserve thousands of documents and video accounts of torture and executions.

In Iraq, one could find episodes in history of America operating at its best and worst. The Shia in the south would never forget America's abandonment of them after apparently encouraging an uprising in which Shiites expected military support.

But, on the other hand, the American operation to provide humanitarian relief to the Kurdish people in response to Saddam's attacks, led by Jay Garner, was an example of America at its best. Not surprisingly, the Kurdish people trusted and admired us. The success of that mission was occasionally cited in Washington as an example of America working effectively with the Iraqis. It was presented as a possible model for postwar humanitarian relief operations should Saddam be removed.

After Americans established a no-fly zone protecting the Kurds, they wasted no time building their own institutions. They went to work building hospitals, schools, and universities. They had advanced civil society, even women's groups and an independent media. They had a thriving culture. These were people who knew about rights and responsibilities. It seemed almost as though they were building their institutions to spite Saddam.

The toughness and self-reliance of the Kurds was also viewed by neighbors as a source of potential instability. For one, Kurdish populations stretched across Turkey, Iran, and Syria. Within Iraq there was a fear that the Kurds would insist on immediate independence, seizing the oil-rich city of Kirkuk and declaring it the Kurdish capital—effectively ripping apart Iraq before it was ever assembled as a nation. Saddam had engaged in what was called the "Arabization" of Kirkuk, whereby he effectively drove out the original mix of Turkmen and Assyrian residents and replaced them with people he could control.

The Kurdish hospitality was simply beyond description. Town after town greeted our traveling party with large groups of people who had walked or traveled in pickup trucks significant distances in mountainous territory just to show respect. Even small villages situated in little ravines at hairpin curves in the road would stop our convoy and present gifts and flowers. We stood there face to face, and they smiled warmly and appreciatively. I was more moved and humbled, actually overwhelmed, to be an American and to represent my country than I ever could have imagined.

The Kurds are said to share partial ancestry with Europeans, and I had the strange sense that I was among distant cousins. They are rich in customs and folkways, with their own unique blend of music, dance, and art. At almost any social event, people form circles and immediately start line dancing.

After many brief stops we arrived in Suleimania. Awaiting me were nonstop meetings with officials, interactions with the media, and a town hall meeting packed with hundreds of curious Kurds, all eager to hear us discuss the future. I was positive and hopeful in my remarks, thanking them for their courage, which far exceeded ours. But frankly, my gut tightened when I thought about how things were actually going in Baghdad.

The next day was filled with visits to youth programs and facilities, with each site involving its own ceremony complete with brief talks, the presentation of gifts, and lavishly choreographed demonstrations by children at various stages of their athletic skills. One meal followed another, including one that began under the stars at 10 p.m. Long tables were joined together and covered end to end with freshly cut vegetables, lamb kebab, various blends of hummus, and flatbread. My hosts had organized special performances of dancers and singers performing Kurdish folk music. Some in the Kurdish towns still wear the traditional pants with baggy legs tightly drawn at the ankles and with a colorful cummerbund.

There were endless meetings, often late into the night. No encounter was too small for the media to record. It felt awkward being treated like a head of state. They took me everywhere. I saw a street fair flowing with food and colorful dresses, and a soccer match in one of their finer stadiums, where I was escorted to the seat of honor in the viewing stand. I was even taken to a wedding, which was a lavish traditional affair with the oldest and youngest dancing together in circles. Only the teenage boys formed their own circle to practice a slightly more lascivious variation of the dance. It was an encounter with tradition seen by very few Americans.

These were a joyful and courteous people. It was painful on the several occasions when they made their needs known and I had little to promise. They had great needs in the area of libraries, computers for youth centers, and equipment for sports centers. In one youth center, the concrete floor was broken through to the earth below, and the only weightlifting equipment they had were homemade barbells.

This was about youth and their future, one of the reasons I came. Although I had taken a truckload of sports equipment and donated soccer balls from Baghdad, we had no budget for reconstruction. I offered modest cash donations at various stops taken from our limited emergency budget. But basically I just reassured them that the Kurds would not be ignored or treated like second-class citizens when it came to the reconstruction of Iraq. I also encouraged them to take matters into their own hands and start developing their region. If anyone could build a strong economy and democratic society without a lot of external help, surely they could.

Whatever the future held, the Kurds were genuinely grateful for their freedom from Saddam. Those northern towns positively adored George Bush. Many banners proclaimed "George Bush, our Liberator, our Hero." I took a digital picture of the banner and emailed it to the White House; I knew the chief occupant probably needed the encouragement.

The Kurds loved us because we were Americans. They didn't want us to leave. They wanted us to stay and run Iraq, teaching it about freedom and democracy, something that actually seemed close to their hearts. I didn't have the heart to tell them that I and most of my senior colleagues would be rotating out of the country within a month or two.

Chapter 10

The Moral and Political Question

Did We Do the Right Thing?

THE TOUGHEST DAY OF ALL in my two years' experience started one morning when the first visual images of abuses in Iraq's Abu Ghraib prison made their way onto CNN. For those who were doubtful about America's moral purposes in Iraq, this event seemed to produce a certain clarity. One of the questions I had been asking myself was, "Are we good enough to do this?" By that, I meant is it possible or likely that we can touch the evils in that land and remain unstained by them? That same prison was notorious under Saddam

Team members celebrate with a traditional meal at one of Iraq's finest restaurants: clockwise from lower left, Mark Clark (CPA), Ahmed al-Samarrai (NOCI), Mounzer Fatfat (CPA), Ammar Shawkat (CPA), and myself. Sadly, al-Samarri, my good friend, and twenty-three others were seized by gunmen at the conclusion of a speech he gave on July 15, 2006. (To date, he and the others who were kidnapped are still missing.)

for the worse kinds of atrocities. I often wondered if one of the lasting effects of Osama Bin Laden's attacks might be changing us as a people, for good or for bad. Would those changes leave our reputation throughout the world worse, not better?

Abu Ghraib produced a lot of soul searching. Yes, we're an imperfect country. But how does one explain or even comprehend Abu Ghraib? It seemed to expose all the worst about Americans and our presence in Iraq: our incompetence, lack of commitment to rule of law, cultural decadence, and the suspicion that at least a few carried a seething condescension toward Iraqis, Arabs, and Muslims.

Looking back, I believe the best day—the high-water mark—of the Iraq war was the day Saddam Hussein's statue was dragged to the ground by an American Abrams tank. The sight of ordinary Iraqis finding cathartic relief by hitting the bronze replica of the fallen tyrant with their shoes will forever remain a symbol of that spring liberation. By the time I left Iraq in late summer, it was obvious we had come a long way.

But those early days of euphoria, when all of the country's rage was directed toward humiliating Saddam and praising their liberators, were short-lived. Many Iraqis, fearful of what they saw happening around them and aware that Saddam, his sons, and many of his top lieutenants were still at large, stayed in their homes and never really joined in the jubilation. It was too early to give up one's fear and apprehension.

The law-abiding Iraqis who stayed in their homes were a long way from rising up and embracing a new future of democracy. First there was the bone-chilling torment of Saddam's police state, then weeks of the American bombing producing what one observer described as "constant skull-splitting explosions." That was followed by looting, kidnapping, and killings, all generating a state of fear on the streets that never really went away. According to some estimates, Saddam had released as many as 150,000 thieves, murderers, and rapists onto the streets of Baghdad.

There were other historic high marks in the march to democracy: two constitutions and two elections, the symbol for which was the famous ink-stained finger. Iraqis had gained the franchise and had a constitution that guaranteed individual rights and protection from abuse.

But constitutions and elections are not enough. They are more the crowning symbols of a functioning democratic society than they are the origins of it. Democracy cannot take root in the midst of violence and deepening factions. In fact, rapid democratization can and does fuel divisions and even

A central square in downtown Baghdad. The stone structure with the mural was once used for a public hanging of forty Iraqis.

violence. Violence completely stunts the growth of democratic citizenship, as people retreat inward, withdraw from public life, and place their confidence for safety in tribal affiliation. As Iraqis themselves became responsible for functions of state, government became more and more divorced from the reality of daily life for Iraqis.

The ordinary Iraqi could only now associate the danger and mayhem with the American occupation. America's failure to preserve order was interpreted as reckless neglect or intentional. It seemed to many that they had traded one form of terror for another. The descent was fairly precipitous. In many ways, we confirmed the worst fears among Iraqis about Americans. It is very hard to appreciate how the American government is perceived in that part of the world.

The looting and mayhem caused the first rise of doubts. When the looters were permitted to ransack the National Museum of Antiquities, in particular, Iraqis were outraged. They felt as though we were deliberately allowing criminals to make off with their nation's most cherished artifacts, destroying their culture. The activity was seen as the handiwork of an enemy. These events played against a backdrop of hostile attitudes in the region.

From a public relations standpoint, the odds were against us from the beginning. With anti-Americanism fueled by extremist propaganda and their sympathizers in the Arab world and with circumstances on the ground working against us, many Iraqis came to suspect that America had mixed motives for being there. Was the Iraq liberation one step in America yielding to the temptation of imperial overreach?

It is hard to appreciate from a distance how deeply the suspicions in the Middle East run toward the United States; many wonder if our whole war on terror and the drive toward regime reform in that region are aimed broadly at Muslims. To the extent that our efforts are viewed as anti-Islam, our actions only fuel the embrace of Islamic identity as a defense.

From the reports we received at headquarters, there was genuine jubilation in many towns following the removal of Saddam. Tribal leaders and ordinary Iraqis alike seemed to welcome the liberation. But what they were hoping for more than anything in the aftermath was normalcy, something they had never really experienced. Normalcy meant living in peace, pursuing normal life realities like opportunity and education, and not having to fight continuously to simply survive.

Their assumption that we Americans could and would deliver normalcy held other doubts about our intentions in check. They believed Americans could do anything. Many had outlandish expectations of how we would rapidly deliver an American way of life; one even asked in all seriousness if we would be bringing in a Disney theme park. That was the outlook. Americans were miracle workers.

These expectations would and could never be met, regardless of our performance. Except for the privileged enclaves of Baghdad's educated and politically connected elites, Iraq was a thoroughly broken country. Nothing really worked, and that was before the postwar looting and mayhem. No amount of money or American ingenuity operating under the most hospitable circumstances on the ground would give them back the decades of development they lost. Nations aren't built like Disney theme parks.

Not surprisingly, it wasn't long before we started receiving reports that Iraqi leaders and sheiks were wondering what we were doing. The miracles weren't happening. Some asked pointed questions about our purposes and agenda, and a few began to believe they were being tricked. Saddam was gone, yet the atmosphere of danger remained, services were worse than before the war, and the national government had been demolished. They had hoped things would be different, they said. What the Iraqis observed during the early weeks of ORHA's operation was indecision and uncertainty, with little clarity on who would be in charge of post-Saddam Iraq. They perceived what we knew—that it was never the intent of ORHA or CPA to exercise firm authority or truly transform Iraq.

I was honored to give some introductory remarks at ceremonies for a special competition between Iraq and U.S. military soccer teams.

The plan was to finish the cleanup job in three to four months and hand political authority over to an interim body of Iraqis, organized and presumably led by Washington's handpicked leader Ahmed Chalabi, a selection Jay Garner and his team did their best to resist. That group would take temporary charge of the government ministries, draft a constitution, and hold elections.

America's job would be finished. That was the clear message that military commanders and civilian administrators alike received. Everyone expected to go home in fairly short order.

Ambassador Bremer, who would be blamed for acting like an imperial viceroy, had little choice but to take firm control of the political chaos and call it an occupation, because that's what it was. The act of formalizing the occupation was really little more than calling the reality on the ground by its right name. It was an act of simply telling the truth.

Many Iraqis would come to feel betrayed, first by our failure to provide order and authority, and then by our use of ultimate authority—occupation. By the early fall of 2003, polls showed that two-thirds of Iraqis saw the Coalition Provisional Authority as an "occupying power." Only 15 percent described America's military as a "liberating force." A mere 5 percent believed we were there to "assist the Iraqi people."

Reference is often made to "the fog of war." All the while Iraq was sinking, there was a great need to keep up appearances of progress. There was constant pressure to herald a new start after every event and spin coalition success.

None of the historic high points proved to be high-water marks for very long. The capture of the deck of cards criminals. The death of Uday and Qusay. The capture of Saddam. The killing of Musab Zarqawi, Osama Bin Laden's lieutenant in Iraq. Iraq just kept lumbering along without leadership and without order. No one seemed to have the means to make something of it.

Every day there were updates and announcements on how many schools had been repaired and hospitals upgraded. Electricity, which was at one-fifth pre-war levels and never really rebounded, was always on the verge of "major improvement."

It was almost impossible to assemble reliable reports on anything because the professional means did not exist to investigate the facts in that environment. It was even harder for people in Washington to know what to make of the information they were receiving. We were 8,000 miles away from home, in a time zone eight hours removed, trying to run a country at least eighty years behind our own.

Many in Washington slowly concluded that CPA had become a big motion machine, a government in its own right, isolated and unaccountable, believing too much in our own press.

Iraqi culture changed before our eyes as well. In secular-leaning Iraq under Saddam, the corrupt and violent Ba'athists were also unsympathetic to ultra traditionalism and Islamic extremism. Before we arrived, Baghdad had nightclubs and bars where whisky flowed freely. There were a few movie houses and live performance theaters. Women dressed in modestly fashionable clothes and had their hair styled in beauty shops. Now, Baghdad was in some ways becoming a grimmer place. Everywhere you looked there was more black—more women wearing black abayas and more black banners. Stylish Westernized women reported that they had to be careful. Shops were bombed or closed; ordinary amusements were increasingly frowned upon.

In the vacuum that existed around us, Iraq was changing. It took too long for CPA to acknowledge how deep the frustration of Iraqis was. It took far too long for senior officials in Washington to appreciate how difficult the situation was.

"Boots on the Ground"

If all of the complex problems in postwar Iraq could be reduced to one simple factor, it was "too few boots on the ground." The comments most indelibly sealed in my memory from the early weeks in Iraq came from ordinary Iraqis on the streets near the Ministry of Youth and Sport. Several times during the early weeks I went to the ministry headquarters to survey the building, traveling in an armored vehicle for protection. The Iraqis mistakenly assumed that we were arriving to provide security. With looting still occurring in the background, one Iraqi after another commented, "I haven't seen a soldier in days." As far as the eye could see in any direction, there were no police, no soldiers, and no order.

In my judgment, the looting started a chain of events from which we never regained control. If there was any one setback for which there was no excuse, it was the looting. All of the pre-war analysis that had been assembled from prestigious think tanks indicated that, based upon previous experience, people in oppressed lands tend to lash out in a fury in the explosive post-liberation environments. This was a problem waiting to happen. No one could have been oblivious of that fact.

People living under authoritarian governments are used to someone being in charge. When it becomes apparent that the floodgates are open for plundering, raping, and killing, anything can happen. In the cathartic explosion following liberation, it is common for freed captives to attack any symbol of the previous oppressive order, especially property. How could we not have known that?

The mayhem and destruction produced by looting was not merely a security problem. It had profound consequences for establishing a new political and social order. It made us look powerless and blithely indifferent to what would follow the war. It fueled a deep suspicion that we were not serious about building a strong, unified Iraq and had other purposes in mind. If we weren't committed to a strong, independent nation state with proud symbols of national government, why should the ethnically splintered elements of Iraqi society be so committed? Whatever goodwill we might have had evaporated before our eyes in the aftermath of the rape of Iraq by looting.

Looting happened because of the "light touch, brief stay" doctrine guiding the mission from the beginning. The avoidance of duty resulting from "light touch" in the case of looting was arguably a violation of international law. In a postwar environment such as Iraq following the fall of Saddam, the occupying power assumes full responsibility under international occupation law for civil order and for meeting all of the security needs of the people. This obligation was not met.

For every vital task, we needed more troops than we had. We needed troops for urban order, for curbing crime, for reining in the militia. We needed troops to protect vital oil and electricity infrastructure. We needed troops for the civilians to carry out their dangerous missions. We needed troops to rapidly train Iraqi military forces.

A lack of security was the biggest impediment to reconstruction. Many firms eventually found it impossible to carry out projects on time or according to contract terms. More and more reconstruction money was diverted to hiring security guards.

In many cases the breakdown of basic services happened when unprotected infrastructure was hit by saboteurs. Stealing component parts or shooting holes in transformers or other vital pieces of equipment was as big a factor as any in keeping Baghdad in the dark.

We needed troops for border control. Failure to control the borders for almost the first full year was a major contributor to the movement of foreign Jihadist fighters into Iraq. It was always a puzzle as to why more troops weren't sent when the evidence of their need was obvious to anyone who was there. It wasn't the case that they didn't exist, as some have argued. Before the war, 250,000 troops operated outside of the United States, approximately 120,000 in Europe alone.

The failure to provide adequate security was a major factor in the rapid emergence of an insurgency. Both the military and civilian planning were tied to the flawed "brief stay, light touch" premise. The core objective in the military operation was to produce the rapid collapse of the Iraqi army. According to the original plan, the military was not asked to pacify the country by eradicating regime remnants. Doing so could have made a major difference. Numerous conversations with military officials in the CPA compound confirmed that coalition forces were too rushed to get to Baghdad when they should have stopped and flushed out the remaining enemy. One stated it bluntly and brutally: "there should have been 50,000 more casualties among Saddam's fighting forces than there were." That did not seem the humanitarian or prudent thing to do at the time, but the price would be pervasive violence and heavy loss of civilian life later.

For the same reasons, coalition forces had no means either to destroy or supervise all of the ammo and weapons depots. At the end of a war, there is supposed to be peace. Normally, the enemy is vanquished and whatever is left of it agrees to a settlement. But there was no peace or end to the violence in Baghdad, and that is because of the premises guiding the mission. Responsibility for the remaining existence of a sizable enemy and its access to RPGs, land mines, and machine guns must be borne by the coalition forces. Before long, millions had AK-47s. Some were distributed by Saddam to his trusted allies, and millions more were stolen from unguarded arsenals. The war was never over. Regime loyalists simply faded away into a new phase of resistance.

Would more troops have made a difference? Yes, especially if they could somehow be delivered right away, not months or years later. If Rumsfeld had followed the war plan as it was originally drawn up, sufficient troops would have been available immediately, according to Garner. But even if additional troops had been committed in the spring of 2003, they would not have arrived until late in the year.

Perhaps it was an "optics problem." The whole operation already looked too much like an American occupation. Plus, increasing American troops, already the dominant force in the coalition, might dissuade other allied countries from committing more troops. And others just assumed that we would pass through this stage fairly quickly, that the "bitter enders" who were causing all the trouble would be killed or just go away.

The more likely reason was that the military doctrine operating at the Pentagon precluded facing up to postwar military requirements; that would have been tantamount to "boots on the ground" nation building.

As some who participated in internal debates have recounted, Secretary Rumsfeld actually wanted far fewer troops for the mission than were eventually sent.

Even the troops that were on the ground during the first two months reported being confused over their actual mission. If they didn't act like they were setting up for a long stay, it was because they would be going home soon. If it didn't look like they were responding to the early signs of an insurgency, it was because they weren't sent in to fight a multi-year war with an insurgency. They were sent to liberate and leave.

Armed Factions: The Wild West

The basic requirement of the sovereign state is to maintain a monopoly on violence. No state is viable without a capacity to control the use of force. Under Saddam, the Ba'ath government had a monopoly on guns. Following our arrival, the culture of guns was one of the first things to take on a democratic dimension of power sharing—just about everyone had one.

From the beginning, guns and general banditry were huge problems. Frequently references were made by colleagues to our own "Wild West" history in describing the scenes around us. For as long as I was in Iraq, the level of shootings surprised us all.

The most harmless was so-called celebratory fire in which Iraqi males would fire into the night on special occasions such as weddings or victories on the soccer field. But even this shooting killed and injured a lot of people.

One form was common crime, involving common criminal acts like theft and armed robbery. The more serious form of common crime involved kidnappings, car-jackings, and extortion to fund criminal enterprises and subversion. This was organized crime styled after the American mafia, and involved stealing oil, trucks, and state property.

The descent into fear and violence happens when every unarmed group decides it is justified in arming itself as defense against other armed groups, whether for self-defense or political purposes. In effect, the factions within society engage in an arms race, each fully expecting that things will get worse. The pattern is very difficult to reverse.

Where did all of the mortars, RPGs, and explosive devices come from? There is evidence that in the year before the war, Saddam moved large volumes of weapons and equipment from place to place throughout Iraq, including houses, farms, and warehouses, in order to avoid destruction in the event of an invasion. He also released massive amounts of weaponry to

Ambassador Bremer meets with International Olympic Committee leaders in his office. Great attention was given to guiding Iraq through an Olympic reorganization process in the hope that they could qualify for participating in the 2004 games in Athens. The Iraqi soccer team came in fourth, narrowly missing a bronze metal.

the privileged elements around him—senior Ba'ath party, government, and military loyalists.

In the chaos of the invasion, and with the lack of constraints after the invasion, control over these weapons was lost. Securing the sites of these weapons was yet another casualty of too few troops. In the month or two after the war, an open market for weapons evolved. It was not uncommon to see street sales displaying RPGs or mortars along with eggs, fruit, and other agricultural items.

From the beginning, disarming Iraq proved to be a near impossibility. Some militia already enjoyed semi-independence—for example, the Pesh Merga, the tough fighting force of the Kurds, which had been used to resist Saddam Hussein's army. The only way to prevent militia from multiplying would have been to dismantle the Shiite and Kurdish militia early on, a step that proved to be impractical and politically unfeasible.

Today, Iraq is crawling with weapons. Just about everyone has an AK-47, a Russian Kalashnikov, or a pistol. The central government has been disinclined to confront the problem of armed militia because the armed groups in question are associated with the dominant parties that rule Iraq.

Given the fractured history of the country, most of these groups can think of no good reason to give up their arms and have every reason to keep them. Working out a political compromise is compounded when ethnic and sectarian divisions run through all major institutions. Not only are political factions armed, the new Iraqi army is struggling to overcome incompetence, corruption, and divided loyalties. It is hard for Iraqi police and soldiers to fight their cousins in the militia.

THE SETBACKS CAME EARLY. The most unprincipled and menacing of the Shiite religious leaders was Muqtada al-Sadr. As early as the third week in May of 2003, he had organized protests in the streets of Baghdad that attracted over ten thousand agitated Shiites demanding an end to "foreign administration" and the immediate adoption of the laws of Islam. Most of us also noted the frequent condemnation of the Iraqi exiles by al-Sadr's followers. They simply were not legitimate, and probably would have been violently attacked if they had been given broad power.

Muqtada al-Sadr was probably a criminal. An Iraqi judge had unearthed convincing evidence that he had been directly involved in the April assassination of a respected ayatollah. Al-Sadr should have been stopped early on through a massive show of force. All of his operations should have been closed down. But like so many decisions in a confusing environment, it would have been controversial and consequential. So, Washington balked. Some in the military balked. Foreign governments were complaining about unjustified arrests. The media was unforgiving. I watched Bremer try to negotiate those circumstances and it seemed impossible. Muqtada al-Sadr won the time he needed and was never brought to justice. Instead, he became one of Iraq's least respected yet most ruthless power brokers.

Not only was Muqtada al-Sadr never stopped, but according to one observer, he "metastasized like a malignant tumor in the body politic of Iraq." The insurgency was a big enough problem. Muqtada's forces virtually became a second front, with foreign fighters and his own movement playing off each other's successes against a common enemy. Muqtada would graduate continuously to higher and more destructive forms of aggression. At one point, he seized towns in the south, playing off public hostilities toward the occupation, and even Sunni paranoia about what their future held.

Al-Sadr projected the image of the shrill, hateful fanatic, but more resembled a street thug ready to slaughter his way to power than join in an emerging democracy. It is doubtful he has ever been caught smiling or engaging in small talk. His affect radiated a crazed and vengeful lust for power. His plan for Iraq was some variation on Islamic theocracy, perhaps not completely fashioned after the Taliban in Afghanistan, but certainly imposing traditional Islamic law (called Sharia), implemented through Sharia courts, not civilian or secular jurists. Al-Sadr pretty much outmaneuvered Sistani, preeminent Shiite ayatollah from Najaf, and with that action doomed the thought that coalition forces would have a moderate and reliable friend in the Muslim community.

The militias were only the armed extension of the country's deep divisions and divided loyalties. As violence involving bandits and militia escalated, much of the country fell increasingly eager to use criminality and brutality. At one point CPA estimated that there were as many as 60,000 to 100,000 armed militia belonging to nine different groups. Thousands of tribal sheiks had armed followers. Why risk going back? How can you go back? What did it matter to defend the small unit?

At one point CPA's own compound in Kut was taken over by al-Sadr forces; they burned and looted everything in the building. Other facilities in Najaf, Hilla, and Karbala came under heavy assault and had to be defended. On a fairly regular basis, buildings that had been repaired and restored to coalition control, including policy stations and government buildings, were overrun by al-Sadr's henchmen.

The Rush to Democracy

The Iraqi experience has raised deep questions about the prospects for swift democratization following regime change. The early results have reinforced the case for skepticism. How precisely does a country with Iraq's painful history transition out of that kind of past? It was never really clear.

We had hoped to build what Ambassador Bremer called "a decent, lawful and democratic political order" in Iraq, if at all possible. Most on the team harbored at least some doubt about the country's readiness for the ambitious democratization that was about to be offered. Certainly the status quo of dictatorship was taking the region nowhere. And why not give Iraqis a chance to build a hopeful democratic future? Maybe in a region in which democracy was almost nonexistent, democratization would take root and become the wave of the future.

But how much did these battered children of dictatorship really know about democracy? Democracy isn't something you just give people. Of course they would be happy to enjoy new rights and protections from abuse. But did they know the meaning of equality, universal rights, and the responsibilities of citizens in a free society? If given the vote, will they think about the big picture or mostly act out the dictates of tribal society?

Some felt that a transitional Iraqi authority should have been established and granted immediate sovereignty. Although that is an appealing idea on the surface, the experience of the past three years makes it clear that legitimate authority could not have been created by us, nor was it going to simply bubble up out of the roiling politics around us.

Iraqi exiles had little credibility. The governing council that CPA established had little credibility. And our general credibility evaporated quickly and increasingly became dependent upon the military's role, which was grudgingly accepted as the only way to hold the country together.

Others felt that elections should have been pursued immediately. Elections could not be held for a long time. In addition to the lack of public order, there simply was no electoral administration in place to conduct a census, register voters, or develop competent political parties. This was not like calling a special election in an American congressional district. Some form of election could have been held, but it could not have been rendered free or fair by established international standards.

The Iraqis didn't want to place authority again in the hands of one person. But the alternative to centralized autocratic power could quickly become a debilitating fragmentation. How especially would all of this work out when it came to poor, uneducated rural Iraqis for whom life had stood still for centuries?

Of all the skepticism voiced by public policy scholars, the greatest doubt concerned how ready the Iraqi people themselves would be for democracy. Even Iraqi exile Kanan Makiya, a strong advocate for the war,

A bombed Agriculture Ministry structure.

openly expressed his skepticism—not that the Iraqis weren't ready to part with Saddam but whether they were ready to replace him with democracy grounded in pluralism and rule of law. In interviews he expressed deep concern about what would happen next.

After roaming the Iraqi countryside following the war, he talked and wrote about his assessment of the human raw material that the new society would have to deal with. He found the people deeply wounded, paranoid toward other Iraqis, and not really sure who or what to follow. Under Saddam, they were taught submission and obedience, not good habits of mind for practitioners of democracy. Now they would need to take initiative and learn to reason and deliberate. They weren't ready for this challenge.

Many had at best a superficial notion of what democracy was all about. Their notion of rights was weak. They understood the part about securing protection from an all-powerful ruler. But what about exercising power once they took it in their own hands? For the long-oppressed Shia in particular, the temptation to grab majority rights while overlooking minority rights and reversing the cycle of oppression was probably too great.

Lives that had been tyrannically manipulated under Saddam were now upended and thrown into chaos by the liberation. Politically speaking, it was a revolutionary environment. Not only did groups like the Shiite militia move into the vacuum, taking over hospitals and schools, but people yielded their loyalty to the known and trusted—the factions. They had survived through millennia by their strong tribal bonds. Advocates of democracy often dismiss local tribal leaders as "warlords" who are incapable of adopting democratic practices.

Too little was known or appreciated about the underlying power structure of Iraq. For centuries and through long periods of occupation and hostile rule, the sheiks held communities together and preserved the customs and rules of communal life. Particularly in rural areas of Iraq, it was tribal law that was still practiced to punish transgressors.

We never really appreciated the depth of tribal connections or the power of sheiks. Many imagined them as the kinds of parochial power brokers that would be replaced in the large universal and secular democratic system that we would be creating. No state-building effort was bound to succeed without treating local elites, the sheiks, as major stakeholders. It was their authority, after all, that in many ways was affected by a new democratic state. To succeed in a larger democratic experiment, they would have to be drawn into the process.

Even Saddam realized that governing would be easier if he could build a system to maintain the loyalty of the 7,000 Iraqi sheiks. Sheiks had the power to make things happen or prevent them from happening. Colonel Alan King, who was assigned to conduct outreach to the sheiks, found them eager to cooperate if only the coalition was trustworthy and kept its promises. When it appeared that the coalition was a trustworthy partner, the sheiks were helpful in arranging the surrender.

The drift toward fragmentation was strongly encouraged by the anarchy. The less order that existed in the streets of Iraq, the more Iraqis turned toward Islam for order and protection. The lack of democratic order and the embrace of authoritarian religion went hand in hand. The power of clerics quickly came to exceed the power of political leaders.

The drift away from a national democratic society and toward parochialism and tribalism only reinforced some of the most backward tendencies that many in the West are slow to understand, let alone acknowledge, as barriers to democracy. To question the capacity of residents of the Middle East was said to be patronizing and condescending.

The experience in Iraq confirmed the doubts of those nation-building scholars who seriously question the priority given to popular elections. Do elections necessarily lead to the creation of democratic society and good governance, or is it more the case that they are an outgrowth of good governance? It is possible, as the experience of Iraq demonstrates, for popular elections conducted too early to exacerbate the underlying ethnic fault lines and even contribute to violence. The creation of new democratic institutions with a modicum of rule of law should precede elections.

Democracy advocates tend to overestimate Iraqi capacities for democracy. That causes them to discount the steep learning curve that comes with the introduction of electoral democracy. To voice doubts about capacities of a particular ethnic group has less to do with innate ethnic characteristics than with embedded cultural practices and historical circumstances.

Iraqis were a lot less polite than we tend to be in describing their own intolerance and lack of forgiveness. They often made references to their own shame and honor culture, which is used by some to legitimize revenge. Among the less educated Iraqis, it remains "an eye for an eye, tooth for a tooth" society in which modern notions of justice don't apply.

Georges Sada, former military aide to Saddam and CPA advisor, said that at the base of the conflicts among Iraqis is a failure to love other people. Each is interested in money, position, and power for his own group. "The Sunnis love their people; the Shia love their people; the Kurds love their people; but there is no love between them. In many cases, there is animosity that goes back centuries." Under Saddam, they were taught that hatred, violence, and distrust was an established way of life. Somehow, he said, they need to "relearn the lost art of forgiveness." [1]

This culture of vengeance was what they knew; it was encouraged by the country's history, by life under Saddam, and by the chaotic circumstances that followed the war. Iraqis were also traumatized and needed healing of mind and relationships.

Some of the Iraqi exiles advocated creating a truth and reconciliation commission, which would take charge of all of the psychologically sensitive business in a country reeling from tyranny and war. Such a commission would include trying the top criminals while re-integrating others back into society, and gathering up records of atrocities—all in the name of the people who had suffered.

Others, like Chalabi, argued strenuously for more radical de-Ba'athification, which we would learn too late was probably more about vengeance and personal power agendas than it was about restorative justice. This was not the kind of delicate business that any exile, decades removed from the country, could possibly undertake. Iraqi exiles were united by little more than their hatred of Saddam, and were as divided among themselves by egos and conflicting agendas as the local Iraqis. Most Iraqis regarded them as irrelevant.

Recognizing the problem of Iraqis coming to terms with their pain and anger, the CPA established a commission in 2004. Many Iraqis went to considerable lengths to describe their state of psychological disrepair. They believed they had been intentionally ruined by a dictator. They described the experience of being brainwashed and its lasting disabling effects. None of this reparative work—the "soft" work of healing and mending a nation—was done in a systematic way while it could have made a difference. There was too little time, and far bigger challenges dominated.

In addition to the personal scars and remaining fears, very little held Iraq together as a nation state. As is often remarked, Iraq is a patchwork of a country bordering six nervous neighbors. Persian Iran, with whom Arab Iraq carried out an eight-year war under Saddam, resulting in an estimated half-million Iranian casualties, was four times the size and three times the population of Iraq. Iran's Shiite Muslims share a kindred spirit with Iraq's majority Shiites. These allegiances, already more significant than national boundaries, would become more dominant factors in the region.

Saddam's authoritarian rule suppressed hotly simmering hostilities. The Kurds, a more secularized and Western people in the north, were deeply suspicious of Shia intentions to create an Islamic state. How do foreigners forge a new nation out of former Ba'athists, theocratic-leaning Shia clerics, secular-leaning Kurds, and angry Sunnis?

The coalition believed that since the abuses of the central state were the big problem in the past, perhaps a decentralized system of federalism in which power was dispersed and shared was the answer. According to Garner, the idea was taken to Condoleezza Rice and her response was, "There will be no federalism." What Washington wanted, believing it would solve the potential problem of fragmentation, was an American-style democracy and a strong central state.

Iraq lacked a pluralistic civil society, an independent media, and political parties, all of which are part of the machinery of a normally functioning democratic society. Under Saddam, the Ba'ath party either destroyed or controlled everything that would normally function under civil society, such as associations of women, academics, and artists. Professional associations were manipulated and forced to serve as propaganda tools. Everyone was forced to be an accomplice of the regime in order to practice their trade.

Given time and sufficient experience through small-scale projects in local settings, Iraqis could learn about democracy and take ownership of their own lives and communities. The CPA did contract with firms such as

Research Triangle International (RTI) to provide extensive training in the basics of citizenship. This was important work and did help Iraqis appreciate the importance of sound governance centered on open and transparent public service, and other things. By instructing Iraqis in how to organize nongovernmental organizations (NGOs), the democracy training also included helping to develop civil society.

Numerous Iraqi civil society organizations were, in fact, launched. Several democracy centers were put in place, especially throughout the south. It was all good work, but in retrospect not sufficient to get Iraqis ready for democratic society. The process of building democratic and civic institutions comes through internal practices and experience gained over decades. These are not processes that normally take root in the chaotic environment of war and deep social conflict.

How might things have gone differently? What difference might more resources and more effective democratization policies have made? Could a more aggressive approach toward planting civil society as a middle way between authoritarian government and Islamization have made a difference? Could Iraq have been prevented from balkanizing into separate parts? Could the rush to Islamization have been prevented?

An honest assessment of these questions also requires some skepticism that current conditions were avoidable. Much of the social implosion within Iraq is arguably an inevitable byproduct of dismantling a sovereign state. It is questionable whether the kinds of outcomes that were required could have been engineered by a Western superpower.

The likelihood is that in any post-Iraq periods, greater interest will be taken among democracy advocates in strengthening states. Tyrannical states can be dangerous, but, as we are learning, so can collapsed or failed states. In fact, in the environment of collapsed institutions of sovereignty, forces no less dark or dangerous are able to gather.

The opportunity for democracy can be presented by removing a tyrant, but democracy can't be created by an outsider power. It can emerge only through a country's own internal development over a long period of time.

WMDs: The Weapons That Weren't

The decision to invade was based upon the intelligence information available at the time; its reliability could be determined only by entering Iraq.

The existence of these weapons and the imminent threat they were alleged to represent in Saddam's hands served as the major pretext for the war. So, naturally, most of the postwar debate about the rightness or wrongness of the invasion of Iraq has been about Iraq's lack of WMDs and what we now think about the Iraq liberation in light of their absence.

The journey toward doubts and second thoughts about the Iraq war among Americans probably started when they first learned that Iraq didn't have WMDs after all. Americans remain as confused and dismayed over the false claims of WMDs as anything else. How, they wonder, could the world's superpower with the most sophisticated and well-funded intelligence agencies be so misled?

If Iraqis were now using their freedom to build a civilized order and American troops were packing for home, the issue of WMDs might even fade entirely from consciousness. Were it not for the chaos and cost of the war, the WMD issue would not matter that much. Instead, the WMD issue may define the war in history. The absence of WMDs combined with the postwar chaos has led many to question the competence and judgment of the administration and to wonder why the American people weren't informed straightforwardly about these realities from the beginning.

The absence of WMDs in Iraq will stand as a lasting tribute to Saddam's craftiness. Saddam, who had been conning and manipulating America for much of his life as Iraq's ruler, decided to try to bamboozle America one more time. It was a rather spectacular case of successful deceit. The failure of WMDs to materialize represented an intelligence breakdown, not just for the United States but for European and even Arab intelligence agencies, all of whom believed that he still possessed them.

At some point in the 1990s, unbeknownst to anyone, including apparently most of his inner circle, Saddam got rid of his WMDs. All the while, however, he cleverly nurtured the belief around him that they were being secretly held. Numerous military insiders who survived Saddam have given eyewitness reports of major efforts at evasion.

Mahdi Obeidi, who was responsible for developing Saddam's top secret centrifuge program, has detailed Saddam's sophisticated schemes of deceit. He described the experience of having to rapidly dismantle the component parts of an entire centrifuge facility on the eve of America's bombing campaign in January of 1991 to drive Saddam's forces out of Kuwait. Just before the air attack on Baghdad, the component parts were packed, handed over to the special security forces, and stored in suburban buildings and farmhouses. Large deposits of raw materials were allegedly buried in the farmland north of Baghdad. Other materials were allegedly held in schools, private homes, businesses, and trucks that moved from place to place.

Georges Sada, another senior military figure under Saddam who survived and has spoken out, maintains that when large stockpiles of weapons were destroyed by UN inspectors in 1991 and 2003, many tons of raw materials escaped destruction. Special measures were taken to hide biological and chemical weapons along with laboratories and equipment. He maintains that in June 2002 large supplies of chemical weapon components and equipment were sent under cover of humanitarian aid to Syria (when a dam collapsed and destroyed several villages). Saddam sent in 747s loaded down with humanitarian supplies. The flights also carried shipments of chemical toxins and contraband technology.

At another point Saddam ordered all of the supplies gathered up and destroyed, hoping to prove their destruction to inspectors. After the 1991 dismantling, the program apparently went through fits and starts but never really regained potency. He kept his nuclear commission alive pretending that it was ready for mobilization.

At one point in the 1990s, Saddam kept large collections of documents and design materials in a chicken farm owned by his son-in-law, Hussein Kamel. When UN inspectors were tipped off and discovered the material, Saddam was forced to admit that he had ambitions for a nuclear program.

Hemmed in but not wanting the world to know it, he turned instead toward a self-indulgent spending spree on palaces and kept his military and WMD scientists divided and confused as to what really existed. Even they believed that Saddam was working on recovering WMD capacity somewhere out of their own sight. At the time of the liberation, Obeidi was the sole possessor of the centrifuge blueprints.

Colonel Alan King, who served with the army's 3rd Infantry Division, was told by the Iraqi atomic industry leader that the reason for the American invasion went away in 1998. It was apparently around this same time that all of the raw materials, machines, and facilities used for developing the centrifuge program were removed or destroyed. Saddam persisted in maintaining a defiant stance and leaving the strong impression that he was hiding something. From 1998 on, Saddam refused to allow inspectors into Iraq.

Exactly how and why Saddam did this will probably be debated for a long time. At some point in the 1990s—thanks to the combined effects of sanctions, U.S. bombings, and inspections—Saddam's internal weapons production system fell into dysfunction, leaving Iraqi weapons producers and their designers demoralized. Lacking a system to build and maintain the weapons, the remaining inventory was apparently destroyed.

Mahdi Obeidi wrote about the complete sense of denial that pervaded Saddam's inner circle until the very end. During Saddam's latter years, as his actual military capacity declined, he became more grand in his delusions. He had everyone pretending that although the armament factories had become completely dysfunctional, they would quickly be restored on Saddam's orders because that's how things worked with Saddam.

It was a twisted world under Saddam, a world of layer upon layer of deceit. Saddam lied to his senior officials, they lied to him, and they lied to one another. As Obeidi put it, "everyone lied in order to survive."[2] Georges Sada described it this way: "these men were eager to assure Saddam that two plus two is nine, because that's what he wanted to hear." Feeding Saddam's fantasy of omnipotence was probably the surest route to survival.

The status of weapons during the 1990s was integrally linked to Saddam's extensive network of covert partners in evading UN sanctions and personally profiting from the Oil for Food program. Saddam was able to move enormous sums of supplies and equipment through a corrupt network of collaborators who made large sums of money off the elaborate schemes. Mingled within contracts for food, furniture, and other basic household supplies were shipments of military parts and equipment from Russia and France—anything from rocket engines to missile guidance systems. Saddam is personally alleged to have made tens of billions in profits from the schemes. It is entirely possible that Saddam himself became intoxicated by his own system of corruption.

In the strangest twist, Saddam could easily have used this reality to save himself. By allowing international inspectors in to validate that his chemical weapons had actually been destroyed, he would probably still be in power. He didn't do that apparently because he believed the United States would never act on its threats to invade.

And he didn't do it out of fear of displaying weakness to his many enemies, at home and across the border in neighboring Iran and Syria. By posturing, he could continue to intimidate and harass at will. He maintained the pretense of having them in order to deter Iranian aggression or internal uprisings against him.

Among the many questions raised, on political talks shows and around office water coolers, is whether the United States would have invaded knowing what it knows now. Quite clearly, congressional support would not have materialized. But in objective academic terms as well as in the context of our popular debate, would it still have been justified?

By any standard, Saddam would still have remained one of the world's most dangerous dictators, even without WMDs, given his long history of abuses. However, absent a "serious and imminent threat" to the United States, we might have delayed the invasion, allowing for a larger coalition of international partners to take shape.

Allowing Saddam to survive would have preserved the very uncertain status quo in Iraq and the Middle East. Iraq could have turned again against neighbors and the United States. Most Iraqi scientists interviewed maintained that Saddam's clear intent was to survive and eventually to return to his aggressive weapons program. He clearly had developed and used chemical weapons in the past, and he had gone to great lengths at various times to develop the basic technology for a nuclear program.

Equally uncertain was what relationship he might have developed with the growing Islamic extremist movement. There was no strong evidence at the time of links between Saddam and organized terrorist movements. He had even struggled with Islam in attempting to build a secular-leaning Ba'athist state. Still, he was capable of shifting his alliances depending upon the changing political winds. The possibility of Saddam providing weapons to the wrong people in tactical alliances against enemies was certainly plausible.

Making policy with the benefit of 20/20 hindsight is an interesting academic exercise, but it's not a luxury that exists in the real world where decisions have to be made. Was it ever possible to know without invading that dangerous weapons did not exist? What difference might it have made in the decision if all that was known was that Saddam possessed small amounts of nerve gas and was prepared to release it to terrorists for use against America and her friends? The invasion would probably still have occurred.

Postwar Planning

It was the president's decision alone to invade; chances are he would have eventually done so anyway, for a variety of reasons that will be debated for years to come. Liberating Iraq may have been a certainty for the six months prior to the March 21 invasion, but the postwar rebuilding effort was never approached with the same certainty.

In the campaign of 2000, the administration was on record opposing nation building. Even after 9/11, nation building remained a term that was uncomfortable to many. The lion's share of attention was just on getting rid of Saddam.

Perhaps the avoidance of postwar planning—the nation-building part—was the administration's way of avoiding the subject. Those who were the most strongly pro-war were the same ones who had been most strongly resistant to the idea of nation building. So, not surprisingly, they were the least inclined toward addressing questions about postwar reconstruction or occupation. From numerous private conversations, the evidence suggests that "the details" really were of secondary concern.

Any assessment of postwar operations must start with an acknowledgment that a few things did go right. There was no severe malnutrition, Iraqi refugees did not swamp neighboring countries by the millions, the oil fields were not set ablaze, and public health did not collapse. Perhaps most remarkably, severe economic dislocation did not occur as the CPA steered Iraq through a transition to a new system of banking, currency, and employment. One could have expected wild inflation.

Many of the emergency conditions that worried planners the most just did not materialize. But the problems that did emerge immediately had to do with the fundamentals of postwar stabilization, the big macro issues of order, security, and political authority. All of which was symbolized most powerfully by the pervasive looting.

Those truly responsible at the Pentagon for postwar planning either really didn't know what to expect—a reasonable assertion—or simply didn't care much because they believed the Iraqis would solve problems themselves. The latter is a less forgivable offense. Either way, the result was the same: slim attention to the resources and commitment needed to make the postwar reconstruction and recovery work.

According to one telling comment, there was no pretense of planning even on these higher-end problems. Undersecretary of Defense for Policy Doug Feith told *Atlantic Monthly* reporter James Fallows, "you will not find a single piece of paper . . . if anybody ever went through all of our records—and someday somebody will, presumably—nobody will find a single piece of paper that says, 'Mr. Secretary or Mr. President, let us tell you what postwar Iraq is going to look like, and here is what we need plans for.' " Feith continued, "The notion that there was a memo that was once written, that if we had only listened to that memo, all would be well in Iraq, is so preposterous." [3]

General Garner got next to no instructions. Planning documents, if they existed, were not even handed off to us while we were in Kuwait

City. Garner would later learn that significant planning had been taking place within the bowels of the Pentagon on de-Ba'athification. But he was not informed of it at the time. In many ways, Feith was only reflecting the culture at the Pentagon at the time. Rumsfeld's focus, according to Feith, was on strategically managing uncertainty.

There were limits on knowledge, limits on intelligence, and thus limits on our ability to predict. As it turns out, that perspective was somewhat justified by the facts. But in most planning organizations, these "unknowables" would have produced deep conservatism in the working assumptions. In other words, expect the worst; leave nothing to chance. The stakes of failure are enormous.

The doubts and uncertainties, in other words, could have been invoked to produce a redoubling of effort to increase the chances of success by having sufficient troops on standby and having adequate military police to take control of the streets, among other things.

ORHA was also cut off from much of the forethought given to the postwar phase by other entities. Thousands of pages of analysis had been done by outside groups and the State Department's "Future of Iraq" Project. All of them raised sobering questions about potential consequences. To address these questions openly, however, before the invasion was to be implicitly against the war. The fear apparently was that if those doubts gained public momentum or were allowed too close to senior advisors or the president himself, the war might not ever be launched.

The strategic planning was not directed toward addressing the uncertainties because it was not the intention to have Americans stay and confront problems. Who needs a detailed contingency plan if we didn't intend to stay long and postwar activity would be transferred to the Iraqis, more specifically the ex-patriots led by Chalabi?

It was in this environment that ORHA was born. ORHA was created by Presidential Order 24, which assigned responsibility to the Pentagon to meet humanitarian, reconstruction, and administrative needs in Iraq after the war. The idea was that ORHA would focus exclusively on humanitarian concerns and reconstruction. It would be very lean and rely heavily on contractors who would presumably stay to complete the mission, working in concert with the new Iraqi government after we went home.

It certainly wasn't created to exercise political authority in Iraq, as was reflected in its initial rank. In terms of its place in the command structure, it was a hybrid organization with uncertain rank, at best a branch on the tree, not the trunk. Garner reported upward to General Franks at CENTCOM as well as to Secretary Rumsfeld (and often his underlings).

The focus of military planning was on winning the war. The focus of ORHA planning was on cleaning up humanitarian problems and rebuilding after the war. Jay Garner was told by a senior official, "we win the war and you rebuild." Those were the two elements that received priority attention.

The element that was lacking was a postwar plan for stabilization and governance of the country. The assumption seemed to be that governance, including law and order, would more or less take care of itself. This strategic uncertainty existed at the highest level of the U.S. government, and could not be concealed for long. It was perceived almost immediately.

The postwar plan was constructed on a flawed premise, and ORHA and its successor CPA were products of it. General Garner, and Ambassador Bremer after him, inherited circumstances that were largely impervious to their control. The issues were profoundly complex:

- How do you deliver and maintain order without fueling backlash against America?
- How do you stabilize a country and deliver services in the midst of an insurgency for which neither the civilian nor military teams went to Iraqi prepared to face?
- How do you plan for competent Iraqi administration when the Iraqis are not ready for prime time?
- How do you build a democracy without a civil society or middle class?
- How do you give the Shiites their rightful place as a majority while reassuring the Sunnis that they will not be oppressed?
- What do you do with the senior Ba'athists, intelligence services, and secret police commanders you send into retirement?
- How do you get a new military and police force to defend a stable, legitimate government that does not exist, especially when many of their relatives belong to militias?
- If you call back much of the previous government, army, and police, how do you train them to be honest professionals, avoiding corruption and cronyism?
- How do you create jobs when a private enterprise system doesn't exist and when everything from food to housing and fuel was subsidized?
- How do you privatize industries or jump-start trade when the entire country depends on state-run enterprises to survive?

- How could a Western occupying power effectively deal with a traditional tribal society?

Finding the right answers to these questions was essential for creating a new democratic society and government. Each involved a delicately balanced scale; the slightest tilt in the wrong direction could create trouble. At the most basic strategic level, the United States was between the proverbial rock and a hard place. To stay and occupy would stir up resentment, and to leave precipitously would have guaranteed civil war.

And time was not on our side. An adequate contingency plan might have included a request before the war for the authorization for standby reconstruction money. We arrived in Baghdad in April; five months later in September the $18 billion in "emergency funds" for infrastructure and economic improvement was passed. By the time CPA left in June 2004, $400 million out of the supplemental had been spent, and only $186 million on reconstruction, because of the difficulties the U.S. government was having accelerating the contracting process. This means that the first full year following the liberation, the most politically delicate period, passed without significant investment in reconstruction.

The two policies that have received the most criticism and will undoubtedly be subjects of intense debate for decades to come were the decisions by Ambassador Bremer to de-Ba'athify the Iraqi government and dissolve the army. Those were consequential decisions, but they have been wrongly singled out in the postwar debate as though they alone have determined Iraq's fate.

It is simplistic to suggest that a more balanced approach to de-Ba'athification or dissolution of the army would have made much of a difference. The criticism wrongly implies that there is an easy way to put a highly militarized society on a new path. None of the options was convincing.

The original plan, according to Pentagon sources, was apparently to get rid of the Republican Guard and other elite services but keep the regular army, which approached 400,000 in number. Similarly, the original policy on the civil service side was to get rid of perhaps 30,000 to 50,000 out of a workforce that numbered millions.

The plan apparently was to redirect as many as 300,000 Iraqi soldiers to reconstruction purposes. A major effort was made to encourage them to abandon their posts and not fight the coalition forces. As tanks were rolling north, Central Command dropped leaflets telling Iraqi soldiers to go home to their families and not to fight. Many apparently did just that. Many in the army had disappeared by the time coalition forces captured Baghdad.

General Abizaid reported that no Iraqi military units remained intact. The bases were abandoned and many were looted beyond repair. Acting on senior defense advisor Walter Slocomb's advice, Bremer officially dissolved the army.

How many of these soldiers, who had been conscripts receiving poor pay, were prepared to return and join a new workforce is anyone's guess. It is true that many came forward and indicated a desire to serve, and were probably not accommodated as they should have been. According to CPA advisor Paul Hughes, nearly 100,000 had indicated a desire to be integrated back into a civilian reconstruction corps. Others were almost immediately inclined to make trouble for the coalition, according to reports.

The criticisms assume that many of the troublemakers from Saddam's regime wanted to come back after the war and would have obliged us if only we had reached out to them. They also assume that with the right programs Iraqi soldiers could be rehabilitated and made loyal to the new regime. However, as we have since learned, even many former soldiers and police who did return after a period were more loyal to their tribes or political parties than to the state they were trained to serve.

Even with the best plans, tens of thousands of potential recruits— senior Ba'athists; Saddam's secret police, the Mukhabarat; and thousands more from Fedayeen Saddam—would still have drifted into the shadows of Iraqi society, far more than necessary for an effective insurgency.

Included among the critics of Bremer's de-Ba'athification policy are those who supported the original political transition plan that would have had Chalabi and the exiles put in power and made responsible for de-Ba'athification. Had that occurred, the removal of Sunni Ba'athists would likely have resulted in greater alienation and the real possibility that the country would have been in a state of civil war within several months.

An insurgency might have been difficult to prevent. And it was even harder under the circumstances to defeat, once it started. As is often remarked, insurgents have the easy part. All they need to do to succeed is ensure that we fail. Their first objective is to simply create a hostile environment that makes restoring services and repairing institutions difficult. Their second is to draw troops, who in this case were sent there to engage in classical combat, into an engagement with a different kind of enemy.

Military tactics that are the product of that flawed concept of mission can quickly backfire. The coalition force's job was to defeat an enemy, but in the course of finding and eliminating that enemy, lots of things got broken and people were humiliated and enraged. In tribal societies, honor and pride are everything. For every successful raid in which one insurgent is destroyed, several new ones are created. Even with all of the benefits of hindsight, the decisions appear no less complicated.

There is evidence to suggest that Saddam was planning all along to have at least the loyal elements of his military, secret police, and intelligence services fade away and become an insurgency. It has been confirmed that in the week or two before Baghdad fell, he released thousands of common criminals onto the streets, provided weapons to senior Ba'athists, and moved large supplies of gold and cash to locations where they could be used to finance a revolt. After all, Saddam and his Ba'ath party came to power three decades earlier by means of an insurgency.

These risks were all well known before the liberation. Colin Powell's widely affirmed doctrine was to (1) line up broad support; (2) amass enough force to leave no doubt about the military outcome; and (3) determine how it will end. The military outcome was never in doubt. But neither was there ever much doubt that the third part, the endgame, would be tough.

All of the risks were knowable and inherent in the decision to liberate and should have been part of the calculation. All of the problems were evident instantly after liberation and would have been compliant to at least some correction. Failing to make immediate corrections pretty much guaranteed that we would end up paying a far greater price.

Should We Have Done It?

As I stated from the beginning, with or without WMDs, many of us saw a moral case for delivering the Iraqi people from a tyrant who had oppressed and slaughtered them. Saddam himself was a weapon of mass destruction, against his own people, his neighbors, and civilized standards.

As we visited the sites of slaughter and the mass graves, and listened to the stories of survivors of torture, there was an overwhelming sense that this was the right thing, the moral thing, to do. Yes, I said, I would do this all over again. I especially will long remember the inexpressible look of gratitude that I saw in the eyes of the Kurds, who had suffered so much.

The drumbeat that Iraq was a mistake is overwhelming, especially coming from so many who on other occasions, such as Darfur, condemn their country for doing too little. As I was writing this book in the fall of 2006, one daily East Coast newspaper simultaneously focused on the fallout from Iraq and the growing international drumbeat for the U.S. and international community to take decisive action on Darfur, where hundreds of thousands of victims of Sudanese oppressors had already died, and just as many made refugees. It was an odd juxtaposition as I thought about the morality of military force. It was simple in the case of Darfur: do something, and do it by force if necessary. Why wait?

The more I thought about it, the more puzzling it all felt. Of course the Iraq case was different in that it focused on claims of an imminent and serious security threat. But that is where the differences stopped. In the five years before the March 2003 invasion of Iraq, much of the debate focused on Saddam the tyrant who gassed his own people and routinely used grotesque torture on them. The condemnation of his systematic violation of basic human rights was eloquent, it was bipartisan, and it came from liberal as well as conservative journals. And it was right.

Were there mistakes? Of course. The descriptions presented in these pages represent only a portion of them. Assumptions were too rosy. The intelligence failures were profound. Everything seemed rushed. Placing faith in extremely unpopular exiles, chief among them Ahmed Chalabi, who never really stood a chance of getting political traction as a postwar leader, was embarrassing to watch. Postwar planning was far too casual, and there seemed like a blithe indifference among some to the difficulty of the task. The disinterest, especially in the dangers of ethnic and sectarian conflict, reflected a dismaying lack of knowledge of the Middle East.

There were minor sins, and there was a major sin. The stubborn refusal to welcome input from people who had studied all of these issues deeply (for example, the "Future of Iraq" Project) strikes me as arrogant.

OF COURSE, THE ALTERNATIVE QUESTION IS: what if we hadn't removed Saddam? Where would we be today? In many ways the removal of Saddam was probably inevitable. All of the factors and forces pointed inexorably in that direction. What we have learned could fully be learned only by doing it. In other words, the postmortems should not be offered as though 20/20 hindsight was an option.

Saddam had weapons of mass destruction at one point and he used them. He just didn't have them at the time of the invasion, a reality that has caused many to feel deceived and betrayed. Throughout his life and until the end, he possessed the hope and intention of returning to the program some day. Long after the program had ended, Saddam still kept hundreds of scientists busy maintaining up-to-date information on nuclear technology. Saddam was a real threat; the only part that was false was the claim of imminence.

The most interesting discussion following Iraq will likely be held by political scientists and social theorists. It is impossible to plant a democratic state in the absence of a meaningful political society; only with rule of law is power legitimate.

Democracy is not possible without a strong civil society—voluntary associations and advocacy groups led by citizens, political parties, independent judiciaries, and a free media. A premature rush to democracy—without first building broad multi-ethnic voluntary associations that inculcate democratic habits—actually sets back the goals of democratization. Iraq remains in its infancy as a newly constituted sovereign state, and only time will tell if the hard-won advances will prove sustainable.

Epilogue

I am certain that had we taken all of Iraq, we would have been like the dinosaur in the tar pit—we would still be there, and we, not the United Nations, would be bearing the costs of that occupation.
—Gen. H. Norman Schwarzkopf, commander, Coalition Forces, Operation Desert Storm, 1991

IN 1991, GENERAL SCHWARZKOPF FORETOLD the steep price in American treasure and blood of eventually finishing the job of liberating Iraq from Saddam Hussein's oppressive regime. We could see with our own eyes the mass graves in the Shiite south and Kurdish north where Saddam deposited thousands of the Iraqis he slaughtered after the liberation of Kuwait. I share the opinion that these graves were a result of America's failure then to finish the job of securing all of Iraq, thus emboldening a corrupt and destabilizing dictator, one with a penchant for invading his neighbors and building dangerous weapons.

In this Iraq war, the military liberation and postwar occupation would be compared to Vietnam in its social and political divisiveness and national costs. With the extraordinary complexities of realities on the ground in the early postwar period, it is hard to imagine the American government undertaking a more daring or dangerous intervention. In the postwar years, Iraq has passed through several distinct seasons, but the mental image that remains for many American's was shaped by the carnage and chaos of the early years. At the lowest point in the operation in 2006, Iraq seemed to be edging toward all-out civil war, with American forces caught in the middle.

Now Americans are making mental room for new images. Visitors to Iraq today offer mixed observations, with far more good news in the picture. For instance, the surge that was implemented starting in early 2007 has produced clear, positive results. Violence is down 80 percent, and military deaths were down to twenty-five a month by the end of 2008. There are many successes to

My work required paying attention to the needs of the entire country, which meant frequent trips out of the secure confines of the presidential palace. When security on the ground did not permit ground travel, we traveled by Blackhawk, as seen above after landing in the Kurdish north.

report, such as in Anbar province, once the site of the most intense fighting but now among the most peaceful provinces thanks to the success of more finely tuned counterinsurgency measures introduced by American military.

New York Times reporter Dexter Filkins recently described his return to Iraq: "When I left Baghdad two years ago, the nation's social fabric seemed too shredded to ever come together again. The very worst had lost its power to shock. To return now is to be jarred in the oddest way possible: by the normal, by the pleasant, even by hope." Two years ago, the neighborhood where he stayed was "shuttered, shattered, broken and dead." Baghdad was a "grim, spooky, deserted place."[1]

But in spite of surge-inspired progress, observers have noted that Iraq remains a deeply divided country with a very weak state. The phrase used most frequently is "fragile," the progress "reversible." Iraq's central government is too feeble, dysfunctional, and divided to maintain order or perform essential functions.

There are any number of possible developments that could bring sectarian rivalries to a rapid boil. Particularly worrisome is a sectarian standoff in Iraqi politics. The age-old habits of looking out first for one's own tribe and sect are becoming more deeply ingrained. Peace will be challenged in the effort to resettle millions of Iraqis who fled the country during the war. Ethnically divided Kirk, which sits on top of Iraq's main oil field, could easily disintegrate.

In short, our stated goal—a free, stable, and independent Iraq—will take a lot more time to accomplish. The debate over whether the costs were worth it may never be settled, with every American left to decide for themselves. Finally, I hope this book has shed light on our country's experience in Iraq and offer insight and wisdom for the future.

Appendix A

Proclamation to the People of Iraq

I, Lieutenant General David McKiernan, Commander of all Coalition Ground Forces in Iraq, affirm to the citizens of Iraq the Coalition's commitment to restoring security, stability and rapidly repairing Iraq's damaged infrastructure. As the head authority in Iraq, I call for the immediate cessation of all criminal activity to include acts of reprisal, looting, and attacks on Coalition forces. Those who commit criminal acts, will be apprehended and be subject to criminal prosecution. I expect the support and assistance of the proud people of Iraq to restore stability to Iraq. To this end, I charge the citizens of Iraq to immediately return to work. Citizens who have served in leadership positions must identify themselves to Coalition forces to assist in the building of a new Iraqi government.

The Coalition, and the Coalition alone, retains absolute authority within Iraq. The Coalition will remain in control until it transfers its authority to a new firmly established and internationally recognized Iraqi Government. Individuals or organizations may not claim control of property, civil institutions or represent themselves as civil or military authorities without the explicit endorsement of the Coalition. Furthermore, the wearing of any distinguishing uniforms denoting a position of civil or military authority, specific group or organization is not authorized unless sanctioned by the Coalitio Likewise no one is authorized to speak as my representative or for Coalition forces. Those choosing to represent themselves in this manner will be considered a disruption to the stability of Iraq and treated as criminals. Additionally, all checkpoints and traffic control points, both established and planned, are not authorized unless directed and supervised by Coalition forces.

Together the noble people of Iraq and the Coalition will endeavor to reestablish a viable nation state and a model of success to the international community.

David D. McKiernan
Lieutenant General, United States

Appendix B

UNITED STATES CENTRAL COMMAND
OFFICE OF THE COMMANDER IN CHIEF
7115 SOUTH BOUNDARY BOULEVARD
MACDILL AIR FORCE BASE, FLORIDA 33621-5101

CCCC   28 April 2003

MEMORANDUM FOR Director, Office of Reconstruction and
                Humanitarian Assistance (ORHA)

SUBJECT: Delegation of Authority

As the Coalition Provisional Authority responsible for the
temporary governance and civil administration of the State of
Iraq, I authorize you, on my behalf, to reestablish, reorganize,
provide oversight, and reform the Iraqi central government
ministries and infrastructure for the benefit of the people of
the State of Iraq.

                                        TOMMY R. FRANKS
                                        General, USA

CC: Commander, CFLCC

Appendix C

U.S. DEPARTMENT OF DEFENSE
OFFICE OF RECONSTRUCTION AND HUMANITARIAN
ASSISTANCE
CFLCC-ORHA
APO AE 09304

May 2, 2003

To: Ministry of Youth

From: Director, Office of Reconstruction and
         Humanitarian Assistance

Subj: Appointment

On behalf of the Coalition Provisional Authority, I am authorized to oversee the reestablishment of Iraqi central government ministries and infrastructure.

I hereby appoint Don Eberly as the Senior Ministry Advisor from the Office of Reconstruction and Humanitarian Assistance to the Ministry of Youth to act on my behalf in matters related to that Ministry. In that capacity, he will supervise the activities of this Ministry on behalf of the Coalition Provisional Authority.

As public servants, you have a responsibility to Iraq and to the Iraqi people. I expect your full cooperation and adherence to Mr. Eberly's supervision.

Jay Garner, Director
Office of Reconstruction
and Humanitarian Assistance

Appendix D

The leadership of the party and revolution has paid a great attention to the youth sector which is considered one of the most prominent vital elements in the movement of the new Iraqi society which its pillars have been fixed by the militant leader the President Saddam Hussein. The support of H.E. the President to this sector has a great influence in mobalizing youth and developing youth activities in all sports, technical, cultural, and scientific fields.

The Ministry of Youth has a great share of this support and the big results were represented in constructing youth centers, stadiums, indoor swimming pools, sports gymnasiums, scientific centers where different activities are organized; these activities help in encouraging youth to contribute positively in the comprehensive development programmes, defending the country against invaders, and foiling imperialist and zionist conspiracies.

The youth centers and other specialized centers, and sports clubs are considered an essential materials to develope and refine the talents of youth through. The supervision of the Directorates General each according to its specialization in addition to the Directorates of Youth which are distributed through out the country.

Directorate General of Sports and Games

It is one of the important directorates general in the Ministry of Youth. It organizes activities and

sports games in the clubs and youth centers which are distributed through out the country in order to invest the free time, and provide medical and social welfare to achieve the highest levels of physical fittness and mental capability. It also open training, refreeing courses to technical cadre who work in its sports institutions. The following Directorates are attached to the Directorate General of Sports and Games:

The Directorate of clubs and sports federations, Directorate of training, Directorate of sports and games, Directorate of mass sport, Directorate of sports medicine.

Directorate of Sports Medicine

It is a medical institutions in charge of providing medical care to all sportsmen. It's duty is fulfilling medical checkings, and tests as well as declaring the extent of the sportsmen capabilities to practice different sports games, and ensure medical treatment for them.

Directorate General of scientific welfare

It is one of the Ministry's establishments which is concerned in spreading out scientific education and encouraging scientific talents and abilities and exerting no effort to develope and exploit them in a way which serve the society and implant the spirit of creative ability of development, and orginality in the fields of electricity, electronic, chemisstry, life sciences, embalmment, physics, photography, radio, and wirless. There are six scientific welfare centers now in the country distributed in six governorates; and the directorate now has developed methods, modern devices, advanced labs, in addition to specialized technical cadre.

Planetarium

The planetarium is one of the scientific projects which aims at spreading out astronomic and space awarness and reviving Arab heritage which is full of science. Every day the plantarium receives many students and visitors. It's sinternal diameter is 30 m and its capacity is 300 persons.

Directorate General of Culture And Arts

The Directorate General of Culture and Arts is one of the important Directorates in the Ministry. It supervises the preparation of youth mentally, nationally, and socially; it also generalize and spread out beauty values, as well as developing artistic practices which are connected with the revolution's aims. The Directorate General of Culture and Arts plans to draw up youth information policy which contributes in confronting the attempts of imperialistic cultural invasion which aims at influencing youth attitudes, also immuniz-

العلاج الطبيعي

فنون تشكيلية (رسم)

ing the youth against the western trends and practices. The above Directorate General supervise on the cultural and artistic activities in the youth centers which include posters, cultural lectures, developing the talents in the field of plastic art and others.

The Center of Culture and Arts

It is a specialized center in Baghdad aims at taking care of talented youth, developing their skills, and uprising their artistic standard. Different plastic, theatrical, musical arts are practiced there in addition to sewing, photography, opening courses of specialization for youth. Another center of culture and arts are constructed in Babylon under the name of "AL/FAYHAA center for culture and arts"

National Institute for Youth

The National Institute for Youth is one of the prominent youth establishments in the Ministry. It aims at preparing theotrical, and practical qualified youth leadership to work in the different youth sectors regionally and nationally, developing youth abilities in the mobalization fields of culture, science, technique, education, and sport, in a way that make these youth leaderships qualified to perform their national responsibilities; in addition to preparing and publishing researches and studies directed to youth and enriching the contribution of youth in the movement of changing the society. The institute include specialized professors in the field of youth and sport. It is the only institute which is specialized in these fields in the middle east.

The Directorate General for Youth training

The Direcstorate General for youth Training aims at preparing and training youth, educating them mntally, developing their physical abilities, refine these abilities in order to be capable of taking their national responsibilities to confront destiny challanges through the following activities:-
Courses in gliding, aviation by engine, olympic shooting, bow and arrow; there are also special airports allocated for youth activities and an olympic shooting field.

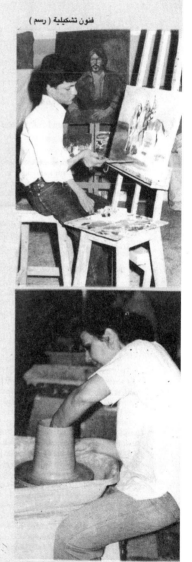

فنون تشكيليه (خزف)

Olympic Shooting Field

It's location in Baghdad, and it is one of the important olympic fields in the middle east; local, Arab, and international championships are held there with different shooting weapons as pistols, rifles, bow and arrow and others.

Directorate General of Follow up and Planning

This Directorate prepare technical, and economical studies for youth and sports projects. It implements these projects in cooperation with the Ministry of housing and reconstruction, and Ministry of local rule as well as following up the implementation of items included in the investments' plans. This Directorate provide statistical information concerning sport, cultural, scientific, technical, training, and camps activities.

Directorate General of Administration

It applies service regulation, legal affairs, organizing contracts, agreements and preparing the budget assessments of the Ministry and its youth institutions.

Youth Centers

They aim at organizing youth activities, exploding youth hidden energies to use them for the benefit of progress and building process, planting revolutions' genuin principles and values in the youth brains, and deepening the youth belonging to the country and helping them to get rid of negativism and indifference within a frame of work of unity and intellectualism, and aim, braised on sound morality and balanced emotions. The youth centers embody the programmes of the Directorates General through youth practices which are organized in the centers for the sons of Saddam Qadisyah, the new generation of the revolution. There are various sports games as football, basketball, volleyball, handball, table tennis, boxing, wrestling, athletics, shooting, martial arts, karate, judo, taikiwuondo, fencing, swimming, mass sport, in addition to science, plastic art, musical arts, theatre, cinema, festivals or national occasions.

رعاية علميه

Notes

Introduction

1. "Iraqis and Americans: One Land, 2 Realities," *New York Times* (October 29, 2006).

2. "Ten Months of Ten Years," *New York Times* (November 29, 2006).

Chapter 1: Prepping for Deployment

1. As the history is being written on Iraq, it is becoming clearer that the preponderance of military opinion was one of skepticism, at least toward the timing, approach, and core assumptions of the operation. Several generals generated career-ending controversies by publicly stating their criticisms. Like the civilians on my side of the planning process, the military commanders wanted some assurance that, if we were going to do it, they be given the tools and resources necessary to achieve success. They weren't against it as much as they insisted that the exceedingly high stakes required a hard-headed examination of real requirements to succeed.

2. Bob Woodward, *State of Denial* (New York: Simon & Schuster, 2006), 113.

3. I am certainly not the only one who saw that. Four years later, Rudy Giuliani and Newt Gingrich wrote in the *Wall Street Journal*, "Iraqis need to establish a civil society. Without the support of mediating civic and social associations—the informal ties that bind us together—no government can long remain stable, and no cohesive nation can be maintained. To establish a civil society, Iraqis must rebuild their basic infrastructure. Iraqis must take control of their destiny by rebuilding houses, stores, schools, roads, highways, mosques, and churches." "Getting Iraq to Work," *Wall Street Journal* (January 12, 2007).

Chapter 2: Camping Out in Kuwait

1. Except for very low-level workers, I never met a single senior person who worked for Uday. Not one. They had all disappeared into the anonymous and shadowy world of Saddam's deposed regime. The ministry

itself functioned under a minister, but he refused to see me. When we sent Lt. Col. Alan King over to arrange contact, the minister said, "Tell Mr. Eberly that I work for Saddam and I have no interest in helping him. You would have to come with a tank and haul me away for me to do that."

2. "Plan to Secure Postwar Iraq Faulted," *Washington Post* (May 19, 2003), A01.

Chapter 3: Wheels Up to Baghdad

1. For a brief period, the Al Rasheed was considered. It did have some advantages; the luxurious hotel by Iraqi standards was located near the palace in what was then called the international zone. But it was rejected as being a potential target. The Al Rasheed was a high building with a soft exterior, completely surrounded by block after block of heavily populated Iraqi neighborhoods. As feared, the Al Rasheed did come under attack some months after we arrived, injuring some CPA staff who were quartered there.

2. Although the palace had hundreds of bedrooms, only a small number were actually available to us in the beginning of the operation. Only a small section had been cleaned and cleared of rubbish, broken glass, rotten food, et cetera. Many other rooms and sections of the palace were reserved for the expected arrival of additional personnel.

3. When Rumsfeld was asked about the looting at an April 11, 2003, press conference, he replied, "Stuff happens! . . . [I]t is a fundamental misunderstanding to see those images over and over and over again of some boy walking out with a vase and say, 'Oh my goodness, you didn't have a plan.' That's nonsense. They know what they're doing and they're doing a terrific job. And it's untidy, and freedom's untidy, and free people are free to make mistakes and commit crimes and do bad things. They're also free to live their lives and do wonderful things, and that's what's going to happen there."

4. The factors that would likely complicate the postwar experience were studied and analyzed to incredible depth and breadth—for example, the "Future of Iraq" Project (which was rejected by the OSD), Rand Corporation studies, Center for Strategic and International Studies, USAID study groups, and a variety of smaller research projects as well as a long list of independent scholars. They all pointed to the same concerns—among them, deep ethnic fault lines that would immediately become exposed.

5. "Blind Into Baghdad," *Atlantic Monthly* (January/February, 2004), 54.

Chapter 4: Civilizations Collide

1. William R. Polk, *Understanding Iraq* (London: IB Taurus Publishing, 2005), 89.

2. Mahdi Obeidi, *The Bomb in My Garden* (Indianapolis, IN: Wiley Publishing, 2004), 10.

3. Georges Sada, *Saddam's Secrets* (Mobile, AL: Integrity Publishers, 2006).

4. Eric Davis, *Memories of State: Politics, History and Collective Identity in Modern Iraq* (Berkeley, CA: University of California Press, 2005).

5. Ed Davis "Baghdad's Buried Treasure," *New York Times* (April 16, 2003).

6. "Duty to the Future: Free Iraqis Plan for a New Iraq," U.S. State Department, 2003.

7. Who exactly might be a security threat would not be possible to determine. We were told that U.S. intelligence did not reach too far down below the top. The security procedures training from Forte Meade quickly came to mind. We were told that any threats would probably come in close quarters, in the form of surprise attacks or booby traps. We were strictly instructed not to set foot on surfaces that were not hard such as grass or dust.

8. I was told that the ministry was a prime military target because it had come to serve a serious indoctrination purpose. A variety of senior Ba'ath party leaders and even military advisors worked in the upper floors of the building, seeking to make Iraq safe for continued rule by Saddam and his sons. Their jurisdiction included overseeing the most violent youth movement in Iraq: the Youth Fedayeen.

Chapter 6: The Sketchy Postwar Plan

1. "Blackouts Return, Deepening Iraq's Dark Days," *Washington Post* (July 3, 2003), A01.

2. "An Educator Learns the Hard Way," *Washington Post* (June 21, 2004), 1.

Chapter 8: The Sociopathic Son

1. Pamela Constable, "After Uday, Iraqis Release their Rage," *Washington Post* (July 24, 2003), A7.

2. She became one of my and Ambassador Bremer's most admired and trusted friends. We were embarrassed later when attempts were made to procedurally exclude her. Eventually, she was subjected to the Iraqi rumor machine and was thrown off the committee.

3. Ahmed won overwhelmingly and took the reins of the committee. Ultimately, he became president of the new National Olympic Committee of Iraq. Ahmed was a patient and caring man who deeply respected his fellow Iraqis.

4. Nico Price, "Oasis of Hedonism in Nation of Poverty," *Associated Press* (April 15, 2003).

5. Robert F. Worth, "Uday's Trove: To Remember or Forget?" *New York Times* (July 26, 2003).

Chapter 9: Youth are Iraq's Future

1. Josh White and Griff Witte, "To Stem Iraqi Violence, U.S. Aims to Create Jobs," *Washington Post* (December 12, 2006), A01.

2. This was a tricky question because it was actually Iraqi government property, which was regulated under international law. Plus, we needed a uniform policy for all ministries, something I pushed for and eventually received.

Chapter 10: The Moral and Political Question

1. Georges Sada, *Saddam's Secrets* (Mobile, AL: Integrity Publishers, 2006), 277–78.

2. Mahdi Obeidi, *The Bomb in My Garden* (Indianapolis, IN: Wiley Publishing, 2004), 98.

3. "Blind Into Baghdad," *Atlantic Monthly* (January/February, 2004), 45–46.

Epilogue

1. Dexter Filkins, "Back in Iraq, Jarred by the Calm," *New York Times* (September 21, 2008).

Index